Enterprise Risk
Management

# Enterprise Risk Management

## A GUIDE FOR GOVERNMENT PROFESSIONALS

Dr. Karen Hardy

Foreword by
Allen Runnels

Published by Jossey-Bass
A Wiley Brand
One Montgomery Street, Suite 1200, San Francisco, CA 94104-4594—www.josseybass.com

**_Library of Congress Cataloging-in-Publication Data_**

Library of Congress Cataloging-in-Publication Data has been applied for and is on file with the Library of Congress.

ISBN 978-1-118-91102-0 (cloth); ISBN 978-1-118-91103-7 (ebk.); ISBN 978-1-118-91112-9 (ebk.)

Printed in the United States of America
FIRST EDITION
*HB Printing*        10  9  8  7  6  5  4  3  2  1

# CONTENTS

# FIGURES, TABLES, AND EXHIBITS

## Figures

## Tables

# FOREWORD

Karen Hardy understands the value proposition associated with the practice of enterprise risk management (ERM). With this book, oriented toward informing the federal workforce about ERM, she has contributed significantly to expanding the body of knowledge about this extremely important subject. The insights she shares can help encourage and empower the federal workforce at all levels to identify, assess, and manage risk effectively. She writes from both thought-leader and practitioner points of view and focuses upon the need to advance the practice of enterprise risk management in the federal government. She gives readers specific examples of what the practice of risk management looks like in agency operations, and she also includes information about tools available to help manage risk. For the few current champions of risk management in government, this book lays the groundwork for enabling them to obtain buy-in from their agency leadership. For agencies without a champion, it provides an easy-to-read road map that answers the basic question of why organizations should adopt the practice of ERM.

As risk in government becomes more dynamic and complex, managers must become more enlightened and equipped to effectively plan for it, anticipate it, and manage it. The huge balance of the federal debt and the lack of political cooperation to resolve it have led to the sequestration of federal funds, driving drastic reductions in resources available to agencies to accomplish their missions. Federal executives and managers have been asked to do more with less for the last several years, a situation that generates even more risk in the execution of government programs and services. In her book, Karen Hardy asserts that for agencies to best navigate their way through these uncertain times and effectively accomplish their missions, they need to develop an enterprise-wide approach to risk management wherein *everyone* in the organization becomes a risk manager.

Karen Hardy has done a stellar job of introducing the subject of ERM to the federal workforce. She seamlessly guides the government risk manager through an extraordinary step-by-step review of all the pieces that make up ERM as a management tool. Her book should be mandatory reading for the federal workforce, because it can fill a huge knowledge gap regarding the value of ERM in contributing to the effectiveness of government. Those tasked with designing, implementing, and sustaining ERM at their agencies will find her book a much-needed reference in their ERM toolbox. Without her book, the practice of risk management in government would lack a key perspective from a real practitioner who not only writes about the subject matter but also is applying it. Karen gives readers an opportunity to understand the value of ERM for best accomplishing agency missions and programs, and, more important, how to apply it in their organizations.

Thanks to Karen Hardy for her efforts in making such a tremendous contribution to the practice of enterprise risk management in government.

Allen Runnels
President
Association for Federal Enterprise Risk Management

# PREFACE: MANAGING RISK IN THE CURRENT FEDERAL ENVIRONMENT

It has been said that the only thing constant is change and the risks and opportunities that come with it. Over the past century, we have seen constant change in every aspect of life. Traditions that were once seen as mainstays and permanent fixtures in our society are now distant memories. Thanks to changes in technology and social norms, the ways in which we live and interact with our families, businesses, and communities continue on a path of rapid evolution. Key indicators of this change include simple, yet transformational events that we may have taken for granted. Consider the once-popular radio disc jockey; to a great extent, these announcers have been replaced by iTunes playlists. For many, the iPod has erased memories of the CD player, and books have been transformed into electronic delivery devices such as the Kindle. People by the millions are unplugging from telephone landlines and instead connecting with cell phones—allowing 24/7 access from almost anywhere in the developed and developing world. Telephone booths are now on display in museums rather than on street corners, and drones are fast becoming the next big delivery service. Even the system for manufacturing products has changed. With development of the new 3D printing technology, the use of factory assembly lines will no longer be limited to big car manufacturers in Detroit or Michigan. Rather, manufacturing will be personalized and accessible to ordinary individuals, such as doctors, dentists, and small business owners. On a larger scale, these individuals may soon be able to replicate and customize organs, tools, parts, and other products in minutes—and within the confines of their private garages and offices.

Government is not exempt from this constant change, which produces both risk and opportunity. However, as agents of change, the federal workforce must be aware of the environmental factors that will influence the context in which agency risk and opportunity will be managed. These factors include, but are not limited to, the political environment, budgetary constraints, workforce culture, policies, and laws and regulations, to name just a few.

## ENVIRONMENTAL FACTORS

When Theodore Roosevelt set the foundation of the Civil Service Reform Act of 1883, one of his presidential goals was to modernize, expand, and reform the federal government. This included establishing a hiring system for America's workers based on fairness and equal access and protection.[1] Certainly, Roosevelt considered the political environment as well as the risk that came with pursuing such lofty goals, yet the risk of *not* reforming the system would have meant forfeiting historic transformational opportunities.

Based on a merit system, Roosevelt's philosophy regarding government reform was based on three principles:

- Opportunities should be made equal for all citizens.
- Only those who have merit should be appointed to federal jobs.
- Public servants should not suffer for their political beliefs.

Under his leadership as both civil service commissioner and U.S. president, Roosevelt led efforts to investigate fraud and political abuse in government. During his administration, there was also great expansion of the federal government, including new laws protecting the health of Americans, regulating the pharmaceutical industry, and increasing the workforce. From 1901 to 1909, the federal workforce more than doubled, from 110,000 to 235,000 employees. That pales in comparison to the number of employees hired into the civil service system since the days of Roosevelt. However, the continuum of reform and modernization that began over one hundred years ago continues to resonate throughout government today. A snapshot of measurable changes can be seen in the employment trends impacting the federal service regarding age, salary, and education. As of September 2012, the federal government employed more than 2.6 million people in the executive branch versus 699,000 in 1940.[2] By 2011, the average salary for all federal employees was $75,296, and cabinet-level agencies employed the majority of that workforce. As a whole, the federal workforce is growing better educated. The majority of federal employees have obtained at least a high school degree and nearly half at least a college degree.[3] More than 40 percent of the employees added from 2004 to 2012 had at least a bachelor's degree; an additional 53 percent had at least a master's.[4]

## Policies, Laws, and Regulations

In addition to seeing demographic changes, over the years since the Civil Service Reform Act the federal government has instituted many new policies, laws, and regulations that have redefined how our government works—most notably the passage of the U.S. Patriot Act, Chief Financial Officers Act of 1990, Government Performance and Results Act (GPRA) of 1993, American Recovery and Reinvestment Act (ARRA), and the Federal Manager's Financial Integrity Act of 1982 (FMFIA). All were instituted to address and manage some level of risk and opportunity inside and outside the government. These and other policies, laws, and regulations have shaped the ways in which government operates and executes its internal day-to-day activities as well as monitors and regulates industry. Issuance of such policies also demonstrates the government's political willingness and need to respond to changes in society as a whole. For example, in response to the Enron acts of fraud and abuse, the government created the Sarbanes-Oxley Act of 2002 (SOX), which President Bush signed into law on July 30, 2002. He characterized it as "the most far-reaching reforms of American business practices since the time of Franklin Delano Roosevelt." The Act mandated a number of reforms to enhance corporate responsibility and financial disclosures and to combat corporate and accounting fraud.[5]

On February 13, 2009, in direct response to the economic crisis and at the urging of President Obama, Congress passed the American Recovery and Reinvestment Act (ARRA) of 2009—commonly referred to as the "stimulus" or the "stimulus package." Not long after that, the president signed the Recovery Act into law. The three immediate goals of the Recovery Act were to:

- Create new jobs and save existing ones
- Spur economic activity and invest in long-term growth
- Foster unprecedented levels of accountability and transparency in government spending

The Recovery Act intended to achieve those goals by providing $787 billion in:

- Tax cuts and benefits for millions of working families and businesses
- Funding for entitlement programs, such as unemployment benefits
- Funding for federal contracts, grants, and loans

Eventually, ARRA's original expenditure estimate of $787 billion was increased to $840 billion. To achieve the goal of transparency, the Act required recipients of Recovery funds to report on a quarterly basis how they were using the money. Today, all the data affiliated with Recovery Act spending is posted on Recovery.gov so the public can track how the money is being spent.[6]

A year after ARRA was passed, the Dodd-Frank Wall Street Reform and Consumer Protection Act was signed into law on July 21, 2010, by the Obama administration. The legislation set out to reshape the U.S. regulatory system in a number of areas, including but not limited to consumer protection, trading restrictions, credit ratings, regulation of financial products, corporate governance and disclosure, and transparency.[7]

## Culture

While the demographics and policies of the federal workforce may have shifted drastically over the last century, the dedication, purpose, and level of service given by federal government workers have remained constant. In a 2013 Federal Employee Viewpoint Survey, administered by the U.S. Office of Personnel Management (OPM), civil servants showed an unwavering commitment to the missions of their organizations as well as a sense of pride and satisfaction in their work despite difficult and uncertain times. The survey also served to strengthen belief in the federal workforce at a time when their relevance and value is questioned by Congress and other opponents in the court of public opinion. OPM Director Katherine Archuleta emphasized that despite these obstacles, the results showed "employees are ready and willing to meet the challenges they face and are steadfastly accountable for achieving results and knowing what is expected of them on the job."[8]

This confirmation of the resiliency of the federal workforce is a significant and reassuring observation, given the magnitude of their tasks and the extensive role they play in delivering, managing, and overseeing core programs and services on which our nation depends. More important, the value of public service could not have been more evident than during the 2013 government shutdown. When a group of veterans was not able to get full access to visit the War Memorial in the nation's capital, a renewed respect for the level of service that federal employees provide to the nation resonated throughout the country. The federal workforce remains engaged and committed: over 90 percent of employees continue to be willing to put in extra effort, are constantly looking for new ways to do their jobs better, and feel their work is important.[9]

Given this scenario, there is every indication that the public sector has the right stuff to get the job done during times of ever-increasing change, and that the workforce is ready to manage the risks and opportunities that come with its responsibilities.

## Challenges for Public Administrators

Leading scholars define public administration as "all processes, organizations, and individuals associated with carrying out the laws and other rules adopted or issued by legislatures, executives, and courts."[10] As the arena in which government employees work, public administration itself has changed in response to complex and often uncertain national and global political environments.[11]

We can clearly see how government's role has expanded exponentially. This includes its involvement in civil and voting rights "and extended presidential powers needed to respond to natural disasters, cope with economic downturns, reduce federal spending, and respond to military crises."[12] As noted by Milakovich and Gordon, "The challenges facing administrators accountable for implementing public programs today have become even more daunting— requiring more effective expenditures of scarcer public resource and increased commitment from all public servants."[13] The task won't be easy, so organizations such as the American Society for Public Administration (ASPA) will need to play a key role in helping to navigate the ethical framework for the public administration professional. Established in 1939 to help government employees navigate the political and managerial aspects of government operations, ASPA advances excellence in public service through a code of ethics to develop the spirit of responsible professionalism and increase awareness and commitment to ethical principles and standards (see Table P.1). While there are similar organizations advancing the practice of public administration, ASPA's well-defined list of guiding principles serves the public sector workforce well as they oversee and execute government performance.

## Table P.1
## American Society for Public Administration Code of Ethics

1. Advance the Public Interest. Promote the interests of the public and put service to the public above service to oneself.

2. Uphold the Constitution and the Law. Respect and support government constitutions and laws, while seeking to improve laws and policies to promote the public good.

3. Promote Democratic Participation. Inform the public and encourage active engagement in governance. Be open, transparent and responsive, and respect and assist all persons in their dealings with public organizations.

4. Strengthen Social Equity. Treat all persons with fairness, justice, and equality and respect individual differences, rights, and freedoms. Promote affirmative action and other initiatives to reduce unfairness, injustice, and inequality in society.

5. Fully Inform and Advise. Provide accurate, honest, comprehensive, and timely information and advice to elected and appointed officials and governing board members, and to staff members in your organization.

6. Demonstrate Personal Integrity. Adhere to the highest standards of conduct to inspire public confidence and trust in public service.

7. Promote Ethical Organizations. Strive to attain the highest standards of ethics, stewardship, and public service in organizations that serve the public.

8. Advance Professional Excellence. Strengthen personal capabilities to act competently and ethically and encourage the professional development of others.

*Source:* American Society for Public Administration. Reprinted with permission.

## The Political and Budget Environment

Scholars have noted that "the politics of administration involves agency interactions with those outside the formal structure as well as interactions among those within administrative agencies."[14]

Arguably, two of the biggest risks that public servants face stem from the political and budget arenas, where interaction is a key ingredient to agency success. Politically, the consistent gridlock of Congress over the past few years has made the government worker's task more unpredictable. The level of uncertainty in funding programs and projects and the cuts to the levels of discretionary spending continue to make budgets a moving target, making it harder for agencies to nail down agency-specific goals and objectives. While the push-and-pull dynamics of congressional inner workings may be temporary, the realization of long-term financial constraints is not.

At the end of fiscal year 2012, the total federal debt was about $16.1 trillion.[15] In its Fiscal Update for 2012, the Government Accountability Office (GAO) acknowledged that addressing the long-term federal fiscal challenges will likely require difficult choices affecting both government revenue and spending—challenges for which there are no quick or easy solutions. GAO noted that many of the long-term drivers, including health care cost growth and the aging population, have already begun to affect the federal budget.[16] Within its simulations of long-term federal deficits, GAO projected that spending for the major health and retirement programs will increase in coming decades, putting greater pressure on the rest of the federal budget. The GAO reported that for the first few decades this spending is driven largely by the aging of the population, with the oldest members of the baby boom generation already eligible for Social Security retirement benefits and for Medicare. The number of baby boomers turning sixty-five is projected to grow in coming years, from an average of about 7,600 per day in 2011 to more than 11,000 per day in 2029.[17]

Another budgetary risk that continues to have a profound impact on government performance and operations is that of continuing resolutions (CR). Annually, Congress faces difficult decisions on what to fund, with the available resources, among competing priorities and interests. When these decisions aren't agreed upon within a certain time frame, CRs are used as a stopgap measure to keep the government operating. Historically, continuing resolutions have created budget uncertainty; they have complicated agency operations as well as produced inefficiencies. Because CRs provide funding only until agreement is reached on final appropriations, they create uncertainty for agencies about both when they will receive their final appropriation and what level of funding will ultimately be available. In all but three of the last thirty years, Congress has passed CRs to provide funding for agencies to continue operating until agreement is reached on final appropriations. The biggest risks to agencies when CRs are enacted stem from the provisions and restrictions that prohibit agencies from beginning new activities and projects. This forces agencies to take only the most limited funding actions and makes it difficult to pursue their missions and plans for the future. Though the effects of CRs vary by agency and program, overall the residual impacts have been disruptive, resulting in operational challenges such as delayed hiring, a shifting of grant and contract award cycles, and the need to perform additional work to manage CR constraints.[18]

## The Upside of Risk

Not all change in government has been negative. There have been positive outcomes as well as opportunities to expand missions and ensure sufficient services for American citizens. In the middle of the twenty-first century's first decade, the merging of several intelligence agencies (for example, the FBI, CIA, U.S. Marshal's Service) was proposed to Congress to create what is now the Department of Homeland Security (DHS). The DHS was established in response to a national safety and security breach, but it also brought with it bountiful opportunities to create a more streamlined agency responsive to threats and natural disasters. Over time, the biggest benefit anticipated from the restructuring was a reduced risk of terrorism for the nation.

The transition to a more effective homeland security approach was also part of a larger transformation that the government needed to undertake to meet the expectations of the American people for timely, high-quality, and cost-effective public services. Within nine months of the events of September 11, 2001, the Bush administration and Congress responded with important and aggressive actions to protect the nation. The establishment of DHS was seen as a remedy to long-standing issues and concerns in the government's domestic security functions by instituting greater consolidation and agency coordination. Given the global challenges the government will face in the coming years, the consolidation was considered a unique opportunity to create an extremely effective and performance-based organization to strengthen the nation's ability to protect its borders and citizens against terrorism.[19]

# INTRODUCTION

Since the first introduction of this material in 2009, the practice of risk management and, more so, that of enterprise risk management (ERM), has expanded in the federal space. For example, the Association for Enterprise Risk Management (AFERM) has been established solely for those who oversee risk management in federal agencies. The AFERM mission is to advance the practice of ERM in the federal government through thought leadership, education, and collaboration.[1] AFERM provides specific programs and opportunities to educate members and stakeholders on the benefits, tools, and leading practices of federal ERM. AFERM also fosters collaboration with organizations and stakeholders to promote laws, regulations, and policies to establish federal ERM in the various agencies and departments. In addition, an International Risk Management Standard (ISO 31000) was adopted by the American National Standards Institute (ANSI), and the FederalERM.org website saw its membership exceed seven hundred government online subscribers. *Government Executive* magazine recognized the FederalERM.org website as "an informal network to help employees learn new skills."[2]

There has also been a modest increase in the frequency with which job postings for chief risk officers (CROs) and risk management officers (RMOs) have been advertised on USAJOBS.gov (see Table I.1). Job titles such as risk management specialist have been identified as a new emerging occupation with a bright outlook. According to the Department of Labor,

## Table I.1
## Agency Hiring Activities

| | |
|---|---|
| Department of Education | Chief Risk Officer |
| Department of Housing and Urban Development | Chief Risk Officer |
| Federal Thrift Retirement Investment Board | Chief Risk Officer |
| Veterans Administration | Chief Risk Officer |
| Federal Home Loan Bank | Chief Risk Officer |
| Internal Revenue Service | Chief Risk Officer |
| National Credit Union Administration | Chief Risk Officer |
| Federal Deposit and Insurance Corporation | Chief Risk Officer |
| Centers for Medicare and Medicaid Services | Deputy Administrator for Risk Management and Chief Risk Management Officer |
| Government National Mortgage Association | Senior Vice President/Chief Risk Officer |
| Department of Interior | Risk Management Officer |

The Chief Risk Officer

A Chief Risk Officer (CRO)[3] is a C-level management position recently created for managing risk at an enterprise-wide level. CROs have been put in place mostly in the financial industry, but are believed to spread into other industry sectors in the future. This position has created a level for current risk managers to aspire to and a way for them to become involved in a more strategic role within the enterprise.

A CRO should provide information to other C-level managers as well as to the board about whether or not current strategic decisions include the most up-to-date risks that the enterprise faces on a financial and strategic level. Risk managers are already trained to identify and manage risks, but will they cooperate with the CRO? The Risk & Insurance Management Society (RIMS) believes that the creation of this role will benefit risk managers by making their role more strategic. Their role will transform to encompass more issues to allow them to improve their risk identification and mitigation skills.

Although current risk managers are skilled mostly in operational risk, those who have welcomed ERM have developed more financial skills that will be.

necessary to become Chief Risk Officers. Current economic conditions have heightened financial issues awareness such as liquidity and solvency, making risk managers a great value to their companies because they are better suited to manage financial risks in strategic decisions

According to some, risk managers may be at a disadvantage because they are skilled in risk identification, but often report to higher management and are not skilled at making decisions. CROs will be required to be skilled decision makers and also to work with the board and other C-level management to form strategic plans. Peter den Dekker, president of FERMA (Federation of European Risk Management Associations) believes that current risk managers will be more suited for ERM roles instead of Chief Risk Officers. Successful CROs will need strong quantitative backgrounds and will need to embrace a global view of the company. As he points out, a company who has a CRO may not necessarily be managing risk to the appropriate level. The position may help some companies, but may give others false assurance that risks are being monitored successfully.

From a different perspective, Julie Graham, a CRO for a nonfinancial corporation, asserts that risk managers have exactly what it takes to become CROs. If they incorporate financial and management skills with their ability to communicate and employ judgment, they possess the basis of qualities needed to be successful as a Chief Risk Officer.

*Source:* The listing of CROs hired in government agencies is taken from a random selection of USAJOBS .gov job announcement postings and organizational charts. "The Chief Risk Officer" is from http://erm .ncsu.edu/library/article/cro-emerging-trends/#.UwV-iMKYbVI.

"bright outlook" occupations are those that are expected to grow rapidly in the next several years, will have large numbers of job openings, or are new and emerging occupations.[4] According to the U.S. Department of Labor's O*NET OnLine, the risk management specialist occupation is projected to

- Grow much faster than average (employment increase of 29 percent or more) over the period 2010–2020
- Offer one hundred thousand or more job openings over the period 2010–2020

The speed with which these developments have transpired in the federal environment makes this book especially timely for several reasons:

1. There is a growing demand for knowledge and understanding of ERM and its application to public sector organizations.

2. There is a lack of available information focused on the practice of ERM and how it benefits public sector organizations.

3. A solid blueprint for utilizing ERM in public sector organizations, namely federal agencies, is sorely needed to guide those who champion risk management practice.

4. There is no single resource guide available that summarizes information about ERM and risk management in general for the government workforce.

Finally, the Obama administration's focus on accountability and transparency has also prompted a renewed focus on risk and controls. This publication aims to satisfy these needs.

In recent years, the federal government has been on the receiving end of new legislation and regulations that require it to better manage risk and improve controls in discrete areas. Generally, to meet the requirements of each of these new mandates, agencies have engaged in many compliance-driven activities. This stove-piped approach to compliance is costly and does not optimize value. This book explores how federal C-suite executives, as well as financial and operational managers, can help guide their agencies to take a more holistic approach to risk management by implementing an ERM system. This approach can help reduce the total cost of compliance by proactively mitigating risk, while helping agencies achieve greater value from their risk management activities.

Although the current focus on risk management for most federal CFOs and financial managers stems from the revised OMB Circular A-123, these are only two requirements among the many that federal agencies must address. Agencies are also required to report their results in implementing the Federal Managers' Financial Integrity Act (FMFIA) of 1982, the Improper Payments Information Act (IPIA) of 2002, and the Federal Information Security Management Act (FISMA) of 2002, among others. Virtually all of these requirements are ultimately geared toward one objective—improved risk management—so an agency's response to risk provides reasonable assurance that the organization will achieve its strategic objectives.

This dramatic increase in compliance requirements, coupled with the realization that compliance cannot be effectively achieved just by having discrete compliance programs in various business units, now makes it critical for organizations to move toward an enterprise-wide risk management approach. Holistic ERM starts with a focus on possible events and their classification into opportunities and risks.

Keeping track of these possible events requires good data and data governance managed at the enterprise level. It also requires a taxonomy or classification scheme of the most important risks to the entity and a common language for understanding those risks. Improved data management allows the enterprise to take advantage of modern analytical methods to quantify the impact of risk. Data analysis also enables the enterprise to gain an overall view of current risk as well as trends and potential future risks.

It's clear that implementing an ERM approach makes sense and yields benefits to an organization. It is my hope that federal executives will find this book useful to them as an introduction and guide to enterprise risk management.

## STATE OF RISK MANAGEMENT IN GOVERNMENT

At a September 2011 annual summit on Federal Enterprise Risk Management, J. Christopher Mihm, managing director for strategic issues at the U.S. Government Accountability Office (GAO), summarized the state of risk management in the federal government and a path for moving forward (*note:* "Recent Risk Events" is reproduced at the end of this introduction):

> In a relatively short amount of time, enormous progress has been made in the area of risk management in government. Due to major efforts by many risk managers in the public and private sectors, risk management both as a discipline and a way of thinking has deepened and expanded significantly. Risk management has moved from its traditional domains into areas such as IT, financial management, contracting, health and safety programs, and homeland security. In concept and language, risk management is moving

more into the routines of other federal program and functional management areas.

The nature of risk is evolving as well and its dynamics originate from a variety of sources [see "Recent Risk Events"]. Characteristics of this evolution include the following:

- Risks can emerge more quickly;

- Greater transparency about risk is needed;

- Public knowledge of risk occurs more quickly; and

- There are higher expectations that risk will be addressed more quickly

With this newfound awareness, can risk management play a vital role in helping line managers understand and address the performance and accountability challenges associated with government issues?[5]

To help answer that question and to realize the true potential of risk management in government, Chris Mihm cited several additional actions that must be taken.[6]

First, there must be ongoing momentum and commitment to "continue to expand the discipline across programs" and at an enterprise level. Too often, "Federal managers take massive risks every day but too often do not consider and manage them as such." Without the proper level of awareness, managers will not properly identify and manage risk effectively.

Second, there must be internal and external commitment to "help managers understand and calculate the risk inherent in the status quo." Anecdotal observations and assumptions of risk made without a degree of calculation would undermine the value of risk management in an organization. The more specific the descriptions of risk made available to managers, the better they will be able to articulate the impact it will have.

And finally, actions speak louder than words. Current and future risk practitioners must demonstrate to managers "how they can use risk management to help address governance challenges." It will be necessary to engage managers early on in action-oriented activities that show how risk management can improve their operations or performance.

## HOW THIS BOOK SHOULD BE USED

This book is an update to the research report "Managing Risk in Government: An Introduction to Enterprise Risk Management," published by the IBM Center for the Business of Government in 2009 and 2010. The practice of and interest in ERM in government has expanded since the original publication of that report, and this book is a reflection of the growth in this area.

Overall, ERM continues to be a tall order for federal risk managers to fill. To ensure success, all federal executives, managers, and employees in general need a blueprint for defining and executing effective risk management in their organizations. Readers should consider this book as a road map for sorting through the key elements that make up ERM success. It is designed to guide risk managers and champions of ERM through a practical thought process using highlighted, real-world work examples. For those in the workforce who have not been designated a specific role in ERM practice in their organization, this book provides a basic educational foundation that will equip any employee with an understanding of risk management.

This book will not answer all the questions about enterprise risk management, nor is it possible to cover all aspects of the subject in one publication. However, the reader will gain a better understanding of the key topics commonly related to ERM design and implementation. This book was written as a resource that can be shared with all employees, no matter what their role in an organization, because a basic understanding of the subject matter is the beginning of an evolving process. Readers are encouraged to maximize use of the book, tools, and other related resources available to reinforce the principles shared and increase awareness and practice of ERM.

## EMERGING RISKS TODAY

Nothing seems to define or capture the absolute essence of risk better than the events that emerge from some level of uncertainty. It is then that as a society we are wholly able to grasp and understand risk in its purest sense. Unfortunately, it is when risk has materialized that our greatest sense of awareness is heightened, affording us the opportunity to gain a better understanding of the origins of uncertainty. It allows us to reflect, for a moment, on all the variables that may have contributed to the act or occurrence and permits us to assess why it happened and whether it could have been prevented.

In our society we are surrounded, daily, by events and occurrences that give us the privilege of understanding and defining the "why" and "how" of these instances when they take place. Ideally, we walk away with a better understanding of the root causes and then move forward to fortify ourselves against future challenges. We live in a society in which risks are all too real—that is, when the dangers for which we feel at risk materialize, we see and hear about them. Repeated exposure to such events socializes us to feel uncertain, though we are not always aware that this is happening. In this societal framework, we begin to understand that risks managed in our organizations are often similar to the risks we see playing out in our external environment.

In 2010, the United States witnessed what became the costliest oil spill in the country to date. On April 20, 2010, an explosion from a well site at which the mobile offshore drilling unit (MODU) Deepwater Horizon had been drilling resulted in a spill of national significance in the Gulf of Mexico. As a result of the explosion, oil flowed into the Gulf of Mexico at an estimated rate of between 12,000 and 19,000 barrels per day, according to the National Incident Command's Flow Rate Technical Group, making it one of the largest, if not *the* largest spill in U.S. waters. BP, which leased the Deepwater Horizon at the time of the explosion, made efforts to contain the leak. During the later congressional testimonies, it was reported that the total cost of cleaning up this massive and potentially unprecedented spill, repairing the untold damage to the environment, as well as the potential impact to the livelihood and the economic status of the region, will be undetermined for some time. However, it was estimated that the spill cleanup and related damage claims would be in the tens of billions of dollars—well beyond the costs of the Exxon *Valdez* spill. Federal officials have predicted that this spill and future spills all have the potential to result in considerable costs to the private sector, as well as to federal, state, and local governments.

This was a disaster on a national scale. Of course, we as individuals are not exempt from exposure to risk, accidents, or chance. Thus, the management of risk in an organization naturally evolves from knowledge common to everyone.

In society, we experience direct and indirect exposures to risk. Regardless of the type of exposure experienced, we can learn from it and better prepare for future challenges and occurrences. What have recent events taught us about uncertainty and the management of risk, and how can we apply that knowledge in the quest to incorporate effective risk management in our organizations?

"Recent Risk Events," later in the chapter, provides a comprehensive list of the wide variety of risk events that have taken place, to help us answer these questions. Through these examples, we can conclude that failures in the systemic process of identifying and managing risks led to consequential impacts on reputation, financial investments, public trust, health, safety and security, and the environment.

Through these events, we have learned that risk impact can be far reaching and felt across borders. To take some specific examples described in "Recent Risk Events," the international incident involving horse meat discovered in the United Kingdom underscored major safety issues and highlighted the extensive reach of the global food supply chain. We also learn that risk must be identified and mechanisms must be put in place to manage the unexpected. For instance, the Mine Safety and Health Administration's (MSHA) extended authority to issue additional violation notices will help mitigate risks associated with the monitoring of safety problems by mine operators. The U.S. Department of Labor rule will serve as a red flag for mines that repeatedly fail to meet safety requirements and will force them to correct problems before workers are allowed to return to the work site. And finally, we learn that contingency plans for continuity of operations must be sufficient to reasonably ensure the safety of the general public. After a fire in the engine room disabled the Carnival *Triumph* cruise ship, more than 4,200 passengers and crew were left adrift without power in the Gulf of Mexico. Passengers were forced to sleep in hallways, and food supplies ran low before the ship was finally towed to port in Mobile, Alabama.

But we also learn to recognize how the proactive management of risk can have a positive impact. GAO's audit of the National Archives and Records Administration (NARA) identified several opportunities for the agency to improve its management of key risks through electronic records archiving. As a result, the nation will be positioned to have a stellar records management system in place, saving billions of dollars in management systems over time. Likewise, the National Institutes of Health, through a GAO audit of its Risk Management Program, is better positioned to support science administratively, as risk is managed through a process that meets specific framework criteria.

The approval of the American Recovery and Reinvestment Act (ARRA) was intended to infuse the U.S. economy with desperately needed funds. The risks associated with issuing multimillion-dollar grants and contracts as required by ARRA in such a short period of time were great; however, the opportunity to stimulate the economy and make economic gains was projected to outweigh the risks. State and local governments were able to use stimulus funds to repair major transportation systems and boost local economies as well. This in turn created grants that were extended to small businesses to help support these initiatives, boosting economic development at the micro level.

These are just a few examples of the activities the federal government has proactively launched to manage the positive aspects of risk. Others include creation of the GAO High Risk List.

## TOP GOVERNMENT RISKS

In 1990, GAO began a program to report on government operations that it identified as "high risk." Since then, generally coinciding with the start of each new Congress, GAO has reported on the status of progress to address high-risk areas and updated the High Risk List. In 2013, the GAO removed the high-risk designation from two areas—Management of Interagency Contracting and IRS Business Systems Modernization—and designated two new high-risk areas: Limiting the Federal Government's Fiscal Exposure by Better Managing Climate Change Risks and Mitigating Gaps in Weather Satellite Data. These changes brought GAO's 2013 High Risk List to a total of thirty areas.

The GAO High Risk List is particularly useful to risk managers, chief risk officers, and agency executive leadership in general because it serves as an independent review for flagging risk areas in government that may be missed by agencies. Overall, GAO's high-risk program has served to identify and help

| Table I.2 Changes to GAO's High Risk List, 1990–2013 | |
|---|---|
| Original High Risk List in 1990 | 14 |
| High-risk areas added since 1990 | 41 |
| High-risk areas removed since 1990 | 23 |
| High-risk areas consolidated since 1990 | 2 |
| High Risk List in 2013 | 30 |

*Source:* www.GAO.gov.

resolve serious weaknesses in areas that involve substantial resources and provide critical services to the public. Since the high-risk program began, the government has taken high-risk problems seriously and has made long-needed progress toward correcting them. In a number of cases, progress has been sufficient for GAO to remove the high-risk designation. A summary of changes to GAO's High Risk List over the past twenty-three years is shown in Table I.2.

## CRITERIA

When legislative, administration, and agency actions result in significant progress toward resolving a high-risk area, GAO removes the high-risk designation. Key to determining whether the high-risk designation can be removed are the following five elements: (1) a demonstrated strong commitment to, and top leadership support for, addressing problems; (2) the capacity to address problems; (3) a corrective action plan; (4) a program to monitor corrective measures; and (5) demonstrated progress in implementing corrective measures.

To determine which federal government programs and functions should be designated high risk, GAO considers whether the program or function is of national significance or is key to performance and accountability. GAO also considers which of the following the risk represents:

- An inherent problem, such as may arise when the nature of a program creates susceptibility to fraud, waste, and abuse

- A systemic problem, such as may arise when the programmatic, management support, or financial systems, policies, and procedures established by an agency to carry out a program are ineffective, creating a material weakness

  Further, GAO considers qualitative factors, such as whether the risk

- Is a matter of public health or safety, service delivery, national security, national defense, economic growth, or privacy or citizens' rights

- Could result in significant impaired service, program failure, injury or loss of life, or significantly reduced economy, efficiency, or effectiveness

In addition, GAO also considers the exposure to loss in monetary or other quantitative terms. At a minimum, $1 billion must be at risk in areas such as the value of major assets being impaired; revenue sources not being realized; major agency assets being lost, stolen, damaged, wasted, or underutilized; improper payments; and contingencies or potential liabilities.

Before making a high-risk designation, GAO also considers corrective measures planned or under way to resolve a material control weakness and the status and effectiveness of these actions. To determine which federal government programs and functions should be designated high risk, GAO uses the self-titled guidance document *Determining Performance and Accountability Challenges and High Risks*.

In February 2011, GAO detailed thirty high-risk areas. Sufficient progress has been made to remove the high-risk designation from the following two areas:

• *Management of Interagency Contracting*. Improvements include (1) continued progress made by agencies in addressing identified deficiencies, (2) establishment of additional management controls, (3) creation of a policy framework for establishing new interagency contracts, and (4) steps taken to address the need for better data on these contracts.

• *Internal Revenue Service Business Systems Modernization*. The IRS made progress in addressing significant weaknesses in information technology and financial management capabilities. The IRS delivered the initial phase of its cornerstone tax processing project and began the daily processing and posting of individual taxpayer accounts in January 2012. This enhanced tax administration and improved service by enabling faster refunds for more taxpayers, allowing more timely account updates and faster issuance of taxpayer notices. In addition, IRS has put in place close to 80 percent of the practices needed for an effective investment management process, including all of the processes needed for effective project oversight.

Although these two areas have been removed from the High Risk List, GAO will continue to monitor them.

GAO has added two areas in 2013:

• *Limiting the Federal Government's Fiscal Exposure by Better Managing Climate Change Risks*. Climate change creates significant financial risks for the federal government, which (1) owns extensive infrastructure, such as defense installations; (2) insures property through the National Flood Insurance Program; and (3) provides emergency aid in response to natural disasters. The federal government is not well positioned to address the fiscal exposure presented by climate change; it needs a government-wide strategic approach with strong leadership to manage related risks.

• *Mitigating Gaps in Weather Satellite Data.* Potential gaps in environmental satellite data, beginning as early as 2014 and lasting as long as fifty-three months, have led to concerns that future weather forecasts and warnings—including warnings of extreme events such as hurricanes, storm surges, and floods—will be less accurate and timely. A number of decisions are needed to ensure that contingency and continuity plans can be implemented effectively.

Notable progress has been made in the vast majority of areas that remain on GAO's High Risk List. This progress is due to the combined efforts of Congress, through its oversight and legislation; the Office of Management and Budget (OMB), through its leadership and coordination; and the agencies, through their efforts to take corrective actions to address long-standing problems and implement related GAO recommendations.

## PROFILES OF SELECT HIGH-RISK AREAS IN GOVERNMENT

The U.S. federal government is the world's largest and most complex organizational entity, with about $3.5 trillion in outlays in fiscal year 2012 funding a broad array of programs and operations. GAO maintains a program to focus attention on government operations that it identifies as high risk due to their greater vulnerability to fraud, waste, abuse, and mismanagement or the need for transformation to address economy, efficiency, or effectiveness challenges. Solutions to high-risk problems, such as those listed in this section, offer the potential to save billions of dollars, improve service to the public, and strengthen the performance and accountability of the U.S. government:

• *Strategic Human Capital Management.* Addressing complex challenges such as disaster response, national and homeland security, and economic stability requires a high-quality federal workforce able to work seamlessly with other agencies and levels of government and across sectors. However, current budget and long-term fiscal pressures, coupled with a potential wave of employee retirements that could produce gaps in leadership and institutional knowledge, threaten the government's capacity to effectively address these and many other evolving national issues. The Office of Personnel Management (OPM), individual agencies, and Congress have all taken important steps in recent years that will better position the government to close current and emerging critical skills gaps that are undermining agencies' abilities to meet their vital missions. Although progress has been made, the area remains high risk because more work is needed in implementing specific corrective strategies for addressing critical skills gaps and evaluating their results. GAO added this area to its High Risk List in 2001.

• *Managing Federal Real Property*. The federal government faces long-standing problems in managing federal real property, including effectively managing excess and underutilized property, an overreliance on leasing, and protecting federal facilities. The government has given high-level attention to this issue and has made progress in real property management, but the underlying challenges that hamper reform remain. Specifically, the government continues to lack consistent, accurate, and useful data to support decision making. In addition, competing stakeholder interests regarding the disposition of excess real property and legal requirements such as those related to environmental cleanup also present challenges. The Federal Protective Service (FPS) has struggled to effectively target limited resources for protecting federal facilities.

• *National Flood Insurance Program*. The National Flood Insurance Program (NFIP) is a key component of the federal government's efforts to limit the damage and financial impact of floods; however, it likely will not generate sufficient revenues to repay the billions of dollars borrowed from the Treasury to cover claims from the 2005 hurricanes or future catastrophic losses. This lack of sufficient revenues highlights what have been structural weaknesses in how the program is funded. The Biggert-Waters Flood Insurance Reform Act of 2012 addresses a number of these weaknesses, but the extent to which the changes included in the act will reduce the financial exposure created by the program is not yet clear. Weaknesses in NFIP management and operations—including financial reporting processes and internal controls, and oversight of contractors—have also placed the program at risk. The Federal Emergency Management Agency (FEMA), within the Department of Homeland Security, is responsible for managing NFIP. Although FEMA has taken some steps to address these issues, it continues to face complex challenges. In October 2012, Superstorm Sandy caused extensive damage in several states on the East Coast, raising the prospect that NFIP would not be able to pay all the resulting claims without borrowing additional funds from the Treasury. In January 2013, Congress passed legislation to temporarily increase NFIP's borrowing authority by $9.7 billion, from $20.7 billion to $30.4 billion, to address these claims.

• *Improving and Modernizing Federal Disability Programs.* Federal disability programs remain in need of modernization. Numerous federal programs provide a range of services and supports for people with disabilities—including forty-five employment-related programs—that together represent a patchwork of policies and programs without a unified strategy or set of national goals. Further, three of the largest federal disability programs—managed by the Social Security Administration (SSA) and Department of Veterans Affairs (VA)—rely to a great extent on out-of-date criteria in making disability benefit decisions. Although SSA and VA have taken concrete steps toward updating their criteria, these disability programs emphasize medical conditions in assessing an individual's work incapacity without adequate consideration of the work opportunities afforded by advances in medicine and technology and in changing job demands. Finally, federal disability benefit programs are experiencing growing disability claim workloads as the demand for benefits has increased in a difficult job market. Thus challenges are likely to persist, despite concerted efforts to process more claims annually. GAO designated improving and modernizing federal disability programs as high risk in 2003.

• *Pension Benefit Guaranty Corporation Insurance Program.* The Pension Benefit Guaranty Corporation (PBGC) insures the pension benefits of forty-three million American workers and retirees participating in nearly twenty-six thousand private sector defined benefit plans through its single-employer and multiemployer insurance programs. PBGC's financial portfolio is one of the largest of any federal government corporation, with more than $80 billion in assets. Yet because of long-term challenges related to PBGC's governance and funding structure, PBGC's financial future is uncertain. At the end of fiscal year 2012, PBGC's net accumulated financial deficit was $34 billion—an increase of over $23 billion from the end of fiscal year 2008, and significantly worse than in 2000, when PBGC reported a $10 billion surplus. PBGC estimates that its financial risk for potential termination of underfunded plans sponsored by financially weak firms is about $295 billion, an amount that has continued to worsen since the economic downturn in 2008. The Pension Protection Act of 2006 (PPA) strengthened some aspects of funding rules, but in response to the recession, subsequent legislation has softened these provisions—initially by phasing in PPA's changes, and more recently through changes in how minimum contributions are calculated. Thus, although Congress has enacted various provisions to strengthen PBGC's governance and PBGC has implemented various measures to improve its operations, weaknesses in the structure of its board and its revenue streams continue to undermine the agency's long-term financial stability. GAO designated the single-employer program as high risk in July 2003 and added the multiemployer program in January 2009.

• *NASA Acquisition Management.* The National Aeronautics and Space Administration (NASA) plans to invest billions of dollars in the coming years to explore space, understand Earth's environment, and conduct aeronautics research. GAO has designated NASA's acquisition management as high risk in view of NASA's history of persistent cost growth and schedule slippage in the majority of its major projects. GAO's work has identified a number of causal factors, including antiquated financial management systems, poor cost estimating, and underestimation of risks associated with the development of its major systems. This area was added to GAO's High Risk List in 1990.

• *Protecting Public Health through Enhanced Oversight of Medical Products.* Millions of medical products are used by Americans on a daily basis at home, in the hospital, and in other health care settings. The Food and Drug Administration (FDA) has the vital mission of protecting the public health by overseeing the safety and effectiveness of these products—drugs, biologics, and medical devices—marketed in the United States. The agency's responsibilities begin long before a product is brought to market and continue after a product's approval, regardless of whether it is manufactured here or abroad. The importance of FDA's role in ensuring our citizens' well-being cannot be overstated. In recent years, FDA has been confronted with multiple challenges. Rapid changes in science and technology, globalization, unpredictable public health crises, an increasing workload, and the continuing need to monitor the safety of thousands of marketed medical products have strained the agency's resources. The oversight of medical products was added to GAO's High Risk List in 2009 because FDA was facing a variety of difficulties that threatened to compromise its ability to protect the public health. Although progress has been made, GAO has found that considerable challenges remain.

• *Protecting the Federal Government's Information Systems and the Nation's Cyber Critical Infrastructures.* As computer technology has advanced, federal agencies and our nation's critical infrastructures—such as power distribution, water supply, telecommunications, and emergency services—have become increasingly dependent on computerized information systems and electronic data to carry out operations and to process, maintain, and report essential information. The security of these systems and data is essential to protecting national and economic security and public health and safety. Safeguarding federal computer systems and the systems that support critical infrastructures—referred to as cyber critical infrastructure protection (cyber CIP)—is a continuing concern. Federal information security has been on GAO's list of high-risk areas since 1997; in 2003, GAO expanded this high-risk area to include cyber CIP. Risks to information and communication systems include insider threats from disaffected or careless employees and business partners, escalating and emerging threats from around the globe, the ease of obtaining and using hacking tools, the steady advance in the sophistication of attack technology, and the emergence of new and more destructive attacks.

• *Revamping Federal Oversight of Food Safety.* The fragmented federal oversight of food safety has caused inconsistent oversight, ineffective coordination, and inefficient use of resources. The 2010 nationwide recall of more than five hundred million eggs because of salmonella contamination highlights this fragmentation. Several agencies have different roles and responsibilities in the egg production system, including the Food and Drug Administration (FDA) and the U.S. Department of Agriculture's (USDA) Food Safety Inspection Service (FSIS), USDA's Agricultural Marketing Service, and USDA's Animal and Plant Health Inspection Service. Three major trends also create food safety challenges: (1) a substantial and increasing portion of the U.S. food supply is imported, (2) consumers are eating more raw and minimally processed foods, and (3) growing segments of the population are increasingly susceptible to food-borne illnesses.

New food safety legislation—the FDA Food Safety Modernization Act (FSMA), which was signed into law in January 2011—strengthens a major part of the food safety system. It shifts the focus of FDA regulators from responding to contamination to preventing it, according to FDA, and expands FDA's oversight authority. Although FSMA has several provisions that require interagency collaboration on food safety oversight, the provisions do not apply to the federal food safety system as a whole or address USDA's authorities, which remain separate and distinct from FDA's. What's more, because FSMA is not yet fully implemented and a number of the regulations required under the law are still under development or review, it is too early to understand in depth the impact of the law on federal oversight of food safety.

• *Restructuring the U.S. Postal Service to Achieve Sustainable Financial Viability.* Amid challenging economic conditions, a changing business environment, and declining mail volumes, the U.S. Postal Service (USPS) is facing a deteriorating financial situation in which it does not have sufficient revenues to cover its expenses and financial obligations. Mail volume has declined from 213 billion pieces in fiscal year 2006 to about 160 billion pieces in fiscal year 2012. USPS has projected that volume will decline to about 144 billion pieces by 2016. Further, volume for first-class mail, USPS's most profitable product, has declined by 30 percent since 2006, and USPS has projected that it will decline by another 23 percent by 2016. This trend exposes weaknesses in USPS's business model, which has relied on mail volume growth to help cover USPS expenses. USPS actions to improve its financial condition have been limited in part by legal requirements, such as those related to changing the frequency of mail delivery and closing unneeded facilities. Unless USPS can move more aggressively to reduce the gap between its costs and revenues, its financial losses will continue to grow as its viability becomes more difficult to manage. In July 2009, GAO added USPS's financial condition to the list of high-risk areas needing attention by Congress and the executive branch to achieve broad-based restructuring.

The source of risk can originate from several places. The RIMS "Recent Risk Events" for 2013 is an example of the variety of risk that can arise and the impact the risk can have.

---

## RECENT RISK EVENTS

*Source:* Reprinted with permission from Risk Management Society (RIMS) 2013.

**Horse meat Discovered in UK Beef.** The Food Safety Authority of Ireland revealed that horse meat was found in frozen hamburgers for sale at several British and Irish supermarkets. Burgers sold at the Tesco chain, in particular, were found to contain as much as 29 percent horse meat. The contamination was traced to multiple U.K. suppliers and millions of burgers were recalled. Swedish furniture maker IKEA also issued a recall when horsemeat was detected in its signature meatballs, while Burger King shifted its U.K. restaurants to German and Italian beef suppliers. The incident underscored the major safety issues and extensive reach of the global food supply chain.

**New Rule Strengthens Mine Safety.** In response to disasters like the Upper Big Branch Mine explosion that killed 29 workers in 2010, the U.S. Department of Labor issued a new rule requiring mine operators to monitor and address safety problems. The rule gives the Mine Safety and Health Administration more authority to issue "pattern of violations" notices to identify mines that repeatedly fail safety requirements and force them to correct problems before workers are allowed to return to the work site.

**Brazil Nightclub Fire Kills 242.** At least 242 people were killed and 168 injured when a fire raged through the Kiss nightclub in Santa Maria, Brazil. An illegal outdoor flare from the band's pyrotechnic display sparked the blaze by igniting acoustic foam on the venue's ceiling. The subsequent investigation revealed that a main contributor to the death toll was that the club was well over capacity and did not have enough emergency exits. The tragedy prompted officials to conduct safety inspections of nightclubs throughout the country.

**The Cruise from Carnival.** After a fire in the engine room disabled the Carnival *Triumph* cruise ship, more than 4,200 passengers and crew were left adrift without power in the Gulf of Mexico. Conditions reportedly deteriorated quickly as food supplies ran low and toilets backed up into cabins, forcing passengers to sleep in hallways and makeshift tent cities on deck. The ship was finally towed to port in Mobile, Ala. Passengers were offered full refunds, free cruises and $500 compensation for the ordeal.

**Meteor Explodes Over Russia.** A meteor measuring 60 feet in diameter exploded in the sky 15 miles over Chelyabinsk, Russia, with a force 30 times greater than that of the atomic bomb dropped on Hiroshima. The resulting shock wave damaged thousands of buildings and shattered windows, injuring 1,500 people, largely from falling glass. Later that day, a 150-foot asteroid passed within 17,500 miles of the earth—closer than some weather and communications satellites. It was the closest approach ever observed for an object of that size.

**Sinkhole Swallows Florida Man.** In a sudden and unexpected tragedy, a sinkhole opened up under the Tampa-area home of Jeff Bush and swallowed him. His body was never recovered. Sinkholes are a common risk in Florida and are formed when water seeps into limestone bedrock and creates cavities that cause the ground to collapse without warning. Another 60-foot-wide sinkhole caused a three-story resort building in central Florida to collapse. Fortunately, no one was hurt.

**Data Breach Exposes 50 Million Accounts.** Web-based note-taking service Evernote was forced to reset 50 million passwords after hackers accessed its database. The daily deal website Living Social also had to improve password encryption measures when hackers exposed the records of 50 million users. In another incident, Adobe initially reported a breach exposing 2.9 million customer accounts that they later found had compromised more than 38 million. Facebook, Advocate Medical Group, the Washington State Administrative Office of the Courts and St. Louis-based grocery store chain Schnucks also experienced data breaches that each exposed at least one million accounts. The Identity Theft Resource Center had identified nearly 500 separate data breaches in 2013.

**New Avian Flu Threatens Humans.** Pandemic fears reignited when health officials in China and Hong Kong notified the World Health Organization that a new strain of bird flu, identified as H7N9, was found in humans. More than 130 human infections and 45 deaths have been reported. Theoretically, when any animal-based virus develops the ability to infect people, the risk of a pandemic increases, but there has been no evidence of sustainable human-to-human transmission thus far.

**Massive Explosion Levels Fertilizer Plant.** A fire at the West Fertilizer Company in West, Texas, triggered an ammonium nitrate explosion that killed 15 people and injured more than 160. At least 150 homes and buildings in the surrounding area were damaged or destroyed, including a nursing home, apartment complex and school. The explosion was so powerful that it registered as a 2.1 magnitude earthquake, according to U.S. Geological Survey readings. Despite property damage costs estimated at up to $100 million, the plant only carried $1 million in liability insurance. OSHA ultimately cited the plant for 24 safety violations, including improper handling of volatile chemicals and insufficient fire prevention measures.

**Bangladesh Building Collapse Kills 1,100.** Questions about corporate social responsibility arose after the collapse of Rana Plaza, an eight-story building in Savar, Bangladesh, that housed garment factories manufacturing clothing for a number of international retailers. More than 1,100 people were killed and 2,500 injured in what is considered the worst garment factory disaster in history. Critics cited unsafe working conditions, especially after reports surfaced that personnel were forced back to work even after complaining of cracks in the building's concrete the day before the collapse. Public outcry urged companies to take a more active role in championing worker safety among their suppliers.

**Tornadoes Tear Through the Midwest.** A devastating series of tornadoes caused nearly $5 billion in damages in the Midwestern United States. An EF5 tornado that touched down in Moore, Okla., on May 20 caused $2 billion in damage alone, killed 23 people and destroyed 1,100 homes. Another EF5 tornado struck Oklahoma, this time near El Reno. Although it was the widest tornado ever recorded—2.6 miles across—its position over largely open terrain resulted in a fraction of the damage suffered in Moore.

**Vermont Fights Patent Trolls.** Vermont became the first state to pass legislation allowing companies to take action against patent trolls—nonpracticing entities that do not create products, but hold patents in order to charge licensing fees or sue other companies for infringement. Vermont's law lets businesses sue patent trolls that have victimized them with bad faith infringement claims. Losing defendants would pay the victim's court costs and up to $150,000 in damages.

**Washington Bridge Collapses.** A 160-foot span of the Interstate 5 Skagit River Bridge in Mount Vernon, Wash., collapsed after a truck carrying an oversize load struck a support truss. The bridge carried more than 70,000 vehicles a day and was part of the main highway route between Seattle and Vancouver. Although an $18 million temporary span was installed to restore traffic flow, the bridge remains one of an estimated 18,000 "fracture critical" bridges in the United States that the Federal Highway Administration says are in danger of collapse if even a single part fails.

**Canada's Costliest Natural Disaster.** The Canadian province of Alberta experienced the worst floods in its history after heavy rains caused widespread river flooding. Four people died and 100,000 were forced to evacuate, including 75,000 in Calgary alone. Total damages are estimated at up to $6 billion, with insured damages exceeding $1.7 billion, according to the Insurance Bureau of Canada, making it the costliest natural disaster in Canadian history. Officials have proposed an $830 million flood mitigation plan that includes building berms and diversion channels to help prevent future disasters.

**Paula Deen Fired from Food Network.** After celebrity chef Paula Deen admitted in a deposition for a discrimination lawsuit that she had used racial slurs, the Food Network cancelled her popular television show and announced it would not renew her contract. At least 11 other companies, including Target, Sears and Walmart, followed suit and severed ties with Deen. Ballantine Books cancelled publication of her latest cookbook, even though advance sales had already made it number one on Amazon's best-seller list. The controversy may have cost Deen more than $12 million in annual revenue, illustrating the hefty price tag that can come with a damaged reputation.

**Firefighters in Arizona Wildfire.** Nineteen members of the elite Granite Mountain Hotshots firefighting team were overrun and killed by flames while attempting to extinguish a wildfire in Yarnell Hill, Ariz. It was the sixth-deadliest firefighter incident in U.S. history and the largest number of firefighters killed in a wildfire since 1933. Overall, drought conditions and high temperatures made an active year for wildfires in the United States. In Colorado, insured losses from the Black Forest Fire alone were expected to total nearly $300 million, and in California, the Rim Fire burned for two months, scorching more than 250,000 acres.

**Asiana Flight 214 Crashes.** Asiana Airlines Flight 214 crashed just short of the runway while attempting to land at San Francisco International Airport. Of the 307 passengers on board, three died in the accident, including one who was killed on the tarmac after being struck by an emergency vehicle. It was the first fatal accident involving a Boeing 777 and the first fatal airline crash in the United States since 2009. Although the cause of the accident is still under investigation, the South Korean airline announced plans to improve its pilot training program to address technical skills, crew communication, fatigue risk, and safety protocols.

**Detroit Files for Bankruptcy.** In the largest municipal bankruptcy in U.S. history, the city of Detroit filed for Chapter 9 protection after incurring long-term debt estimated to be between $18 billion and $20 billion. Many factors contributed to the city's decline, including the struggling U.S. auto industry and a shrinking tax revenue base—the city's population has dropped from 1.8 million to about 700,000 since 1950. Thousands of commercial and residential buildings were abandoned and fell into disrepair, while unemployment and crime rates spiked. Many businesses continue to support the city, however, and the Obama administration pledged millions to help revitalization efforts.

**Train Derailment.** While traveling from Madrid to Ferrol in northern Spain, a high-speed passenger train jumped its track, killing 79 people and injuring 140. The train was traveling at 95 miles per hour—twice the posted speed limit—when it derailed on a curve outside the Santiago de Compostela train station. The conductor reportedly was using his cell phone at the time of the accident and has been charged with 79 counts of "homicide by professional recklessness." It was the second major train accident that month. On July 6, a runaway train carrying crude oil derailed and exploded in the small Canadian town of Lac-Mégantic, Quebec, killing 42 and destroying 30 buildings.

**Largest-Ever Hacking Scheme Busted.** Four Russian citizens and one Ukrainian were charged in a massive hacking and data breach scheme that exposed 160 million credit and debit card accounts and lost hundreds of millions of dollars. According to the Justice Department, it is the largest hacking case ever prosecuted. For the seven years from 2005 to 2012, the hackers stole personal information from the computer networks of retail and financial institutions, including NASDAQ, 7-Eleven, J.C. Penney, JetBlue, Dow Jones and credit card processor Heartland Payment Systems. The data was sold in bulk for $10 to $50 per credit card number to resellers who would then create phony cards for purchases or bank withdrawals.

**MTA Obtains $200 Million Cat Bond.** New York's Metropolitan Transportation Authority had to turn to the catastrophe bond market after its insurance rates skyrocketed in the wake of Superstorm Sandy, which caused nearly $4.8 billion in damages to the city's transit system. The three-year, $200 million cat bond is a first for the MTA, and is designed to protect against future storm surge losses. As of November, overall cat bond issuance for the year exceeded $6.4 billion, according to industry analyst Artemis—a sum greater than for all of 2012 and on pace to match or even surpass the record cat bond sales of 2007.

**British Banks Pay $2 Billion in Identity Theft Insurance Scandal.** Thirteen U.K. banks, including Barclays, Lloyd's Banking Group, HSBC, Royal Bank of Scotland, Santander and MBNA, will pay £1.2 billion ($2 billion) to customers who were sold unnecessary and misleading credit card and identity theft protection insurance. The banks overstated the risks posed by identity theft and neglected to tell customers that they were already covered for losses by bank policy. This comes after British banks had to set aside £15 billion ($24 billion) last year for wrongfully selling customers payment protection insurance.

**NFL Reaches Concussion Settlement.** The National Football League and more than 4,500 retired players agreed to a $765 million settlement to resolve lawsuits over the league's role in concealing long-term effects of concussions. As part of the agreement, the NFL will fund medical exams, concussion-related compensation and medical research. Former players with disorders including ALS, Alzheimer's disease, Parkinson's disease and dementia could each be compensated up to $5 million on a sliding scale, depending on the severity of their condition. This has not put an end to the NFL's concussion issues, however. In September, another group of players filed a new lawsuit against the league and helmet maker Riddell for allegedly hiding the dangers of head injuries.

**Unprecedented Rainfall Floods Colorado.** Record rainfall led to widespread flooding throughout the state of Colorado. Boulder County alone received more rain in five days than it typically does in an entire year. Floodwaters killed at least eight people, damaged and destroyed thousands of homes and spread across more than 2,000 square miles. Miles of roads and bridges were washed out, and multiple oil and gas spills from damaged storage tanks and flooded wells dotted the state. Early estimates from catastrophe modeling firm EQECAT placed damages at more than $2 billion. The losses are largely uninsured, however, as residents in the area do not usually purchase flood insurance.

**Molasses Spill Kills Thousands of Fish.** A 1,400-ton, 233,000-gallon molasses spill was discovered in Hawaii's Honolulu Harbor and the nearby Keehi Lagoon after an underwater pipe burst while pumping the sugary substance into cargo ships bound for California. The spill led to the death of more than 26,000 fish and marine animals. Although molasses is an unregulated product, shipping company Matson Navigation took responsibility for the accident, and state officials indicated they will require companies in the harbor to conduct pipeline inspections and develop spill response plans for all products.

**Fire Destroys Jersey Shore Boardwalk.** Almost a year after Superstorm Sandy, a massive fire burned a six-block section of boardwalk in New Jersey's Seaside Park and Seaside Heights. More than 50 businesses were destroyed. The boardwalk had recently been rebuilt after Sandy caused $8 million worth of damage. Fire officials blamed the blaze on faulty electrical wiring below the boardwalk that was likely damaged by saltwater and sand during Sandy's storm surge.

**Oil Spill Discovered in North Dakota.** A North Dakota farmer discovered one of the largest inland oil spills in U.S. history when he came across a six-inch-high spurt of oil in his wheat field. The 20,600-barrel leak of crude oil was the result of a ruptured pipeline owned by Tesoro Logistics. The company estimated that cleanup and remediation will cost about $4 million. The spill raised concerns about the effectiveness of pipeline regulations, detection standards and public notification practices.

**European Hail, Floods Cost Insurers Nearly $10 Billion.** Insurance broker Willis estimates insured losses from a series of hail storms that struck France and Germany this summer will cost as much as $4.7 billion. Many areas were hit with tennis ball–sized hail, causing extensive damage to houses and vehicles. In May and June, torrential rains caused flooding in Germany, Austria, the Czech Republic and other Central European countries, causing $16 billion in overall losses and $4 billion in insured losses, according to Munich Re.

**Salmonella Outbreak Sickens Hundreds.** The U.S. Department of Agriculture issued a public health alert warning consumers when an outbreak of a virulent strain of salmonella was traced to raw chicken from Foster Farms in California. By the end of October, more than 360 people in 21 states had been infected with the antibiotic-resistant Salmonella Heidelberg bacteria. Although no deaths were reported, almost 40 percent of those infected needed hospitalization. The USDA stopped short of closing the Foster Farms facilities or demanding a recall, but wholesaler Costco recalled more than 23,000 rotisserie chickens due to possible contamination with the same salmonella strain.

**Earthquake Kills 200 in the Philippines.** A 7.2 magnitude earthquake struck the province of Bohol in the Philippines, killing at least 222 people, forcing evacuation of nearly 370,000 and affecting more than 3.2 million. According to the National Disaster Risk Reduction and Management Council, the quake damaged or destroyed more than 66,000 homes and a number of historic churches and caused 2.26 billion pesos ($52 million) in damage to roads, bridges, schools, hospitals and other public buildings. Ground ruptures also caused the formation of a rock wall, 10 feet high in places, stretching for miles across the island.

**Typhoon Wipha Strikes Japan.** At least 18 people were killed and hundreds of homes damaged after Typhoon Wipha triggered mud slides on the Japanese island of Izu Oshima, about 75 miles south of Tokyo. The storm dumped more than 30 inches of rain on the island in 24 hours. Although it missed the beleaguered Fukushima Daiichi nuclear plant, heavy rain caused contaminated water tanks to overflow, increasing area radiation levels.

**JPMorgan Chase Settles Mortgage Case for $13 Billion.** JPMorgan Chase reached a tentative $13 billion settlement with the Justice Department over its questionable mortgage practices prior to the 2008 financial crisis. The deal includes a $5.1 billion payment to the Federal Housing Finance Agency to settle accusations of misleading Fannie Mae and Freddie Mac about the quality of its residential mortgages. Other terms of the settlement remained uncertain, however, as the bank and government argued over specific loss payments and whether JPMorgan could still face criminal prosecution. Since 2010, JPMorgan, Bank of America, Citigroup, Wells Fargo, Goldman Sachs and Morgan Stanley have paid $65 billion in fines and settlements related to the financial crisis, according to analyst SNL Financial—a number that could reach up to $100 billion as additional settlement agreements are reached.

## chapter ONE

# Why Enterprise Risk Management?

The U.S. government has a long history of adapting and adopting successful and prudent business practices from the private sector. In the arena of financial management, this is perhaps best illustrated by the adoption of the Chief Financial Officers Act of 1990, with its requirement that federal agencies pass financial audits.[1] The adoption of enterprise risk management (ERM) is no exception. Although risk management has long been a priority for many organizations, the private sector financial collapse of 2008–2009 has put a spotlight on enterprise risk management as a critical component of an organization's overall health and long-term sustainability.[2]

There is no one set definition of ERM that all organizations abide by. Several organizations, however, have taken the liberty of defining ERM based on their organizational or industry perspectives. Although the definitions vary, they do have some common themes. Each agency should determine which definition fits their organization, in whole or in part.

According to the Committee of Sponsoring Organizations (COSO), ERM is defined as "a process, effected by the entity's board of directors, management and other personnel, applied in a strategy setting and across the enterprise, designed to identify potential events that may affect the entity, and manage risk to be within its risk appetite, to provide reasonable assurance regarding the achievement of objectives."[3]

Embedded in this definition are seven fundamental concepts, which assert that ERM is:

- A process, ongoing and flowing through an entity
- Effected by people at every level of an organization

- Applied in a strategy setting
- Applied across the enterprise, at every level and unit, and includes taking an entity-level portfolio view of risk
- Designed to identify potential events that, if they occur, will affect the entity, and to manage risk within its risk appetite
- Able to provide reasonable assurance to an entity's management and board of directors
- Geared to achievement of objectives in one or more separate but overlapping categories[4]

The Institute of Internal Auditors (IIA) defines ERM as "a structured, consistent and continuous process across the whole organization for identifying, assessing, deciding on responses to and reporting on opportunities and threats that affect the achievement of its objectives."[5]

The Risk & Insurance Management Society (RIMS) defines ERM as "a strategic business discipline that supports the achievement of an organization's objectives by addressing the full spectrum of its risks and managing the combined impact of those risks as an interrelated risk portfolio."[6]

When put into context, the general idea is well put by Pickett: "ERM is a process that works well at all levels in an organization and brings together the business, back office, and top strategic layers in an integrated manner. By definition, a process is immersed in the business and does not sit outside of the real work. ERM is not about setting up a new team to do ERM. It is about getting a process that feeds into the main business lines to add value and make a meaningful contribution to the bottom line."[7]

Furthermore, ERM is an initiative that is championed by the highest level of management and driven down from there into the organization. ERM promulgates that "if risk is built into the equation when setting strategy for the entire business, then risk management can become a holistic process that starts at the top and filters its way down through the enterprise."[8]

In response to the public's demand for change, government managers as well as those in the private sector are looking for ways to weave risk management strategies and tactics into their everyday operations and strategic decisions at the highest level. Federal agencies are now beginning to recognize the need to weigh the probabilities of what could go wrong before it happens, the upside of doing a cost-benefit analysis for mitigating or accepting a risk, and the advantages of discussing, evaluating, and feeding risk into an agency's strategic plan and budget regardless of the mission. ERM is fast becoming an important activity for many agencies to undertake as a solution for bringing together various agency risk activities.

Although traditional risk management has its merits, it is often still carried out in silos and stovepipes within organizations, leaving the "white spaces" between organizational functions open for interpreting the crosscutting impact of risk. ERM challenges the status quo and requires managers and leaders to step out of their organizational comfort zones and into a collaborative environment to not only discuss common risks but uncover latent risks as well. As part of ERM, the white spaces also indicate that there is room to discuss risks that do not necessarily fit into one particular functional area, but it requires perspective from every function to properly address an enterprise-wide issue that could impact the organization's mission and strategic objectives.

## STATUS OF ERM IN THE GOVERNMENT

ERM is in its infancy in the U.S. government. Other governments, such as that of Canada, have long established a national policy for ERM; in the case of Canada, nearly a decade ago. Canada's Integrated Risk Management Framework aims to protect the public interest and maintain public trust. The Canadian framework is part of its larger objective to modernize management practices in order to make the government more citizen-focused and able to meet the changing needs and priorities of its community.[9]

Despite this level of ongoing risk management activity throughout the government, there has been increasing pressure on the government to do a better job at managing risks. Robert Charette, a risk management expert and founder of the ITABHI Corporation, which specializes in organizational risk management issues, writes: "Recent events, like [Hurricane Sandy] and the subprime mortgage financial meltdown, have Americans looking to their government to ensure that these catastrophes are reduced in the future. Furthermore, the public not only demands that government manages the consequences of risk, but that it deals with problems before they turn into catastrophes. Merely reacting to risk is eroding the people's trust in government."[10]

To address this issue, agencies are looking to enhance their management practices and have shown an increased interest in enterprise risk management.

For example, in 2009, for the first time in its seventy-five-year history, the Federal Housing Administration (FHA) hired its first chief risk officer. The initial focus of the chief risk officer was to be the oversight and the coordination of FHA's efforts to concentrate risk management in a single division devoted solely to managing and mitigating risk to the FHA's insurance fund—across all FHA programs.

In addition to adding a chief risk officer, the FHA proposed specific credit policy changes that are largely focused on ensuring responsible lending and risk management for FHA-approved lenders. These changes build on lessons learned in the credit crisis and seek to align the FHA with the administration's goal of regulatory reform. As the FHA's stable of lenders grows, these lenders must have "skin in the game." These credit changes will do that by ensuring they have long-term interest in the performance of the loans they originate.[11]

According to former FHA Commissioner David H. Stevens, "given the size and scope of the FHA and its importance to today's market, these risk management and credit policy changes are important steps in strengthening the FHA fund, by ensuring that lenders have proper and sufficient protections."[12] Both changes are expected to strengthen the agency's reserves and management of risk.

## LIMITATIONS TO ERM

ERM, if done effectively, has the potential to bring the white spaces and current risk activities being undertaken within each silo together in a process that will benefit the organization as a whole and raise the discipline in the organization to a more strategic level. However, there are limitations. Despite concerted efforts to nail down clear and concise definitions, ERM "limitations [will] result from the realities that human judgment in decision making can be faulty, decisions on responding to risk and establishing controls need to consider the relative costs and benefits, breakdowns can occur because of human failures, controls can be circumvented . . . and management has the ability to override enterprise risk management decisions." Furthermore, "these limitations preclude a board and management from having absolute assurance as to achievement of the entity's objectives."[13]

However, there are instances in which ERM can and does help companies perform better. In an ERM study on company performance and risk, it was found that organizations that have embraced ERM have realized a concrete advantage in their risk management competency. The study also found that 93 percent of organizations with formalized ERM programs in place make better risk-informed decisions—a recognized competitive advantage over those that do not have an ERM program.[14] The state of Washington provides an example of how to establish one.

## STATE OF WASHINGTON: 7 STEPS TO ERM

*Source:* State of Washington. Reproduced with permission.

There are many ways to successfully do an ERM process. The 7-Step method is simple, quick and easy to use while incorporating all ERM fundamental principles.

1. State the goal

2. List everything that could keep you from meeting the goal (the risks)

3. Evaluate each risk:
   - Choose a likelihood rating from 1–5
   - Choose an impact rating from 1–5
   - Multiply together and map

4. Prioritize:
   - Use your risk map to identify the most severe risks
   - Decide which risks to concentrate your efforts on (for your designated time period and time, and staff and money resources)

5. Treat/mitigate:
   - Avoid
   - Accept and monitor
   - Transfer
   - Reduce the likelihood
   - Reduce the impact

6. Make a risk register that includes:

   - Treatment plans
   - Measures of success

7. Communicate results:

   - Gather and share best practices
   - Review and refine
   - State your goal in positive terms

People often miss the "not" in a [negatively worded] statement and develop the opposite understanding. If your goal is positively stated, it will be easier to talk about the barriers to not achieving it than to list everything that could prevent you from not doing something.

Be specific and precise in stating your goal so that everyone understands what is being discussed. Whenever possible, make your goal about operational details that people can discuss. Before you begin to gather risks, make sure participants are satisfied with the goal statement, and if it doesn't work, change it.

Programs, people and conditions change. Set a realistic deadline for how long it should take to accomplish your goal. Whenever possible, include everyone who is involved in meeting the goal when you generate the list of risks. These are the people who know what might go wrong.

## RISK MANAGEMENT: WHAT IT IS AND WHY IT MATTERS

Before risk management can evolve into the practice of *enterprise* risk management, the basic fundamentals of managing risk must be well understood and a part of the learning foundation in an agency. This usually starts with establishing a common understanding and definition of risk for the organization. It also involves taking into account the organization's external and internal environmental factors, mission, and strategic objectives, all of which will influence the successful design, implementation, sustainability, and value of ERM for the organization in the long term.

From a broader contextual perspective, those who seek to integrate risk management into their organizational culture and processes must understand the contrasts between the private and public sector. Managing risk is essential for any organization, but in the private sector risk management is a widely accepted practice designed to control risks that could lead to a business failure if not properly managed. Therefore, profit maximization is the intended result. However, the application of risk management is not as straightforward in the public sector. Government managers must manage risk in a complex environment, taking into consideration the diverse missions and multiple objectives of public agencies. Rather than seeking to realize the greatest profit, government leaders must strive to manage risk so that it increases the likelihood of an agency achieving its primary mission and strategic objectives.[15]

## WHAT IS RISK?

Risk is unavoidable. It transcends virtually every human situation and is present in our daily lives and in public and private sector organizations. Although there are many acceptable definitions of risk in use across various industries and organizations, the most common concept in all definitions is the uncertainty of outcomes.[16] (See Table 1.1.)

The various definitions of risk also depend on how outcomes are characterized. For some organizations, risk has been associated only with adverse consequences without taking into consideration the upside (or opportunities) inherent in risk. Yet there continues to be a debate and discussion on what would be an acceptable generic definition of risk that captures both the associated consequences and opportunities. In addition to consequences, one school of thought asserts that, when assessed and managed properly, risk can also lead to innovation. A perspective that supports this notion is the significant role that the federal government's performance improvement officer (PIO) can play in managing risk opportunity. The PIO position was established under an executive order issued by President George W. Bush in 2007, continued under the Obama administration, and then made permanent when the Government Performance and Results Modernization Act passed in 2010.

**Table 1.1**
**Definition of Risk**

| | Risk | Risk Management | Source |
|---|---|---|---|
| Public Service of Canada | "Risk refers to the uncertainty that surrounds future events and outcomes. It is the expression of the likelihood and impact of an event with the potential to influence the achievement of an organization's objectives." | "... a systematic approach to setting the best course of action under uncertainty by identifying, assessing, understanding, acting on and communicating risk issues." | Integrated Risk Management Framework, Treasury Board of Canada Secretariat, April 2001 |
| U.S. Government Accountability Office (GAO) | "An event that has a potentially negative impact and the possibility that such an event will occur and adversely affect an entity's assets, activities, and operations." | "The continuous process of assessing risks, reducing the potential that an adverse event will occur, and putting steps in place to deal with any event that does occur. Risk management involves a continuous process of managing—through a series of mitigating actions that permeate an entity's activities—the likelihood of an adverse event and its negative impact. Risk management addresses risk before mitigating an action, as well as the risk that remains after countermeasures have been taken." | Government Accountability Office, Report # GAO-06-91, December 2005 |
| ISO 31000 | "The effect of uncertainty on objectives" | "Coordinated activities to direct and control an organization with regard to risk" | ANSI/ASSE Z690.2–2011 Risk Management Principles and Guidelines |

As a key executive, and possibly working with an agency's chief risk officer (CRO), the PIO is responsible for streamlining government processes, cutting program costs, and finding best practices that can lead to more effective management of resources. A stated goal of the Obama administration has been to eliminate dozens of government programs shown to be wasteful or ineffective. Some experts have noted that, if approached appropriately, the PIO can capitalize on risk opportunities by identifying those programs that "manage people's risks the best," saving taxpayers millions of dollars.[17] A "success indicator for government programs could be how well they spread, shift and/or reduce public risk as defined by the agency's mission statement. Another measure could include whether the benefits of mitigating the risk outweigh the program's cost," according to Robert Charette. He notes that "in addition, if a program is to be closed down because it doesn't work, the [PIO] could reason that the government was mismanaging the public's risk or that the agency wasn't equipped to oversee the risk in the first place."

Responses to the 2014 ERM Core Competency Survey for public sector risk professionals showed a diverse understanding of risk as well. Nearly 33 percent of the 103 respondents agreed that risk is the "effect of uncertainty on objectives," while 32 percent agreed that risk is a "combination of the probability of an event and its consequence." No respondents viewed risk as an "opportunity to make a profit or increase revenue."

Whether risk represents adversity or opportunity, the bottom line is that there is currently no standard definition of risk being used in the U.S. federal government. Some experts argue that leading risk management begins with establishing a common definition of key risk concepts so that risk management approaches are implemented consistently across an enterprise.

According to Mark Beasley, Deloitte chair and director of North Carolina State University's Center for Enterprise Risk Management, "Providing clear definitions of risk terms (including discussion of whether 'risk' represents both risk opportunities and risk threats) is often the required first step in establishing an enterprise risk management (ERM) process."[18]

In contrast, the Public Service in Canada has gained consensus on a definition of risk as a part of its Integrated Risk Management Framework. Issued in 2001, the framework is a practical guide to assist Canadian public service employees in their decision-making processes.[19] At the organizational level, it helps departments and agencies to think more strategically and improve their ability to set common priorities. At the individual level, it helps all employees to develop new skills and strengthens their ability to anticipate, assess, and manage risk.

But with issuance of the new International Risk Management Standard (known as ISO 31000), this dilemma that the government faces may be resolved. Issued in 2009 by the International Standards Organization (ISO) and adopted by the United States through the American National Standards Institute (ANSI), ISO 31000 is considered a landmark achievement for moving the practice of risk management forward globally. ISO 31000 signified the universal effort to establish an acceptable and common understanding of risk across all sectors and types of organizations. Although the implications of having a universal approach and definition of risk have yet to be determined, there is great optimism that ISO 31000 will be the standard of choice in an area that has many perspectives to consider.

## EVOLUTION OF RISK MANAGEMENT

Effective risk management cannot be practiced in isolation, but needs to be built into existing decision-making structures and processes.[20] In the past, risk management was seen as relating mainly to matters of safety and insurance. Over time, the nature of this systematic approach has evolved, from transactional and functional to strategic.[21]

Previous practices viewed risks as threats and focused on avoidance of negative events, treated risk as a separate function, and continuously managed risk independently within silos. Gradually, organizations began to integrate risk by accepting risk as an expense, shifting their focus to managing risk, and recognizing risk managers as risk owners. Strategically, companies are now working toward a broader view of risk, understanding that risk is an uncertainty, shifting the focus to optimizing risk, and advocating risk managers as risk facilitators and leaders.

Building on the evolution of risk management (see Figure 1.1), ERM recognizes that risks can be threats and opportunities and that they are a corporate-wide daily concern that is embedded in the operations. ERM transforms risk management from a silo approach to a holistic approach, which is coordinated at the highest level in the organization and recognizes the value of tangible and intangible assets. Historically, organizations focused on hazard risk management

## Figure 1.1
## Evolution of Risk Management

| FROM TRANSACTIONAL TO . . . | INTEGRATED TO . . . | STRATEGIC |
|---|---|---|
| **Traditional Risk Management** | **Advanced Risk Management** | **Enterprise-wide Risk Management** |
| • Purchase insurance to cover risks | • Greater use of alternative risk financing techniques | • A wide range of risks are discussed and reviewed, including reputational, human capital, strategic, and operational |
| • Hazard-based risk identification and controls | • More proactive about preventing and reducing risks | |
| • Compliance issues addressed separately | • Integrates claims management, contracts review, special event RM, insurance and risk transfer techniques | • Aligns RM process with strategy and mission |
| • Safety and emergency management handled separately | | • May include "upside risks" (opportunities) |
| • "Silo" approach—risk management is not integrated across the organization | • Cost allocation used for education and accountability | • Helps manage growth, allocate capital and resources |
| • Risk Manager is the insurance buyer | • More collaboration— as departments are willing | • Risks are owned by all and mitigated at the department level |
| | • Risk Manager may be the risk owner | • Many risk mitigation and analytical tools available |
| | | • Risk Manager is the risk facilitator and leader |

*Source:* Arthur J. Gallagher, n.d.

and insurable financial risks. Today, the practice is much more encompassing, covering operational, strategic, financial, and reputation risks.

## TRADITIONAL RISK MANAGEMENT VERSUS ENTERPRISE RISK MANAGEMENT

Most organizations manage risk to some extent. The traditional approach to managing risk focuses on those risks specific to a specific function or job at the organization or individual level. ERM challenges the notion that the best way to manage risks in an organization is through this silo-allocated, fragmented approach, with risk management not integrated across the organization. But at even a level below that concept, organizations must first learn to view risk from a crosscutting perspective internally before it can evolve into a more mature ERM approach.

An organization is unlikely to launch ERM fully without first ensuring that the foundation for basic risk management practice is in place. This means that whether in a single organizational function or a division, employees must be exposed to the basic tenets of risk management from their position in the organization. When employees understand what risk is to them, based first on their specific tasks, they are more likely to understand their contributions to the overall ERM schema that the organization will eventually offer. ERM implementers should take every opportunity to educate employees about risk management from the viewpoint of their current understanding and expand that knowledge through consistent steps of applying risk techniques and tools.

A description of a set of potential risks employees in specific federal government job series are likely to encounter in their work is detailed in Table 1.2. Identification of specific risks to an individual's work makes risk management more relevant, thus serving as a grassroots technique for maturing ERM practice throughout the organization.

ERM provides a portfolio view of risk, assessing risk impact and mitigation that cuts across all functions. When this ERM is conducted, organizations see a true profile of risk in relation to every type of risk, not just to a single type of risk (see Figure 1.2.).

Even though the United States does not have one central national risk management policy, agencies must comply with other policies that require that risk be taken into consideration (see Table 1.3). One such policy is the Federal Manager's

## Table 1.2
## Selected White Collar Occupational Groups, Job Series, and Potential Risks

| Job Series | Group Title | Duties | Potential Risks |
|---|---|---|---|
| 201 | Human Resources Management | This series covers administrative positions that manage, supervise, administer, advise on, or deliver human resources management products or services. | • Extended vacancies<br>• Leadership gaps<br>• Lack of succession plans |
| 506 | Budget Analysis | This series covers positions that perform, advise on, or supervise work in any of the phases of budget administration when such work requires knowledge and skill in applying budget-related laws, regulations, policies, precedents, methods, and techniques. | • Impact of continuing resolutions on program priorities<br>• Sequestration and long-term mission activities<br>• Lack of experienced budget analysts |
| 1102 | Contracting | This series includes positions that manage, supervise, perform, or develop policies and procedures for professional work involving the procurement of items such as but not limited to supplies, services, and construction. | • Inaccurate cost estimations<br>• Lack of debarment monitoring |
| 1176 | Building Management | This series covers positions that involve management of buildings and other facilities to provide organizations with appropriate office space and essential building services. | • Square footage price escalation<br>• Unfunded building renovations<br>• Reductions in work space and staff morale |
| 505 | Financial Management | This series covers positions that manage or direct a program for management of the financial resources of an organizational segment, bureau, department, independent agency, or other organizational entity. | • Outdated systems for tracking improper payments<br>• Improper payments |

(continued)

## Table 1.2
## Selected White Collar Occupational Groups, Job Series, and Potential Risks (*Continued*)

| Job Series | Group Title | Duties | Potential Risks |
|---|---|---|---|
| 341 | Administrative Officer | This series covers positions for which the employees are responsible for providing or obtaining a variety of management services essential to the direction and operation of an organization. | • Outdated administrative policies |
| 340 | Program Management | This series covers all classes of positions with the duties to manage or direct, or to assist in a line capacity in managing or directing one or more programs, including appropriate supporting service organizations. | • Lack of clearly defined objectives<br>• Incorrect performance measures |
| 343 | Management and Program Analysis | This series covers positions that primarily serve as analysts and advisors to management on the evaluation of the effectiveness of government programs and operations or the productivity and efficiency of the management of federal agencies or both. | • Incorrect alignment of organizational structure to mission |
| 2210 | Information Technology Management | This series covers administrative positions that manage, supervise, lead, administer, develop, deliver, and support information technology (IT) systems and services. | • Outdated cyber threat software<br>• Unsecured password protections<br>• Inadequate safeguarding of mobile device data |
| 1109 | Grants Management | This series includes positions that manage, supervise, or lead grant awards, grants administration, and grants closeout. | • Duplicate funding<br>• False certifications<br>• Burn rate, drawdown spikes<br>• Late final reports |

*Source: Handbook of Occupational Groups and Families*, May 2009, Office of Personnel Management (OPM). Potential risk themes selected from random GAO .gov reports and industry-related publications.

## Figure 1.2
## Siloed and Enterprise Approach to Risk Management

| | HR Risks | IT Risks | Facility Risk | Privacy Risk | Financial Risk |
|---|---|---|---|---|---|
| Risks are viewed across all functions at the enterprise level in relationship to each other | ⟷ | ⟷ | ⟷ | ⟷ | ⟷ |
| Risks are managed in silos horizontally and vertically within the organizations | ↕ | ↕ | ↕ | ↕ | ↕ |

Financial Integrity Act (FMFIA) of 1982 and the companion guidelines set forth in OMB Circular A-123, "Management's Responsibility for Internal Controls."

## U.S. FEDERAL GOVERNMENT POLICY ON RISK MANAGEMENT

FMFIA was issued to amend the Accounting and Auditing Act of 1950 and to require ongoing evaluations and reports of the adequacy of the systems of internal accounting and administrative control of each executive agency, and for other purposes.[22] In essence, FMFIA establishes the overall requirements with regard to internal control. For instance, the agency head must establish controls that reasonably ensure that: "(i) obligations and costs are in compliance with applicable law; (ii) funds, property, and other assets are safeguarded against waste, loss, unauthorized use or misappropriation; and (iii) revenues and expenditures applicable to agency operations are properly recorded and accounted for to permit the preparation of accounts and reliable financial and statistical reports and to maintain accountability over the assets." In addition, annually the agency head must evaluate and report on the control and financial systems that protect the integrity of federal programs (Section 2 and Section 4 of FMFIA, respectively). The three objectives of internal control are to ensure the effectiveness and efficiency of operations, the reliability of financial reporting, and compliance with applicable laws and regulations. The safeguarding of assets is a subset of all of these objectives.[23]

The OMB Circular A-123 is issued under the authority of the Federal Managers' Financial Integrity Act of 1982 [as codified in 31 U.S.C. 3512]. The Circular provides guidance to federal managers on improving the accountability and effectiveness of federal programs and operations by establishing, assessing, correcting, and reporting on internal control. According to government policy: "Management is responsible for establishing and maintaining internal control to achieve the objectives of effective and efficient operations, reliable financial reporting, and compliance with applicable laws and regulations. Management shall consistently apply the internal control standards to meet each of the internal control objectives and to assess internal control effectiveness." The Circular A-123 is also prescriptive with its requirements. For instance, when agencies assess the effectiveness of internal control over financial reporting and compliance with financial-related laws and regulations, management must follow the assessment process contained in Appendix A of the Circular. In addition, on an annual basis, management must provide assurances on internal control in its Performance and Accountability Report, including a separate assurance on internal control over financial reporting, along with a report on identified material weaknesses and corrective actions."[24] Both directives require agencies to maintain robust internal control structures that ensure:

- Effective and efficient operations
- Compliance with applicable laws and regulations
- Reliable financial reporting

Despite carrying out these reporting requirements over the years, a volatile environment regarding ethical behavior and fraud in the financial community prompted a reexamination of the existing internal control requirements for federal agencies. This was initiated in light of the new internal control requirements for publicly traded companies contained in the Sarbanes-Oxley Act of 2002. For government, Circular A-123 and the FMFIA statute it implements both became the center of attention for existing federal requirements to improve internal control. Revisions to Circular A-123 in 2004 sought to (1) strengthen the requirements for conducting management's assessment of internal control over financial reporting and (2) emphasize the need for agencies to integrate and *coordinate internal control assessments with other internal control-related activities.* The latter of the two intentions was the critical shift that led to an expanded view of risk in the evaluation of internal controls.

### Table 1.3
### Policies for Managing Various Types of Risk in Government

| Policy | Description | Type of Risk |
|---|---|---|
| Federal Manager's Financial Integrity Act of 1982 (FMFIA) | An act to amend the Accounting and Auditing Act of 1950 to require ongoing evaluations and reports of the adequacy of the systems of internal accounting and administrative control of each executive agency, and for other purposes. | Heavy emphasis on financial risk area, but includes limited focus on administrative, operations, and programmatic risk |
| Federal Information Security Management Act of 2002 (FISMA) | The act requires each federal agency to develop, document, and implement an agency-wide program to provide security for the information and information systems that support the operations and assets of the agency, including those provided or managed by another agency, contractor, or other source. | Information technology risk |
| Federal Financial Management Information Act of 1998 (FFMIA) | Advances federal financial management by ensuring that federal financial management systems provide accurate, reliable, and timely financial management information to the government's managers. | Federal financial management systems risk |
| American Recovery and Reinvestment Act of 2009 (ARRA) | Law passed to stimulate the U.S. economy. | Contract and grants management risk |

## INTERNAL CONTROLS AS ONE PART OF ENTERPRISE RISK MANAGEMENT

There is some misunderstanding about the relationship between internal controls and ERM. Historically, internal controls in the federal financial management community were understood to focus on managing risks associated with financial reporting—one of the many categories in the risk universe of an agency.

The underlying design of an ERM framework not only addresses risks concerning financial reporting but also intends to identify and manage all relevant areas of risks that any given agency is faced with—not just addressing the questions of compliance with the applicable controls prescribed by legislation and regulation. The value of ERM is derived from managing risk through a collective approach that enables executives to manage risk in the context of an agency's mission, as opposed to solely focusing on an isolated piece of legislation or regulation.

Internal control guarantees neither the success of agency programs nor the absence of waste, fraud, and mismanagement, but is a means of managing the risk associated with federal programs and operations.

The theme of the 2004 revision undoubtedly elevated the importance of risk in relation to internal control, as noted in the following passage:

> Instead of considering internal control as an isolated management tool, agencies should integrate their efforts to meet the requirements of the FMFIA with other efforts to improve effectiveness and accountability. Thus, internal control should be an integral part of the entire cycle of planning, budgeting, management, accounting, and auditing. It should support the effectiveness and the integrity of every step of the process and provide continual feedback to management. *Federal managers must carefully consider the appropriate balance between controls and risk in their programs and operations.* Too many controls can result in inefficient and ineffective government; agency managers must ensure an

appropriate balance between the strength of cc
tive risk associated with particular program'
benefits of controls should outweigh the
consider both qualitative and quantitativ
costs against benefits.

Though the revisions to the Circular A.
the risk and internal control environments, gove..
struggle with the challenges of managing risk outside .
management and using the circular as a point of reference. .
ress made, Circular A-123 was still perceived as a policy written st..
financial management community. The document maintained a very pre..
tive focus on financial controls and little direction on how to apply the principles
to nonfinancial areas. With that stigma, it becomes difficult for those who oversee controls over programmatic and administrative areas to implement Circular
A123 where applicable.

By tradition, the main user of Circular A-123 in the government C-suite has
been the chief financial officer (CFO). Most CFOs focus on A-123's Appendix
A, which pertains to internal control over financial reporting. However,
financial reporting is only one of three control objectives under Section 2 of
the FMFIA. The other two are effectiveness and efficiency of operations and
compliance with applicable laws and regulations.[25] The policy requirements
and processes are very prescriptive for conducting risk assessments pertaining to internal controls over financial reporting, but they fall short in (1) out-
lining specific steps for evaluating, testing, and assessing risks associated with
administrative and federal program operations and (2) demonstrating how
risk assessment ties into the overall process for managing risk at an enterprise
level. The shortcomings have left many agencies grappling with approaches
to incorporate these administrative and programmatic requirements, but not
without hope.

In previous CFO annual surveys, some executives wanted to see Appendix A
requirements reduced or unchanged, sensing that a better return on investment
would be the rechanneling of resources to control over program and entity performance and related reporting.[26] CFOs expressed that "Complying with FMFIA
aside, sound controls on operations reduce the risk of poor performance of an

ion. That is more important than getting the financial numbers
should receive as much or more attention as controls over financial
g. It is also where CFOs can broaden their roles and increase the value
dd to an entity."[27]

esponses from previous surveys also cited that not all financial execu-
es were enthusiastic about this prospect. A few were lukewarm to the idea
of integrating internal controls within their entities, citing that they each
"own" their part of the control structure. This stovepipe mentality proved to
be a barrier to improving the integration of internal controls with an entity-
wide risk management approach. However, in a 2013 CFO Survey, a shift in
the CFO community has led to a possible New CFO Management Agenda
that aims to ensure that internal controls and risk management are everyone's
responsibility.[28]

## ESTABLISHING AN AGENCY RISK MANAGEMENT POLICY

When designing a framework for managing risk in an organization, establishing
a risk management policy is a key component that "should clearly state the organization's objective for, and commitment to risk management."[29] A risk management policy typically addresses the following:

- The organization's rationale for managing risk
- Links between the organization's objectives and policies and the risk manage-
  ment policy
- Accountabilities and responsibilities for managing risk
- The way in which conflicting interests are dealt with
- Commitment to make the necessary resources available to assist those
  accountable and responsible for managing risk
- The way in which risk management performance will be measured and
  reported
- Commitment to review and improve the risk management policy and frame-
  work periodically and in response to an event or change in circumstances

Exhibit 1.1 presents a sample Template of a General Risk Management Policy.

## Exhibit 1.1
## Template for a General Risk Management
## Policy in the United States

**[Title of Policy]**

*Background Information:*

[From ISO 31000: Include the organization's rationale for managing risk; links between the organization's objectives and policies and the risk management policy.]

Provide a short description of why risk management is important to the agency. Include the organization's philosophy toward risk management, including any principles.

AUTHORITY: What laws, regulations, or policies authorize the establishment of this policy?

REFERENCES: What other documents, policies, or regulations were referenced to develop the scope of the policy?

SCOPE:

[From ISO 31000: Include the way in which conflicting interests are dealt with.]

Who or what does this policy impact? Does it apply to an entire organization or a subsection of the organization?

POLICY STATEMENT: At a minimum, what do you want people to do? What is required?

ROLES AND RESPONSIBILITIES:

[From ISO 31000: Include accountabilities and responsibilities for managing risk; the way in which conflicting interests are dealt with; commitment to make the necessary resources available to assist those accountable and responsible for managing risk.] Are there specific roles and responsibilities that must be established to support the successful execution of the organization's ERM/risk management program/effort? Roles and responsibilities can be given to offices, boards, individuals, and so on.

TERMS AND DEFINITIONS: Explain all key terms and provide short and concise definitions.

EVALUATION:

[From ISO 31000: Include the way in which risk management performance will be measured and reported and commitment to review and improve the risk management policy and framework periodically and in response to an event or change in circumstances.]

How frequently will the program be reviewed for effectiveness and by whom?

### Table 1.4
### What Components Are in Place at Your
### Organization to Aid in ERM Implementation?

Percentages rounded. Multiple selections allowed.
$n = 103$ respondents

| Choices | Responses |
|---|---|
| Risk management policy | 73% |
| Change management plan | 17% |
| Communications plan | 38% |
| ERM strategic plan | 37% |
| Training and education plan | 46% |
| Identified governance structure | 49% |
| Written endorsements from senior management | 42% |
| Interagency collaborative work groups | 25% |
| IT and database systems; dashboards | 31% |

In a survey of 103 public sector risk professionals, the majority of respondents indicated that a risk management policy is the most common resource in place to help implement ERM.[30] Other common resources include an identified governance structure, training and education plan, and a communications plan. A *change management plan* was the least-common resource in place to aid in ERM implementation (see Table 1.4).

## ERM POLICY AND PRACTICE IN CANADA

Canada is one of forty countries that have adopted and integrated ISO 31000 into their management system. As a management philosophy, it's important for the Government of Canada "to continually improve the way it delivers services to Canadians . . . that its management regime fosters flexibility, [and] seeks opportunity and focuses on results."[31] Canada sees the awareness and application of risk management principles and practices as "integral to such a regime." Hence, the Canadian view is that "effective risk management practice equips federal government organizations [in Canada] to respond proactively to change and uncertainty by using risk-based approaches and information to enable more effective decision-making throughout an organization."[32]

Canada also boasts a comprehensive ERM approach. Referred to as "integrated risk management," it is "a continuous, proactive and systematic process to understand, manage and communicate risk from an organization-wide perspective." In the true sense of ERM, Canada's integrated risk management "is about supporting strategic decision-making that contributes to the achievement of an organization's overall objectives."[33] In terms of policy, "the Framework for the Management of Risk is a key Treasury Board policy instrument that outlines a principles-based approach to risk management for all federal organizations. The Framework reaffirms Deputy Head responsibility in the effective management of their organizations in all areas of work, including risk management and describes the expectations for an effective risk management practice. Of note, the risk management principles of the Framework also apply to all Treasury Board policies, and guide the Treasury Board Secretariat in its management, enabling and oversight roles" (see Exhibit 1.2).

---

### Exhibit 1.2
### Canada's Risk Management Framework Policy

**1. Effective Date**

The Framework for the Management of Risk (the Framework) is effective as of August 27, 2010.

The Framework will be supported by learning resources, which will replace the Treasury Board Integrated Risk Management Framework (2001) and the Integrated Risk Management Implementation Guide (2004).

**2. Context**

In a dynamic and complex public sector context, risk management plays a significant role in strengthening government capacity to recognize, understand, accommodate and capitalize on new challenges and opportunities. Effective risk management equips federal government organizations to respond actively to change and uncertainty by using risk-based information to enable more effective decision-making. In turn, increased capacity and demonstrated ability to assess, communicate and manage risk builds trust and confidence, both within the government and with the public.

*(continued)*

## Exhibit 1.2
## Canada's Risk Management Framework Policy (*Continued*)

For the Government of Canada to continually improve the way it delivers services to Canadians, it is important that its management regime foster flexibility, seek opportunity and focus on results. Integral to such a regime is effective risk management. The principles-based approach to risk management articulated in this Framework provides the flexibility to departments and agencies to tailor management solutions to their mandate and objectives. In addition, it enables strategic, risk-informed oversight and less transactional involvement of the Treasury Board and Treasury Board Secretariat in supporting department and agency management initiatives.

In order to foster this type of risk-informed culture and capacity to fully realize performance improvements within federal organizations, strengthened risk management approaches must be reflected across all business practices. Failure to effectively manage risks can result in increased program costs and missed opportunities, which can compromise program outcomes, and ultimately public trust. In contrast, sound risk management is fundamental to effective public administration as it can lead to a more effective, results-based, and high-performance government.

### 3. Linkages to Other Treasury Board Instruments

As one of the three core frameworks guiding Treasury Board policies and management instruments, the Framework for the Management of Risk provides Deputy Heads with principles to embed risk management as a critical element in all areas of work, at all levels of their organization. The risk management principles outlined in this Framework complement the conceptual model for policy renewal set out in the Foundation Framework for Treasury Board Policies as well as the considerations for managing compliance identified in the Framework for the Management of Compliance.

The Framework for the Management of Risk outlines the risk management principles to guide Deputy Heads in the effective management of their organizations in all areas of work, including policy and program implementation. These principles apply to all Treasury Board policies, including the individual policies of the renewed Treasury Board Policy Suite, and guide the Treasury Board Secretariat in its policy development, enabling and oversight roles. These three core Frameworks are put in place to enable more effective management of federal organizations by promoting accountability [and] transparency and supporting risk-informed decision making, which is recognized as a leading management practice.

Specifically, the principles contained in the Framework for the Management of Risk have shaped the design and choice of implementation approaches for particular Treasury Board policies (e.g., Policy on Internal Audit, Policy on

Internal Control, Policy on Transfer Payments, Policy on Investment Planning), and will continue to be refined and adjusted based on emerging trends and lessons learned from their implementation.

The current list of Treasury Board policies can be found on the Secretariat's web site.

## 4. Purpose

The purpose of this Framework is to provide guidance to Deputy Heads on the implementation of effective risk management practices at all levels of their organization. This will support strategic priority setting and resource allocation, informed decisions with respect to risk tolerance, and improved results.

To achieve this purpose, the Framework provides principles and guidance for Deputy Heads to consider in their role as leaders of sound risk management practices and risk management integration within their organizations. For the purposes of the Framework, departments and agencies are those defined in section 2 of the Financial Administration Act.

Effective risk management, supported by this Framework, and associated learning resources, will enable Deputy Heads to:

- Identify and explain different types of risks at all levels of their organization and how they can be managed;
- Provide guidance on setting risk tolerance levels and making decisions informed by considerations of risk and mitigation strategies, including who should be involved;
- Support learning opportunities in their organization, including informal and formal risk management practices that respond to the needs and culture of their organizations;
- Lead by example by embedding risk management principles and practices in the management of their organization; and
- Align their risk management practices with other Treasury Board management practices and policies.

## 5. Principles

The following risk management principles inform the development of, and apply to, all Treasury Board policy instruments, some of which have embedded risk management requirements specific to their policy coverage. These principles are grounded in federal public service values and ethics, and guide and underpin effective risk management across the federal government. The principles support Deputy Heads, and their departments and agencies, in taking risk-informed approaches to management decisions and in

(*continued*)

# Exhibit 1.2
## Canada's Risk Management Framework Policy (*Continued*)

demonstrating and verifying that risks are successfully identified, assessed and managed within their respective organizations.

To that end, effective risk management in the federal government should:

- Support government-wide decision making and priorities as well as the achievement of organizational objectives and outcomes, while maintaining public confidence;

- Be tailored and responsive to the organization's external and internal context, including its mandate, priorities, organizational risk culture, risk management capacity, and partner and stakeholder interests;

- Add value as a key component of decision making, business planning, resource allocation and operational management;

- Achieve a balance between the level of risk responses and established controls and support for flexibility and innovation to improve performance and outcomes;

- Be transparent, inclusive, integrated and systematic; and

- Continuously improve the culture, capacity and capability of risk management in federal organizations.

In addition, Treasury Board policy instruments and associated oversight activities are aligned with the above and also guided by the following principles:

- Treasury Board policy instruments should target risks linked to achieving federal government management objectives;

- These instruments should be proportional to the degree of impact and likelihood of the risks identified; and

- Oversight should be adjusted to correspond to an organization's demonstrated capacity for managing risk, where circumstances permit.

Learning resources to support the practical application of these principles by departments and agencies, including the 2010 Guide to Integrated Risk Management, are available on the Treasury Board Secretariat's website.

## 6. Roles and Responsibilities

### *Deputy Heads*

Deputy Heads are responsible for managing their organization's risks by leading the implementation of effective risk management practices, both formal and informal. In doing so, Deputy Heads are encouraged to apply the principles outlined above in section 5.

A key role of the Deputy Head is to ensure that risk management principles and practices are understood and integrated into the various activities of their organization. Deputy Heads are also responsible for monitoring risk management practices in their organizations, as well as considering risks that arise when partnering with organizations within and external to the federal public service. This includes ensuring that issues affecting the organization's risk management approach, whether identified through assessments or internal and external monitoring, are examined, reviewed and addressed effectively.

In addition, Deputy Heads play an important role in creating a learning environment that promotes continuous improvement in risk management competencies and capacity within their organization. Through their leadership, Deputy Heads foster a risk-informed organizational culture that supports risk-informed decision making, enables dialogue on risk tolerance, focuses on results and enables the consideration of both opportunity and innovation.

### Treasury Board and Treasury Board of Canada Secretariat (Secretariat)

A key element of the Treasury Board's role, as well as the role of its Secretariat, is to encourage management excellence in government through leadership, guidance, monitoring, review and oversight, pursuant to the authority given in the Financial Administration Act.

To fulfill this role in the domain of risk management, the Treasury Board and the Secretariat provide guidance, tools and expertise to support departments and agencies in implementing a risk-informed approach to management. This also includes performing a leadership role by sharing information and fostering good practices on risk management and risk-informed approaches.

The Secretariat also monitors and assesses departmental and agency performance on risk management through such means as the Management Accountability Framework, and reviews of internal and external audits. These assessments may be used to inform discussions between the Secretary of the Treasury Board and Deputy Heads.

Evidence that a federal department or agency has effective risk management practices in place may lead to Treasury Board and Secretariat oversight being adjusted to an organization's capacity for managing risk, where circumstances permit. Conversely, ineffective risk management may lead to additional controls and oversight. Where necessary, the Secretariat may encourage deputy heads to undertake appropriate remedial measures in support of their responsibilities for the monitoring of risk management within their organization.

## 7. Enquiries

All enquiries regarding this Framework, as well as its supporting guides and tools, should be directed to: Treasury Board and Secretariat.

*Source:* www.tbs-sct.gc.ca.

## LINKING ERM AND INTERNAL CONTROL

Like ERM, internal control is a major part of managing an organization. However, internal control is one part of ERM and is not considered a stand-alone activity. In ERM, internal controls are the mechanisms used to either mitigate or reduce risk exposures in an organization. Because ERM encompasses a broad spectrum of risk that cuts across the entire organizational landscape, it is imperative that sound internal controls are in place to further improve accountability and minimize operational problems. Technically, internal control is defined as "an integral component of an organization's management that provides reasonable assurance that the following objectives are being achieved:

- Effectiveness and efficiency of operations,
- Reliability of financial reporting, and
- Compliance with applicable laws and regulations."[34]

FMFIA requires GAO to issue standards for internal control in government. In response to this requirement, GAO issued the *Standards for Internal Control in the Federal Government*, also referred to as the "Green Book." First published in 1983 and revised in 1999, "The standards provide the overall framework for establishing and maintaining internal control and for identifying and addressing major performance and management challenges and areas at greatest risk of fraud, waste, abuse and mismanagement."[35]

When work is taking place within a control framework, the intersection of risk and internal control is likely to take place at the Risk Assessment, Control Activities, and Monitoring stages of the GAO Internal Control Framework. Likewise, internal control management is apt to intersect at the Risk Evaluation and Risk Analysis stages of the ISO 31000 Risk Management Framework. Ideally, when risks are identified, every effort should be made to pair the relating internal control with the specific risk. At a minimum, it is important to associate specific internal controls with the highest risks in an organization as a best practice. This helps to establish efficiencies for a system of managing risk and control under the umbrella of ERM. Furthermore, the value of the Green Book goes far beyond the scope of internal control. The broad themes of the major factors for each of the five standards are also useful for identifying sources of risk.

Recent changes such as advances in technology, challenges in human capital management, and requirements stemming from financial management legislation have prompted renewed focus on internal control, forging yet another case for revising the Green Book. Consequently, this revision is to take place in the following year to stay in tune with these changes.

## WHAT ARE THE STANDARDS FOR INTERNAL CONTROL?

When managing internal control as part of ERM, the following definition, objectives, and fundamental concepts provide the foundation for the internal control standards.[36]

### STANDARDS FOR INTERNAL CONTROL IN THE FEDERAL GOVERNMENT

**Definition and Objectives:**

*Internal Control:*

An integral component of an organization's management that provides reasonable assurance that the following objectives are being achieved:

- Effectiveness and efficiency of operations,

- Reliability of financial reporting, and,

- Compliance with applicable laws and regulations

Internal control is a major part of managing an organization. It comprises the plans, methods, and procedures used to meet missions, goals, and objectives and, in doing so, supports performance-based management. Internal control also serves as the first line of defense in safeguarding assets and preventing and detecting errors and fraud. In short, internal control, which is synonymous with management control, helps government program managers achieve desired results through effective stewardship of public resources.

Internal control should provide reasonable assurance that the objectives of the agency are being achieved in the following categories:

- Effectiveness and efficiency of operations, including the use of the entity's resources.

- Reliability of financial reporting, including reports on budget execution, financial statements, and other reports for internal and external use.

- Compliance with applicable laws and regulations.

A subset of these objectives is the safeguarding of assets. Internal control should be designed to provide reasonable assurance regarding prevention of or prompt detection of unauthorized acquisition, use, or disposition of an agency's assets.

**Fundamental Concepts:**

*Internal Control:*

- A continuous built-in component of operations.
- Effected by people.
- Provides reasonable assurance, not absolute assurance.

The fundamental concepts provide the underlying framework for designing and applying the standards.

**Internal Control Is a Continuous Built-in Component of Operations:**

Internal control is not one event, but a series of actions and activities that occur throughout an entity's operations and on an ongoing basis. Internal control should be recognized as an integral part of each system that management uses to regulate and guide its operations rather than as a separate system within an agency. In this sense, internal control is management control that is built into the entity as a part of its infrastructure to help managers run the entity and achieve their aims on an ongoing basis.

**Internal Control Is Effected by People:**

People are what make internal control work. The responsibility for good internal control rests with all managers. Management sets the objectives, puts the control mechanisms and activities in place, and monitors and evaluates the control. However, all personnel in the organization play important roles in making it happen.

**Internal Control Provides Reasonable Assurance, Not Absolute Assurance:**

Management should design and implement internal control based on the related costs and benefits. No matter how well designed and operated, internal control cannot provide absolute assurance that all agency objectives will be met. Factors outside the control or influence of management can affect the entity's ability to achieve all of its goals. For example, human mistakes, judgment errors, and acts of collusion to circumvent control can affect meeting agency objectives. Therefore, once in place, internal control provides reasonable, not absolute, assurance of meeting agency objectives.

**The Five Standards for Internal Control:**

1. Control Environment
2. Risk Assessment
3. Control Activities
4. Information and Communications
5. Monitoring

These standards define the minimum level of quality acceptable for internal control in government and provide the basis against which internal control is to be evaluated. These standards apply to all aspects of an agency's operations: programmatic, financial, and compliance. However, they are not intended to limit or interfere with duly granted authority related to developing legislation, rule making, or other discretionary policy making in an agency. These standards provide a general framework. In implementing these standards, management is responsible for developing the detailed policies, procedures, and practices to fit their agency's operations and to ensure that they are built into and an integral part of operations.

In the following material, each of these standards is presented in a short, concise statement. Additional information is provided to help managers incorporate the standards into their daily operations.

**Control Environment:**

Management and employees should establish and maintain an environment throughout the organization that sets a positive and supportive attitude toward internal control and conscientious management.

A positive control environment is the foundation for all other standards. It provides discipline and structure as well as the climate that influences the quality of internal control. Several key factors affect the control environment.

One factor is the integrity and ethical values maintained and demonstrated by management and staff. Agency management plays a key role in providing leadership in this area, especially in setting and maintaining the organization's ethical tone, providing guidance for proper behavior, removing temptations for unethical behavior, and providing discipline when appropriate.

Another factor is management's commitment to competence. All personnel need to possess and maintain a level of competence that allows them to accomplish their assigned duties, as well as understand the importance of developing and implementing good internal control. Management needs to identify appropriate knowledge and skills needed for various jobs and provide needed training, as well as candid and constructive counseling, and performance appraisals.

Management's philosophy and operating style also affect the environment. This factor determines the degree of risk the agency is willing to take and management's philosophy toward performance-based management. Further, the attitude and philosophy of management toward information systems, accounting, personnel functions, monitoring, and audits and evaluations can have a profound effect on internal control.

Another factor affecting the environment is the agency's organizational structure. It provides management's framework for planning, directing, and controlling operations to achieve agency objectives. A good internal control environment requires that the agency's organizational structure clearly defines key areas of authority and responsibility and establishes appropriate lines of reporting.

The environment is also affected by the manner in which the agency delegates authority and responsibility throughout the organization. This delegation covers authority and responsibility for operating activities, reporting relationships, and authorization protocols. Good human capital policies and practices are another critical environmental factor. This includes establishing appropriate practices for hiring, orienting, training, evaluating, counseling, promoting, compensating, and disciplining personnel. It also includes providing a proper amount of supervision.

A final factor affecting the environment is the agency's relationship with the Congress and central oversight agencies such as OMB. Congress mandates the programs that agencies undertake and monitors their progress, and central agencies provide policy and guidance on many different matters. In addition, Inspectors General and internal senior management councils can contribute to a good overall control environment.

**Risk Assessment:**

Internal control should provide for an assessment of the risks the agency faces from both external and internal sources. A precondition to risk assessment is the establishment of clear, consistent agency objectives. Risk assessment is the identification and analysis of relevant risks associated with achieving the objectives, such as those defined in strategic and annual performance plans developed under the Government Performance and Results Act, and forming a basis for determining how risks should be managed.

Management needs to comprehensively identify risks and should consider all significant interactions between the entity and other parties, as well as internal factors at both the entity-wide and activity level. Risk identification methods may include qualitative and quantitative ranking activities, management conferences, forecasting and strategic planning, and consideration of findings from audits and other assessments.

Once risks have been identified, they should be analyzed for their possible effect. Risk analysis generally includes estimating the risk's significance, assessing the likelihood of its occurrence, and deciding how to manage the risk and what actions should be taken. The specific risk analysis methodology used can vary by agency because of differences in agencies' missions and the difficulty in qualitatively and quantitatively assigning risk levels.

Because governmental, economic, industry, regulatory, and operating conditions continually change, mechanisms should be provided to identify and deal with any special risks prompted by such changes.

## Control Activities:

Internal control activities help ensure that management's directives are carried out. The control activities should be effective and efficient in accomplishing the agency's control objectives.

Control activities are the policies, procedures, techniques, and mechanisms that enforce management's directives, such as the process of adhering to requirements for budget development and execution. They help ensure that actions are taken to address risks. Control activities are an integral part of an entity's planning, implementing, reviewing, and accountability for stewardship of government resources and achieving effective results.

Control activities occur at all levels and functions of the entity. They include a wide range of diverse activities such as approvals, authorizations, verifications, reconciliations, performance reviews, maintenance of security, and the creation and maintenance of related records, which provide evidence of execution of these activities as well as appropriate documentation. Control activities may be applied in a computerized information system environment or through manual processes.

Activities may be classified by specific control objectives, such as ensuring completeness and accuracy of information processing.

### Examples of Control Activities:

- Top-level reviews of actual performance
- Reviews by management at the functional or activity level
- Management of human capital
- Controls over information processing

- Physical control over vulnerable assets

- Establishment and review of performance measures and indicators

- Segregation of duties

- Proper execution of transactions and events

- Accurate and timely recording of transactions and events

- Access restrictions to and accountability for resources and records

- Appropriate documentation of transactions and internal control

There are certain categories of control activities that are common to all agencies. Examples include the following:

*Top-Level Reviews of Actual Performance:* Management should track major agency achievements and compare these to the plans, goals, and objectives established under the Government Performance and Results Act.

*Reviews by Management at the Functional or Activity Level:* Managers also need to compare actual performance to planned or expected results throughout the organization and analyze significant differences.

*Management of Human Capital:* Effective management of an organization's workforce—its human capital—is essential to achieving results and an important part of internal control. Management should view human capital as an asset rather than a cost. Only when the right personnel for the job are on board and are provided the right training, tools, structure, incentives, and responsibilities is operational success possible. Management should ensure that skill needs are continually assessed and that the organization is able to obtain a workforce that has the required skills that match those necessary to achieve organizational goals. Training should be aimed at developing and retaining employee skill levels to meet changing organizational needs. Qualified and continuous supervision should be provided to ensure that internal control objectives are achieved.

Performance evaluation and feedback, supplemented by an effective reward system, should be designed to help employees understand the connection between their performance and the organization's success. As a part of its human capital planning, management should also consider how best to retain valuable employees, plan for their eventual succession, and ensure continuity of needed skills and abilities.

*Controls over Information Processing:* A variety of control activities are used in information processing. Examples include edit checks of data entered, accounting for transactions in numerical sequences, comparing file totals with control accounts, and controlling access to data, files, and programs. Further guidance on control activities for information processing is provided below under "Control Activities Specific for Information Systems."

*Physical Control over Vulnerable Assets:* An agency must establish physical control to secure and safeguard vulnerable assets. Examples include security for and limited access to assets such as cash, securities, inventories, and equipment that might be vulnerable to risk of loss or unauthorized use. Such assets should be periodically counted and compared to control records.

*Establishment and Review of Performance Measures and Indicators:* Activities need to be established to monitor performance measures and indicators. These controls could call for comparisons and assessments relating different sets of data to one another so that analyses of the relationships can be made and appropriate actions taken. Controls should also be aimed at validating the propriety and integrity of both organizational and individual performance measures and indicators.

*Segregation of Duties:* Key duties and responsibilities need to be divided or segregated among different people to reduce the risk of error or fraud. This should include separating the responsibilities for authorizing transactions, processing and recording them, reviewing the transactions, and handling any related assets. No one individual should control all key aspects of a transaction or event.

*Proper Execution of Transactions and Events:* Transactions and other significant events should be authorized and executed only by persons acting within the scope of their authority.

This is the principal means of ensuring that only valid transactions to exchange, transfer, use, or commit resources and other events are initiated or entered into. Authorizations should be clearly communicated to managers and employees.

*Accurate and Timely Recording of Transactions and Events:* Transactions should be promptly recorded to maintain their relevance and value to management in controlling operations and making decisions. This applies to the entire process or life cycle of a transaction or event, from the initiation and authorization through its final classification in summary records. In addition, control activities help to ensure that all transactions are completely and accurately recorded.

*Access Restrictions to and Accountability for Resources and Records:* Access to resources and records should be limited to authorized individuals, and accountability for their custody and use should be assigned and maintained. Periodic comparison of resources with the recorded accountability should be made to help reduce the risk of errors, fraud, misuse, or unauthorized alteration.

*Appropriate Documentation of Transactions and Internal Control:* Internal control and all transactions and other significant events need to be clearly documented, and the documentation should be readily available for examination. The documentation should appear in management directives, administrative policies, or operating manuals and may be in paper or electronic form. All documentation and records should be properly managed and maintained.

These examples are meant only to illustrate the range and variety of control activities that may be useful to agency managers. They are not all-inclusive and may not include particular control activities that an agency may need. Furthermore, an agency's internal control should be flexible to allow agencies to tailor control activities to fit their special needs. The specific control activities used by a given agency may be different from those used by others due to a number of factors. These could include specific threats they face and risks they incur; differences in objectives; managerial judgment; size and complexity of the organization; operational environment; sensitivity and value of data; and requirements for system reliability, availability, and performance.

**Control Activities Specific for Information Systems:**

- General Control
- Application Control

There are two broad groupings of information systems control—general control and application control. General control applies to all information systems—mainframe, minicomputer, network, and end-user environments. Application control is designed to cover the processing of data within the application software.

*General Control:* This category includes entity-wide security program planning, management, control over data center operations, system software acquisition and maintenance, access security, and application system development and maintenance.

More specifically:

- Data center and client-server operations controls include backup and recovery procedures, and contingency and disaster planning. In addition, data center operations controls also include job setup and scheduling procedures and controls over operator activities.

- System software control includes control over the acquisition, implementation, and maintenance of all system software including the operating system, data-based management systems, telecommunications, security software, and utility programs.

- Access security control protects the systems and network from inappropriate access and unauthorized use by hackers and other trespassers or inappropriate use by agency personnel. Specific control activities include frequent changes of dial-up numbers; use of dial-back access; restrictions on users to allow access only to system functions that they need; software and hardware "firewalls" to restrict access to assets, computers, and networks by external persons; and frequent changes of passwords and deactivation of former employees' passwords.

- Application system development and maintenance control provides the structure for safely developing new systems and modifying existing systems. Included are documentation requirements; authorizations for undertaking projects; and reviews, testing, and approvals of development and modification activities before placing systems into operation. An alternative to in-house development is the procurement of commercial software, but control is necessary to ensure that selected software meets the user's needs, and that it is properly placed into operation.

*Application Control:* This category of control is designed to help ensure completeness, accuracy, authorization, and validity of all transactions during application processing. Control should be installed at an application's interfaces with other systems to ensure that all inputs are received and are valid and outputs are correct and properly distributed. An example is computerized edit checks built into the system to review the format, existence, and reasonableness of data.

General and application control over computer systems are interrelated. General control supports the functioning of application control, and both are needed to ensure complete and accurate information processing. If the general control is inadequate, the application control is unlikely to function properly and could be overridden.

Because information technology changes rapidly, controls must evolve to remain effective. Changes in technology and its application to electronic commerce and expanding internet applications will change the specific control activities that may be employed and how they are implemented, but the basic requirements of control will not have changed. As more powerful computers place more responsibility for data processing in the hands of the end users, the needed controls should be identified and implemented.

**Information and Communications:**

Information should be recorded and communicated to management and others within the entity who need it and in a form and within a time frame that enables them to carry out their internal control and other responsibilities.

For an entity to run and control its operations, it must have relevant, reliable, and timely communications relating to internal as well as external events. Information is needed throughout the agency to achieve all of its objectives.

Program managers need both operational and financial data to determine whether they are meeting their agencies' strategic and annual performance plans and meeting their goals for accountability for effective and efficient use of resources. For example, operating information is required for development of financial reports. This covers a broad range of data from purchases, subsidies, and other transactions to data on fixed assets, inventories, and receivables. Operating information is also needed to determine whether the agency is achieving its compliance requirements under various laws and regulations. Financial information is needed for both external and internal uses. It is required to develop financial statements for periodic external reporting, and, on a day-to-day basis, to make operating decisions, monitor performance, and allocate resources. Pertinent information should be identified, captured, and distributed in a form and time frame that permits people to perform their duties efficiently.

Effective communications should occur in a broad sense with information flowing down, across, and up the organization. In addition to internal communications, management should ensure there are adequate means of communicating with, and obtaining information from, external stakeholders that may have a significant impact on the agency achieving its goals. Moreover, effective information technology management is critical to achieving useful, reliable, and continuous recording and communication of information.

**Monitoring:**

Internal control monitoring should assess the quality of performance over time and ensure that the findings of audits and other reviews are promptly resolved. Internal control should generally be designed to ensure that ongoing monitoring occurs in the course of normal operations. It is performed continually and is ingrained in the agency's operations. It includes regular management and supervisory activities, comparisons, reconciliations, and other actions people take in performing their duties.

Separate evaluations of control can also be useful by focusing directly on the control's effectiveness at a specific time. The scope and frequency of separate evaluations should depend primarily on the assessment of risks and the effectiveness of ongoing monitoring procedures. Separate evaluations may take the form of self-assessments as well as review of control design and direct testing of internal control. Separate evaluations also may be performed by the agency Inspector General or an external auditor. Deficiencies found during ongoing monitoring or through separate evaluations should be communicated to the individual responsible for the function and also to at least one level of management above that individual. Serious matters should be reported to top management.

Monitoring of internal control should include policies and procedures for ensuring that the findings of audits and other reviews are promptly resolved.

Managers are to:

1. Promptly evaluate findings from audits and other reviews, including those showing deficiencies and recommendations reported by auditors and others who evaluate agencies' operations;

2. Determine proper actions in response to findings and recommendations from audits and reviews; and

3. Complete, within established time frames, all actions that correct or otherwise resolve the matters brought to management's attention.

The resolution process begins when audit or other review results are reported to management, and is completed only after action has been taken that (1) corrects identified deficiencies, (2) produces improvements, or (3) demonstrates that the findings and recommendations do not warrant management action.

## ASSESSING INTERNAL CONTROL STRUCTURES

In "The Role of the Internal Auditor in ERM," in Chapter Seven, we discuss the Inspector General's (IG) role in assessing the effectiveness of ERM programs in government agencies. The OIG process for reviewing ERM in government agencies is still nascent, but the common default tool used to assess the ERM structure has been the COSO ERM Integrated Framework. Because internal control is an intricate part of effective ERM, it is equally important to assess the structure of internal control in an agency as well. After all, internal control is a mechanism for managing risk. Therefore, having strong and effective controls is essential. Similar to the COSO ERM Integrated Framework used by IGs, agencies have the option of using the GAO Internal Control Management and Evaluation Tool (Evaluation Tool) to assess the effectiveness of internal control structures.

The Evaluation Tool is designed "to assist agencies in maintaining or implementing effective internal control, and when needed, to help determine what, where, and how improvements can be implemented."[37] It is intended to "help users reach a conclusion about the agency's internal control as it pertains to the particular standard."[38] Although not mandatory to use, the Evaluation Tool serves to supplement other guidance that federal managers use in assessing the effectiveness of internal control. The strength of the tool is the systematic, organized, and structured approach it creates for assessing the internal control structure. Modifications to the tool are expected to "fit the circumstances, conditions, and risks relevant to the situation of each agency."[39]

The Evaluation Tool is presented in five sections that correspond to the five standards for internal control.

## OVERALL INTERNAL CONTROL SUMMARIES

We now summarize the standards for internal control in federal government.[40]

**Control Environment**. Management and employees have a positive and supportive attitude toward internal control and conscientious management. Management conveys the message that integrity and ethical values must not be compromised. The agency demonstrates a commitment to the competence of its personnel and employs good human capital policies and practices.

Management has a philosophy and operating style appropriate to the development and maintenance of effective internal control. The agency's organizational structure and the way in which it assigns authority and responsibility contribute to effective internal control. The agency has a good working relationship with Congress and oversight groups.

**Risk Assessment**. The agency has established clear and consistent entity-wide objectives and supporting activity-level objectives. Management has made a thorough identification of risks, from both internal and external sources, that may affect the ability of the agency to meet those objectives. An analysis of those risks has been performed, and the agency has developed an appropriate approach for risk management. In addition, mechanisms are in place to identify changes that may affect the agency's ability to achieve its missions, goals, and objectives.

**Control Activities**. Appropriate policies, procedures, techniques, and control mechanisms have been developed and are in place to ensure adherence to established directives. Proper control activities have been developed for each of the agency's activities. The control activities identified as necessary are actually being applied properly.

**Information and Communications**. Information systems are in place to identify and record pertinent operational and financial information relating to internal and external events. That information is communicated to management and others in the agency who need it, in a form that enables them to carry out their duties and responsibilities efficiently and effectively. Management ensures that effective internal communications take place. It also ensures that effective external communications occur with groups that can affect the achievement of the agency's missions, goals, and objectives. The agency employs various forms of communications appropriate to its needs, and it manages, develops, and revises its information systems in a continual effort to improve communications.

**Monitoring**. Agency internal control monitoring assesses the quality of performance over time. It does this by putting procedures in place to monitor internal control on an ongoing basis as a part of the process of carrying out its regular activities. It includes ensuring that managers know their responsibilities for internal control and control monitoring. In addition, separate evaluations of internal control are periodically performed and the deficiencies found are investigated. Procedures are in place to ensure that the findings of all audits and other reviews are promptly evaluated, decisions are made about the appropriate response, and actions are taken to correct or otherwise resolve the issues promptly.

Each section contains a list of *major factors* to be considered when reviewing internal control as it relates to the particular standard. The factors represent some of the more important issues addressed by the standard. The factors are not all-inclusive and will not apply to every agency. What follows is a modified version of the Evaluation Tool. The tool can be accessed in its entirety at www.gao.gov.

## INTERNAL CONTROL MANAGEMENT AND EVALUATION TOOL

**Control Environment:** According to the first internal control standard, which relates to control environment, management and employees should establish and maintain an environment throughout the organization that sets a positive and supportive attitude toward internal control and conscientious management. There are several key factors that affect the accomplishment of this goal. Managers and evaluators should consider each of these control environment factors when determining whether a positive control environment has been achieved.

**Major Factors:**

- The agency has established and uses a formal code or codes of conduct and other policies communicating appropriate ethical and moral behavioral standards and addressing acceptable operational practices and conflicts of interest.

- An ethical tone has been established at the top of the organization and has been communicated throughout the agency.

- Dealings with the public, Congress, employees, suppliers, auditors, and others are conducted on a high ethical plane.

- Appropriate disciplinary action is taken in response to departures from approved policies and procedures or violations of the code of conduct.

- Management appropriately addresses intervention or overriding internal control.

- Management removes temptation for unethical behavior.

- Management has identified and defined the tasks required to accomplish particular jobs and fill the various positions.
- The agency has performed analyses of the knowledge, skills, and abilities needed to perform jobs appropriately.
- The agency provides training and counseling in order to help employees maintain and improve their competence for their jobs.
- Key senior-level employees have a demonstrated ability in general management and extensive practical experience in operating governmental or business entities.
- Management has an appropriate attitude toward risk taking and proceeds with new ventures, missions, or operations only after carefully analyzing the risks involved and determining how they may be minimized or mitigated.
- Management enthusiastically endorses the use of performance-based management.
- There has not been excessive personnel turnover in key functions—such as operations and program management, accounting, or internal audit—that would indicate a problem with the agency's emphasis on internal control.
- Management has a positive and supportive attitude toward the functions of accounting, information management systems, personnel operations, monitoring, and internal and external audits and evaluations.
- Valuable assets and information are safeguarded from unauthorized access or use.
- There is frequent interaction between senior management and operating/program management, especially when operating from geographically dispersed locations.
- Management has an appropriate attitude toward financial, budgetary, and operational/programmatic reporting.
- The agency's organizational structure is appropriate for its size and the nature of its operations.

- Key areas of authority and responsibility are defined and communicated throughout the organization.

- Appropriate and clear internal reporting relationships have been established.

- Management periodically evaluates the organizational structure and makes changes as necessary in response to changing conditions.

- The agency has the appropriate number of employees, particularly in managerial positions.

- The agency appropriately assigns authority and delegates responsibility to the proper personnel to deal with organizational goals and objectives.

- Each employee knows (1) how his or her actions interrelate to others, considering the way in which authority and responsibilities are assigned, and (2) is aware of the related duties concerning internal control.

- The delegation of authority is appropriate in relation to the assignment of responsibility.

- Policies and procedures are in place for hiring, orienting, training, evaluating, counseling, promoting, compensating, disciplining, and terminating employees.

- Background checks are conducted on candidates for employment.

- Employees are provided a proper amount of supervision.

- Within the agency, there are mechanisms in place to monitor and review operations and programs.

- The agency works closely with executive branch oversight organizations.

- The agency maintains a close relationship with Congress in general and oversight committees in particular.

**Risk Assessment:** The second internal control standard addresses risk assessment. A precondition to risk assessment is the establishment of clear, consistent agency goals and objectives at both the entity level and the activity (program or mission) level. Once the objectives have been set, the agency needs to identify the risks that could impede the efficient and effective achievement of those objectives at the entity level and the activity level. Internal control should provide for an assessment of the risks the agency faces from both internal and external sources. Once risks have been identified, they should be analyzed for their possible effect. Management then has to formulate an approach for risk management and decide upon the internal control activities required to mitigate those risks and achieve the internal control objectives of efficient and effective operations, reliable financial reporting, and compliance with laws and regulations. A manager or evaluator will focus on management's processes for objective setting, risk identification, risk analysis, and management of risk during times of change. The following is a list of factors a user might consider.

**Major Factors:**

- The agency has established entity-wide objectives that provide sufficiently broad statements and guidance about what the agency is supposed to achieve, yet are specific enough to relate directly to the agency.

- Entity-wide objectives are clearly communicated to all employees, and management obtains feedback signifying that the communication has been effective.

- There is a relationship and consistency between the agency's operational strategies and the entity-wide objectives.

- The agency has an integrated management strategy and risk assessment plan that considers the entity-wide objectives and relevant sources of risk from internal management factors and external sources and establishes a control structure to address those risks.

- Activity-level (program or mission-level) objectives flow from and are linked with the agency's entity-wide objectives and strategic plans.

- Activity-level objectives are complementary, reinforce each other, and are not contradictory.
- The activity-level objectives are relevant to all significant agency processes.
- Activity-level objectives include measurement criteria.
- Agency resources are adequate relative to the activity-level objectives.
- Management has identified those activity-level objectives that are critical to the success of the overall entity-wide objectives.
- All levels of management are involved in establishing the activity-level objectives and are committed to their achievement.
- Management comprehensively identifies risk using various methodologies as appropriate.
- Adequate mechanisms exist to identify risks to the agency arising from external factors.
- Adequate mechanisms exist to identify risks to the agency arising from internal factors.
- In identifying risk, management assesses other factors that may contribute to or increase the risk to which the agency is exposed.
- Management identifies risks both entity-wide and for each significant activity level of the agency.
- After the risks to the agency have been identified, management undertakes a thorough and complete analysis of their possible effect.
- Management has developed an approach for risk management and control based on how much risk can be prudently accepted.
- The agency has mechanisms in place to anticipate, identify, and react to risks presented by changes in governmental, economic, industry, regulatory, operating, or other conditions that can affect the achievement of entity-wide or activity-level goals and objectives.

- The agency gives special attention to risks presented by changes that can have a more dramatic and pervasive effect on the entity and may demand the attention of senior officials.

**Control Activities:** The third internal control standard addresses control activities. Internal control activities are the policies, procedures, techniques, and mechanisms that help ensure that management's directives to mitigate risks identified during the risk assessment process are carried out. Control activities are an integral part of the agency's planning, implementing, and reviewing. They are essential for proper stewardship and accountability for government resources and for achieving effective and efficient program results.

Control activities occur at all levels and functions of the agency. They include a wide range of diverse activities, such as approvals, authorizations, verifications, reconciliations, performance reviews, security activities, and the production of records and documentation. A manager or evaluator should focus on control activities in the context of the agency's management directives to address risks associated with established objectives for each significant activity (program or mission). Therefore, a manager or evaluator will consider whether control activities relate to the risk-assessment process and whether they are appropriate to ensure that management's directives are carried out. In assessing the adequacy of internal control activities, a reviewer should consider whether the proper control activities have been established, whether they are sufficient in number, and the degree to which those activities are operating effectively. This should be done for each significant activity. This analysis and evaluation should also include controls over computerized information systems. A manager or evaluator should consider not only whether established control activities are relevant to the risk-assessment process, but also whether they are being applied properly.

The control activities put into place in a given agency may vary considerably from those used in a different agency. This difference may occur because of the (1) variations in missions, goals, and objectives of the agencies; (2) differences in their environment and manner in which they operate; (3) variations in degree of organizational complexity; (4) differences in agency histories and culture; and (5) differences in the risks that the agencies face and are trying to mitigate. It is probable that, even if two agencies did have the same missions, goals, objectives, and organizational structures, they would employ different control activities. This is due to individual judgment, implementation, and management. All of these factors affect an agency's internal control activities, which should be designed accordingly to contribute to the achievement of the agency's missions, goals, and objectives.

Given the wide variety of control activities that agencies may employ, it would be impossible for this tool to address them all. However, there are some general, overall points to be considered by managers and evaluators, as well as several major categories or types of control activity factors that are applicable at various levels throughout practically all federal agencies. In addition, there are some control activity factors specifically designed for information systems. These factors and related points and subsidiary points are presented in the following list as examples of issues to be considered. They are meant to illustrate the range and variety of control activities that are typically used.

**Major Factors:**

- Appropriate policies, procedures, techniques, and mechanisms exist with respect to each of the agency's activities.

- The control activities identified as necessary are in place and being applied.

- Control activities are regularly evaluated to ensure that they are still appropriate and working as intended.

- Top-Level Reviews—Management tracks major agency achievements in relation to its plans.

- Management Reviews at the Functional or Activity Level— Agency managers review actual performance against targets.

- Management of Human Capital—The agency effectively manages the organization's workforce to achieve results.

- Information Processing—The agency employs a variety of control activities suited to information processing systems to ensure accuracy and completeness.

- Physical Control over Vulnerable Assets—The agency employs physical control to secure and safeguard vulnerable assets.

- Performance Measures and Indicators—The agency has established and monitors performance measures and indicators.

- Segregation of Duties—Key duties and responsibilities are divided or segregated among different people to reduce the risk of error, waste, or fraud.

- Execution of Transactions and Events—Transactions and other significant events are authorized and performed by the appropriate personnel.

- Recording of Transactions and Events—Transactions and other significant events are properly classified and promptly recorded.

- Access Restrictions to and Accountability for Resources and Records—Access to resources and records is limited and accountability for their custody is assigned.

- Documentation—Internal control and all transactions and other significant events are clearly documented.

**Information and Communications:** According to the fourth internal control standard, for an agency to run and control its operations, it must have relevant, reliable information, both financial and nonfinancial, relating to external as well as internal events. That information should be recorded and communicated to management and others within the agency who need it and in a form and within a time frame that enables them to carry out their internal control and operational responsibilities. In addition, the agency needs to make sure that the forms of communications are broad-based and that information technology management ensures useful, reliable, and continuous communications. Managers and evaluators should consider the appropriateness of information and communication systems to the entity's needs and the degree to which they accomplish the objectives of internal control. The following are factors a user might consider.

**Major Factors:**

- Information from internal and external sources is obtained and provided to management as a part of the agency's reporting on operational performance relative to established objectives.

- Pertinent information is identified, captured, and distributed to the right people in sufficient detail, in the right form, and at the appropriate time to enable them to carry out their duties and responsibilities efficiently and effectively.

- Management ensures that effective internal communications occur.

- Management ensures that effective external communications occur with groups that can have a serious impact on programs, projects, operations, and other activities, including budgeting and financing.

- The agency employs many and various forms and means of communicating important information with employees and others.

- The agency manages, develops, and revises its information systems in an effort to continually improve the usefulness and reliability of its communication of information.

**Monitoring:** Monitoring is the final internal control standard. Internal control monitoring should assess the quality of performance over time and ensure that the findings of audits and other reviews are promptly resolved. In considering the extent to which the continued effectiveness of internal control is monitored, both ongoing monitoring activities and separate evaluations of the internal control system, or portions thereof, should be considered.

Ongoing monitoring occurs during normal operations and includes regular management and supervisory activities, comparisons, reconciliations, and other actions people take in performing their duties.

It includes ensuring that managers and supervisors know their responsibilities for internal control and the need to make control and control monitoring part of their regular operating processes. Separate evaluations are a way to take a fresh look at internal control by focusing directly on the control's effectiveness at a specific time.

These evaluations may take the form of self-assessments as well as review of control design and direct testing, and may include the use of this Management and Evaluation Tool or some similar device. In addition, monitoring includes policies and procedures for ensuring that any audit and review findings and recommendations are brought to the attention of management and are resolved promptly. Managers and evaluators should consider the appropriateness of the agency's internal control monitoring and the degree to which it helps them accomplish their objectives. The following are factors a user might consider:

**Major Factors:**

- Management has a strategy to ensure that ongoing monitoring is effective and will trigger separate evaluations when problems are identified or systems are critical and testing is periodically desirable.

- In the process of carrying out their regular activities, agency personnel obtain information about whether internal control is functioning properly.

- Communications from external parties should corroborate internally generated data or indicate problems with internal control.

- Appropriate organizational structure and supervision help provide oversight of internal control functions.

- Data recorded by information and financial systems are periodically compared with physical assets, and discrepancies are examined.

- The Inspector General and other auditors and evaluators regularly provide recommendations for improvements in internal control, with management taking appropriate follow-up action.

- Meetings with employees are used to provide management with feedback on whether internal control is effective.

- Employees are regularly asked to state explicitly whether they comply with the agency's code of conduct or similar agency pronouncements of expected employee behavior.

- The scope and frequency of separate evaluations of internal control are appropriate for the agency.

- The agency has a mechanism to ensure the prompt resolution of findings from audits and other reviews.

## chapter TWO

# Examples of Risk Management in the Federal Government

Despite a lack of fundamental definitions, the discipline of risk management is not a new concept in the U.S. federal sector. It has been used in private and public sectors for decades. It is a well-established practice dating back to the late eighteenth century, when the government began to develop policies to deal with risks thought to undermine trade and investment.[1] "Government has always been involved in managing risks, even as risk management has not generally been recognized as being a fundamental function of government," says David Moss, a professor of business administration at the Harvard Business School. As government agencies face increased scrutiny regarding accountability, fraud, resources management, performance, and results, more managers are engaging in risk management activities.

Although some risk management methodologies and processes can be complex and may require expert advice and support, other aspects of risk management—such as setting goals and using performance measures to track progress in meeting them—are well understood and widely practiced.[2] Whether the focus is on public risk, financial risk, or operational risk, agencies are managing risks that are in direct alignment with their missions or are effectively engaging the discipline as a common management practice.

## HEALTH RISKS

*Food and Drug Administration (FDA).*[3] The FDA, an agency within the Department of Health and Human Services, consists of seven centers and offices. The FDA is responsible for protecting the public health by ensuring the safety, efficacy, and security of human and veterinary drugs, biological products, medical devices, our nation's food supply, cosmetics, and products that emit radiation. The FDA is also responsible for advancing the public health by helping to speed innovations that make medicines and foods more effective, safer, and more affordable, and by helping the public get the accurate, science-based information they need to use medicines and foods to improve their health.

In line with the agency's responsibilities is the approval of medications and certain other medical products for public use and then continuous assessment of the products' risks and benefits after they have been made available to the public (a process called *post market risk surveillance*). With increased attention to improving the safety and quality of health care, there has been growing interest in leveraging the large amounts of electronic health data being collected on a regular basis to enhance surveillance of post-market risk.

However, increased analytical use of personal health information raises concerns about the privacy and security of that information. According to the National Research Council, medical information is often the most privacy-sensitive information that individuals provide to others about themselves, and protecting the privacy of that information has long been recognized as an essential element in the administration of health care systems. Further, industry groups and professional associations have called for stronger protections for personal health information.

The Food and Drug Administration Amendments Act of 2007 (FDAAA) requires that FDA develop methods for the establishment of a post-market risk identification and analysis system of electronic health data. In response, the FDA announced the start of its Sentinel Initiative in May 2008. The initiative includes planning for the development of an integrated system to analyze electronic health data in order to identify potential risks and assess the safety of medical products after they have been made available to the public.

## SECURITY RISKS

*Department of Defense (DoD).* The DoD uses a risk management approach to protect its forces. For example, it has used risk management to identify threats and vulnerabilities and determine which assets are the most critical and to make management decisions on how to make its bases and related facilities more secure.[4] Risk management was part of the nation's approach to assessing terrorism before the attacks of September 11, 2001. For example, in the 1990s, the Defense Special Weapons Agency assessed risks to evaluate force protection security requirements for mass casualty terrorist incidents at military bases. Companies under contract to federal agencies such as the Department of Energy, the National Security Agency, and the National Aeronautics and Space Administration used risk assessment models and methods to identify and prioritize security requirements. The Federal Aviation Administration and the Federal Bureau of Investigation did joint threat and vulnerability assessments on airports determined to be high risk.

*Department of Homeland Security (DHS).* The threat of terrorism presents a number of risks to our nation's seaports and other types of critical infrastructure. DHS has three component agencies responsible for the security of critical infrastructure related to ports and other facilities:[5]

• *The U.S. Coast Guard* has responsibility for port security overall. The Coast Guard is the lead federal agency for the security of the nation's ports. Its responsibilities include protecting ports, the flow of commerce, and the maritime transportation system from terrorism. As the lead in domestic maritime security, the Coast Guard has a robust presence at the national, regional, and port levels. The Coast Guard protects more than three hundred ports and ninety-five thousand miles of coastline. Coast Guard officials have been able to use expert knowledge or data from risk assessments to select specific alternatives, such as establishing security zones around key infrastructure, improving security around ferries and cruise ships, and coordinating security improvements (such as fences, gates, and cameras) around key infrastructure. Using local risk assessments, the Coast Guard has also developed alternative approaches to prevent attacks and reduce vulnerabilities.

• *The Office for Domestic Preparedness (ODP)* is responsible for providing port security grants to selected maritime facility owners. Between 2002 and 2005, the program has awarded over $500 million in grants to state, local, and industry stakeholders to improve security in and around their facilities or vessels. For fiscal year 2005, grant criteria included the prioritization of projects based on the criticality of ports and proposals that reduce vulnerabilities to certain threat scenarios. These risk-based criteria were not used in prior fiscal years.

• *The Information Analysis and Infrastructure Protection (IAIP)* directorate is responsible for working with other federal, state, local, and private organizations to identify and protect critical infrastructure across the nation. These priorities are then to be used to direct protective measures for port security as well as across all other kinds of infrastructure. IAIP has developed a national database of critical infrastructure assets and a series of benchmark threat scenarios to be used to analyze potential attacks. IAIP has used these scenarios to develop data collection instruments for two types of assets (nuclear plants and chemical plants) to assess their vulnerabilities.

The IAIP also has a key role in applying risk management to ports and other infrastructure. Relative to the Coast Guard and ODP, IAIP's homeland security responsibilities are by far the widest-ranging. The Homeland Security Act of 2002 and Homeland Security Presidential Directive 7 (HSPD-7) charge IAIP with establishing a risk management framework across the federal government to protect the nation's critical infrastructure and key resources. The scope of this effort is immense, and the effort is one of IAIP's central responsibilities.

IAIP's task ultimately involves developing an approach that can inform decisions on what the nation's antiterrorism priorities should be and identifying what strategies and programs will do the most good. More specifically, IAIP is charged with examining and comparing relative risks associated with a multitude of possible targets, ranging from specific structures (such as dams, chemical plants, and nuclear power plants) to major sectors of national infrastructure (such as the banking system, computer networks, and water systems). IAIP is also responsible for developing policies and guidance that other agencies can use in conducting their own risk assessments.

The application of risk management in homeland security is relatively new—much of it coming in the wake of the terrorist attacks of September 11—and it is a difficult task with little precedent. The goals for using it in homeland security include informing strategic decisions on ways to reduce the likelihood that adverse events will occur and to mitigate the negative impacts of and ensure a speedy recovery from those that do. Achieving these goals involves making policy decisions about what the nation's homeland security priorities should be—for example, what the relative security priorities should be among seaports, airports, and rail—and basing spending decisions on what approaches or strategies will do the most good at narrowing the security gaps that exist.

Risk management has been widely supported by the president and Congress as a management approach for homeland security, and the secretary of the Department of Homeland Security has made it the centerpiece of agency policy.

## FINANCIAL RISKS

*Government National Mortgage Association (GNMA).* GNMA or "Ginnie Mae" is a wholly owned corporation housed within the Department of Housing and Urban Development. For nearly four decades, GNMA has made financial risk management one of its core values. This has allowed it to keep pace with, and frequently surpass, private sector financial risk management practices.[6]

The primary mission for GNMA is to "support expanded affordable housing in America by providing an efficient government-guaranteed secondary market vehicle linking the capital markets with federal housing markets."[7] This is accomplished with fewer than one hundred employees and under the leadership of a strong management team. In 2008, the corporation celebrated forty years of "financial stability." GNMA undoubtedly has a mission closer to that of private sector organizations than many government agencies, yet there is a subtle but important distinction: its primary purpose is to support and expand the market for affordable housing, not to maximize profits. FHA loans in particular are typically made to borrowers who would have difficulty getting loans under normal private sector programs. The general perception is that these loans have higher delinquency and default rates than their conventional counterparts.

Because of this, Congress was concerned that private sector secondary market participants would not be willing to bear this risk, and so it created GNMA to ensure that such a market existed. Historically, the mission of GNMA has meant ensuring the existence of a secondary market for FHA/VA-insured mortgages, and GNMA has created an innovative system to meet this mission. GNMA does this by guaranteeing the performance of the issuers of mortgage-backed securities (MBS). The issuers form these MBS's from pools of FHA and VA mortgage loans.

GNMA does not insure individual mortgage loans; that is the mission of FHA or VA insurance and of the MBS issuer. Rather, it guarantees that if the issuer of the MBS goes into default—that is, does not make the promised payments to the investors—the investors are still paid. The mission and operations of GNMA illustrate one of the most important points about risk in general: managing financial risk does not mean eliminating it. In fact, in the case of GNMA this would be virtually impossible; as long as it is operating, it must take on financial risk. What GNMA must do is balance the risk that it takes against the accomplishment of its mission. The only way for GNMA to eliminate all of its financial risk is to not insure any issuers. The key for GNMA is to maximize its mission accomplishment while minimizing the financial risk that it bears.[8]

## TRANSPORTATION SAFETY RISKS

*National Transportation Safety Board (NTSB).* The NTSB is an independent federal agency charged by Congress with investigating every civil aviation accident in the United States and significant accidents in the other modes of transportation—railroad, highway, marine, and pipeline—and issuing safety recommendations aimed at preventing future accidents.[9]

The Safety Board determines the probable cause of:

- All U.S. civil aviation accidents and certain public-use aircraft accidents
- Selected highway accidents
- Railroad accidents involving passenger trains and any train accident that results in at least one fatality or major property damage
- Major marine accidents and any marine accident involving a public and a nonpublic vessel
- Pipeline accidents involving a fatality or substantial property damage
- Releases of hazardous materials in all forms of transportation
- Selected transportation accidents that involve problems of a recurring nature

The NTSB has made great strides in mitigating the results of accidents and is now concentrating on prevention.[10] This is a seemingly unlikely goal for an agency whose primary objective is to investigate accidents after they occur, but the NTSB has invested in this emerging area. One accomplishment has been the development of guidelines to help reduce travel-related risks, which in the case of car crashes take the lives of forty thousand people and injure three million others every year.

Over the last four decades, NTSB has investigated 124,000 aviation accidents and 10,000 crashes involving trains, ships, trucks, and cars. The Board has also found a way to leverage existing products, such as the issuance of safety recommendations after investigations, to help offset and reduce the public's risk when flying, driving, boating, and traveling by rail.

One compelling linkage of risk to mission is the NTSB's creation of the Most Wanted List. Created in 1990, this list includes dozens of suggestions on how to make travel safer. The list has been credited with reducing transportation risks.

## EXTERNAL RISKS

*United States Postal Service (USPS).*[11] Managing risk certainly isn't new to the USPS. The mission of the service is to provide trusted, reliable, affordable, universal service. Each day, the service delivers to 150 million U.S. addresses and countless more worldwide. The service also helps customers build and maintain relationships, share sensitive information, and exchange goods and services. Following disasters and events that affected the mail, such as Hurricane Sandy and the tornadoes in Oklahoma in 2013, customers and employees regularly turned to the Mail Service Updates site on usps.com for service information. For the USPS, on-time delivery is the critical first step in meeting and satisfying postal customer needs. Yet despite the recent events, the USPS has continued the trend of steadily improving performance.

USPS has done a good job of managing external risks to ensure minimum disruption to services. However, its biggest challenges and threats to its continued success lie in the realm of its internal business operations. Overall, the Postal Service spent a total of $6.7 billion in transportation expenses in FY2013. This represents an increase of $105 million or 1.6 percent over FY2012. Long term, the service is facing major operational hurdles that are forcing the organization to reconsider how it manages strategic, financial, and operational risks. For instance, electronic diversion and a tough economic climate continue to reduce volume and revenue. Fortunately, many of its costs—such as a carrier's daily stop at every address—are fixed, regardless of volume, and are manageable. The Postal Service, like its counterparts around the world, continues to face declining letter mail volume as a result of new communications technologies. Yet as much as e-mail, texting, and various forms of social media are flourishing, recent research has shown that physical mail remains relevant. JWTIntelligence, the research arm of advertising agency JWT, conducted a survey of eight hundred Americans and four hundred Britons aged eighteen-plus from February 1–4, 2013. They found that a majority of people in both the United States and the United Kingdom enjoyed sending physical mail, and on the receiving end, people saw real-world mail as a way to forge tight bonds.

Still, the growing revenue/cost gap is a serious threat to the service's ability to provide affordable universal service, an essential element of its core mission. USPS leadership is cognizant of the reality that the severity of the situation and the pace of change demand an agile, flexible organization. To address these issues, USPS has established a new Performance Plan, the organization's strategic plan for building its business and sustaining a strong, viable Postal Service during turbulent times.

*Centers for Disease Control: Credibility/Reputation Risk.*[12] Leadership at the CDC established a holistic risk recognition and mitigation process comprising three key components: ERM, issues management, and credibility risk management. For the CDC, credibility is high priority. Agency leaders believe that how they communicate as an organization should actively be informed by how they are being perceived. To some extent, the CDC has taken into consideration the wisdom of Warren Buffet, who said "It takes twenty years to build a reputation and five minutes to ruin it. If you think about that, you'll do things differently." This may describe the spirit behind CDC's ERM effort in doing things differently when it pertains to maintaining and sustaining their reputation for promoting health and quality of life. "Reputation" is the perception held by interested persons or groups about the agency's characteristics, achievements, and behaviors. From the CDC's perspective, managing the agency's reputation is important because the agency must have the public's trust to do its mission, or risk:

• Increased disease, injury, and death

• Demands for the misallocation of limited resources

• Circumvented public health policies

Conceptually, CDC likens its reputation (everything they do and how they communicate about what they do) to the double helix of DNA—that is to say, both are intertwined. "The building block of everything that makes up [an agency's] identity is expressed by the accumulation of individual events strung together. Like the DNA's double helix, activities that enhance or protect the brand can't be separated. It is the agency's collective behavior and communication that determines its success."[13]

The CDC identifies maintaining high agency credibility (or its reputation) as the primary driver for implementing ERM. All agencies have this intangible asset, but it's fair to say that few emphasize its importance. Other organizations also share this endeavor. Industry experts note that intangible assets such as brand equity and goodwill account for 70 to 80 percent of a company's market value. Yet most companies don't proactively manage reputation risk until after their reputation suffers damage.[14] Even though government agencies are not assessed according to market value, the perceptions of taxpayers, the general public, and political governing bodies have as much impact, just the same.

A *Harvard Business Review* article, "Reputation and Its Risks," noted: "Most companies do an inadequate job of managing their reputations and the risks to their reputations in particular. They tend to focus their energies on handling the threats to their reputations that have already surfaced. This is not risk management; it is crisis management—a reactive approach whose purpose is to limit the damage."[15]

## CASE STUDY: APPLYING RISK MANAGEMENT IN GOVERNMENT: NATIONAL INSTITUTES OF HEALTH

The National Institutes of Health (NIH) mission is to seek fundamental knowledge about the nature and behavior of living systems and the application of that knowledge to enhance health, lengthen life, and reduce illness and disability. It is the primary federal agency for supporting medical research.[16] In fiscal year 2012, the NIH invested over $30.9 billion annually in medical research for the American people. More than 80 percent of the NIH's funding is awarded through almost 50,000 competitive grants to more than 300,000 researchers at more than 2,500 universities, medical schools, and other research institutions in every state and around the world.

The goals of the agency are:

- To foster fundamental creative discoveries, innovative research strategies, and their applications as a basis for ultimately protecting and improving health

- To develop, maintain, and renew scientific human and physical resources that will ensure the nation's capability to prevent disease

- To expand the knowledge base in medical and associated sciences in order to enhance the nation's economic well-being and ensure a continued high return on the public investment in research

- To exemplify and promote the highest level of scientific integrity, public accountability, and social responsibility in the conduct of science

In 2008, GAO initiated a review of the NIH Risk Management Program as part of a larger agency review that focused on extramural research funding and travel and personnel appointment processes.[17] The main focus of this summary is to review the results of the GAO review of the NIH Risk Management Program and highlight lessons learned and best practices.

## Background

In 2006, the agency began to engage in the design of a new risk management framework to replace the previous Management Control Program, which did not comprehensively address risks to the agency's overall operations. This forward-thinking action by leadership put the agency in a favorable position to increase effective management oversight and address emerging risks head-on. In reviewing the design of the NIH Management Control Program and the Enterprise Risk Management Program, GAO compared these designs to the GAO Risk Management Framework. According to GAO, the scope of the audit did not include a review of the agency's new Enterprise Risk Management Program because it was only partially implemented at the time of the study.

GAO was mainly concerned with the completeness of the NIH Risk Management Program design. Although it was an improvement over the Management Control Program, the new Enterprise Risk Management Program did not fully address all of the components of GAO's framework for effective risk management.

NIH's previous Management Control Program was initially implemented in 1999 and updated in 2004. Under the design of this program, risk assessments are performed that relate to specific management control areas, such as functional areas, systems, or processes (for example, intramural research programs) without relating those areas to potential systemic or agency-wide risks. As designed, NIH's Management Control Program did not address several of the components and related key elements included in GAO's framework for an effective risk management program. An effective risk management program should enable management to proactively identify, assess, and mitigate risks.

## Aligning Risk Management Program Designs with GAO's Framework

Agency risk program implementers should take into consideration the GAO Risk Management Framework when designing their programs or initiatives. GAO identified several elements of the former NIH Management Control Program that did not correlate with the GAO Risk Management Framework. A review that looks for such discrepancies can be used to complete an evaluation checklist when considering ERM during the discovery phase. The three components of the GAO framework that every risk management program should address are strategic goals, objectives, and constraints; risk assessment; and information and communication.

Specifically, programs should do the following:

• Link the identification of potential risks with the agency's strategic goals and objectives. The design of a program should require strategic goals and objectives to be set as a precondition for risk management. Without clearly identified strategic goals and objectives, an agency is limited in its ability to effectively identify and address potential risks to its mission, prioritize risk, or identify criteria against which to measure performance.

• Require risk assessments be performed to identify and evaluate potential risks that could adversely affect an agency's ability to achieve its objectives. The design of a risk management program can erroneously call for evaluating the risks in specific functional areas, systems, or processes rather than assessing the risks that could adversely affect the agency as a whole.

• Require pertinent information to be collected from and disseminated to relevant internal and external stakeholders in a form and time frame consistent with the agency's overall risk management needs. The design of a risk program should not allow for inconsistent and incomparable information from internal operational units, which can prevent management from effectively using the information to help ensure that agency objectives are met.

NIH's new program was finally established just shy of the release of major risk management standards, such as ISO 31000, which was issued in December

2009. Given that NIH was ahead in this area, its formal six-step methodology for managing risks was on point:

1. Organize—Identify and train those charged with carrying out risk management activities, and define the risk management structure.

2. Identify and Score—Identify and score risks, review risks for quality and accuracy, and develop the risk baseline.

3. Assess—Document, analyze, and test processes and controls.

4. Remediate—Develop, review, approve, and execute corrective action plans.

5. Monitor—Monitor the risk baseline.

6. Report—Report risk information and results.

The design of the Enterprise Risk Management Program represented an improvement over the 2004 NIH Management Control Program in several key areas. Specifically, the new program allowed for improved identification, assessment, and mitigation of risks agency-wide because it included the following:

• Risk assessments: The new program requires the identification of potential events that could adversely affect the agency and the evaluation of those events based on likelihood of occurrence and impact.

• Oversight by a high-level senior body: The design requires the steering committee to oversee the new risk management program.

• Information and communication: The design requires that pertinent information be collected from and disseminated to relevant internal stakeholders in a form and time frame consistent with NIH's risk management needs. For example, the program requires a consistent methodology for identifying, assessing, and communicating risks across NIH, which will allow for consistent, comparable information from each of the institutes and centers (ICs).

## Insights for Program Enhancements

Additional insights into NIH's program for improvement can be used as a model for other agencies seeking to implement similar programs. It is imperative that agencies ensure that all of the components of the GAO Risk Management Framework are addressed, regardless of the standard or framework they adopt. This is often overlooked due to the lack of recognition the GAO Risk Management Framework receives. But the newest standards made available, such as the ISO 31000 issued in 2009, appear to align with the GAO framework at some level. The following notations made by GAO assisted in improving the NIH program:

- *Strategic Goals, Objectives, and Constraints.* The Enterprise Risk Management Program should require the NIH institutes and centers to set mission-based strategic goals and objectives as a precondition for risk management. This was a critical shortcoming because although the risk design requires risks to be assessed on the basis of their impact on NIH's mission, at that time there was not an NIH-wide strategic plan against which to assess risks. Further, although some ICs and NIH Office of the Director (OD) offices have strategic plans for their organizations, the risk management program as designed should call for risks to be assessed on the basis of their impact on IC or NIH OD office-level missions.

- *Alternatives Evaluation.* Although the NIH Enterprise Risk Management Program identified four different responses from which the agency can select to prevent or mitigate identified risks (creating a new policy, procedure, or control; revising an existing policy, procedure, or control; streamlining or automating an existing policy, procedure, or control; or redesigning the process), the program should also require management to evaluate the risk responses identified to consider (1) the effect on the likelihood of occurrence and impact of a potential risk and (2) the costs and benefits. These types of evaluations could assist management in making an informed decision in an environment that includes constrained resources.

- *Management Selection.* The design of the Enterprise Risk Management Program should require management to document the rationale for selecting a particular risk response. Such documentation could help improve accountability and facilitate analysis of the effectiveness of actions taken.

- *Implementation and Monitoring.* Although the design of the Enterprise Risk Management Program required periodic assessments of the overall efficiency and effectiveness of the risk management program, it did not offer detail regarding how these assessments will be performed. For example, the program should provide details such as the frequency, scope, or methodology for these reviews. Further, the design should require periodic assessments of implemented risk responses.

These types of monitoring activities are critical in helping management to identify problems with the overall risk management program and to determine whether risk responses are preventing or mitigating risks and operating as intended.

- *Internal Environment.* The Enterprise Risk Management Program included many of the elements that define this component. However, the design could be improved by (1) incorporating the importance of ethical values into the risk management program and (2) ensuring that management maintains the competence of its personnel by providing for continuous training to update personnel on risk management practices and techniques.

- *Information and Communication.* The design of NIH's Enterprise Risk Management Program should require the collection and dissemination of pertinent information to relevant external stakeholders in a form and time frame consistent with NIH's risk management needs. For example, although the design requires annual reporting, in aggregate, to HHS on the adequacy of internal control, it does not require communication with other external stakeholders, such as congressional oversight committees.

NIH has since recognized the importance of risk management to its organization and has taken steps toward implementing its new Enterprise Risk Management Program. Specifically, NIH has organized the risk structure at the NIH OD and ICs, identified and trained personnel responsible for managing risks within the NIH OD, and made progress in identifying and scoring risks at both the NIH OD and the ICs, which represent important steps.

On December 17, 2009, NIH officially implemented its risk management program and formally issued NIH Manual Chapter 1750: Risk Management Program.

## Case Study Best Practices

- Mission-based strategic goals and objectives must be a precondition for risk management and risks to be assessed on the basis of their impact on the achievement of these goals and objectives.

- Risk responses must be evaluated to consider the effect on the likelihood of occurrence and impact of a potential risk and the costs and benefits.

- The rationale for selecting risk responses must be documented.

- Additional detail must be provided regarding how the assessments of the overall efficiency and effectiveness of the risk management program will be performed.

- Periodic assessments must be made of implemented risk responses.

- The importance of ethical values must be emphasized.

- Continuous training must be instituted to maintain the competence of personnel carrying out risk management duties.

- Communication with relevant external stakeholders is essential.

## CASE STUDY: NATIONAL ARCHIVES AND RECORDS ADMINISTRATION

Records management activities in the federal government have become more robust since the turn of the twenty-first century. The evolution and upgrades to information technology have created growing volumes of electronic as well as physical records across agencies. In fact, the topic of records management has become so significant that in 2013 OPM issued a draft position classification that establishes a new records management job series. The position would oversee the collection, analysis, protection, and retention of government records. The validity of these trends has directed increased attention to the National Archives and Records Administration (NARA) at a time when the management of records is noticeably becoming a high-risk area.

Records management is a shared risk area across the government. By statute, some of the responsibilities for oversight of federal records management are divided across several agencies. Under the Federal Records Act, NARA shares a number of records management responsibilities and authorities with the General Services Administration (GSA). Under the Paperwork Reduction Act and the E-Government Act, the Office of Management and Budget (OMB) also has records management oversight responsibilities.

Further, the heads of federal agencies are responsible for their agencies' records. The Federal Records Act establishes requirements for records management programs in federal agencies. Each federal agency is required to make and preserve records that (1) document the organization, functions, policies, decisions, procedures, and essential transactions of the agency and (2) provide the information necessary to protect the legal and financial rights of the government and of persons directly affected by the agency's activities. (NARA is assigned responsibilities for assisting federal agencies in this area.) Effective management of these records is critical for ensuring that sufficient documentation is created; that agencies can efficiently locate and retrieve records needed in the daily performance of their missions; and that records of historical significance are identified, preserved, and made available to the public.

Records must be managed at all stages of their life cycle, which includes records creation or receipt, maintenance and use, and disposition. Agencies create records to meet the business needs and legal responsibilities of federal programs and (to the extent known) the needs of internal and external stakeholders who may make secondary use of the records. To maintain and use the records created, agencies are to establish internal record keeping requirements for maintaining records, consistently apply these requirements, and establish systems that allow them to find records that they need. Disposition involves transferring records of permanent, historical value to NARA for archiving (preservation) and destroying all other records that are no longer needed for agency operations.

NARA is responsible for issuing records management guidance; working with agencies to implement effective controls over the creation, maintenance, and use of records in the conduct of agency business; approving the disposition (destruction or preservation) of records; and providing storage facilities for agency records. The Federal Records Act also gives NARA the responsibility for conducting inspections or surveys of agencies' records and records management programs and practices; conducting records management studies; and reporting the results of these activities to the Congress and OMB.

The mission of NARA is "to safeguard and preserve government records, ensuring continuing access to the essential documentation of the rights of American citizens and the actions of their government."[18] Now more than ever, NARA's ability to effectively oversee the government-wide management of records, including its capacity to identify the risk of unlawful destruction of federal records, is of great interest to internal and external stakeholders. Those who have a vested interest in successful government-wide records management want to ensure that NARA has the resources it needs to meet the challenges.

In 2010, the GAO conducted a review of NARA's oversight and management activities, including its risk management function as it related to records management. Here, the GAO review is presented as a case study that provides key insights about the management of an operational risk and the adjustments to a risk management structure that are needed to support mission objectives. The case study exemplifies the importance of alignment of an agency's strategic plan and risk management framework. Both the COSO and ISO 31000, as well as the GAO Risk Management Framework, emphasize the presence of a strategic plan as a precondition to managing risk effectively. And finally, in true ERM form, the case study shows how the management of a risk in one particular functional area can impact operations in another functional area. For example, the risks associated with NARA's acquisition and management of the Electronic Records Archives (ERA) brought challenges to the improvement of electronic records management overall. GAO noted that NARA's management of the requirements for the ERA had weaknesses, noting that "until ERA and its electronic preservation capabilities are fully implemented, there is reduced assurance that NARA can ensure the preservation of all electronic records."[19] Yet, despite these occurrences, GAO acknowledged NARA's overall progress and cited the oversight and management improvements the agency initiated.

The GAO assessment of NARA's management and oversight activities had several focal points:

- To assess NARA's effectiveness in overseeing government-wide records management, an [examination] of its use of the oversight activities—surveys, studies, inspections, and reporting—defined in the Federal Records Act and its process for approving records schedules, was completed. [GAO] examined documents, interviewed agency officials, and obtained input from a panel of experts and from other federal records managers. To comment on NARA's capacity to identify risk of unlawful destruction of federal records, [applicable laws and the results of a NARA survey were reviewed]. Meetings with NARA records management staff were held to identify risk factors.

- To describe NARA's ability to preserve permanent records, GAO met with NARA preservation staff; reviewed NARA's survey of its physical records and its backlog of records needing preservation actions and assessed their reliability; and analyzed NARA's ability to process its backlog. GAO also reviewed external research on electronic records, interviewed staff involved in developing NARA's Electronic Records Archives (ERA) system, and drew on previous reports about the status of ERA.

- To assess NARA's policies, procedures, and plans supporting key management and oversight capabilities, GAO analyzed NARA management, strategic planning, and policy documents against requirements of the Government Performance and Results Act (GPRA) and the [GAO] Risk Management Framework in order to determine whether NARA lines of responsibility were aligned with its strategic plans and whether it was conducting an appropriate risk management program.

- To assess human capital management, [GAO] compared NARA's human capital management capabilities and its human capital strategic plan against the [GAO] Strategic Human Capital Framework. [GAO] interviewed NARA officials and reviewed progress in implementing its human capital plan against the plan's milestones. To evaluate NARA's collaboration capabilities, interviews with policy and planning staff were conducted, and agency policies and procedures related to collaboration were analyzed. GAO obtained a list of NARA collaborative projects, and examined whether collaborative activities specified in the strategic plan were being carried out.[20]

## Identified Risks and Best Practices

The NARA performance audit was conducted from October 2009 to October 2010. There were several key risks identified that needed to be addressed. The following are excerpts from the GAO performance audit listing a few of the risks and select best practices identified to further build on NARA's risk management efforts:

- **Risk No. 1:** NARA has begun to increase its efforts to assess government-wide records management and its reporting of results. Although the Federal Records Act gives NARA responsibility for oversight activities (including inspections, surveys, and reporting), until recently, its performance of these activities was limited. It has now completed its first government-wide records management self-assessment survey, resumed agency inspections after a long gap, and increased its reporting. These new efforts have provided NARA with a fuller picture of government-wide records management, including an assessment by agency of the risk of unauthorized destruction of federal records. As a result, it is in a better position to determine where records management improvements are most needed, develop and update guidance, and hold agencies accountable by publishing assessments of their records management programs. NARA plans to use these oversight activities to develop baselines against which to assess future progress; however, it has not yet developed plans for adequately validating self-reported data or targeting inspections of agency records and records management programs to achieve government-wide results. As NARA continues to build its oversight program, such activities will be important to provide assurance that reported changes from baseline scores reasonably reflect actual performance.

• **Risk No. 2:** NARA also provides oversight through its appraisal and scheduling work with agencies, in which it appraises agency records for their permanent value (among other things) and reviews and approves agency disposition schedules, in accordance with the Federal Records Act. Following an extended effort to get agencies to submit schedules for unscheduled systems containing electronic records, NARA has increased the number of schedules it has approved per year, but nevertheless has an increased backlog of schedules awaiting approval. NARA faces the risk that its success in getting agencies to schedule their systems may result in more schedules being submitted than it can handle in a timely manner. Unless NARA assesses this risk and develops appropriate mitigation plans, the backlog may increasingly hinder agencies' records management.

• **Risk No. 3:** NARA has undertaken efforts to gather government-wide information to help it assess the status of federal records management and risks of unauthorized disposition (including destruction) of records. In September 2009, NARA sent the first of a promised series of annual mandatory records management self-assessment surveys to 242 federal records officers from cabinet-level agencies, agency components, and independent agencies; the survey's goal was to determine how effectively agencies were meeting statutory and regulatory requirements for records management. Agencies were asked thirty-four questions designed to obtain basic information about the agencies' records management programs in five areas: program management, records disposition, vital records, electronic records, and e-mail records. NARA used the data collected to categorize agencies according to the level of risk to records associated with the state of agencies' records management programs. According to NARA, ineffective records management programs are the most significant indicators of risk of unauthorized disposition of records.

NARA's report on the self-assessment survey, released in April 2010, described strengths and weaknesses in agencies' records management programs. It concluded that almost 80 percent of agencies were at moderate or high risk of improper destruction of records; that is, the risk that permanent records will be lost or destroyed before they can be transferred to NARA for archiving or that other records will be lost while they are still needed for government operations or legal obligations. In particular, of the 220 (91 percent) federal agencies and components that responded, 36 percent were at high risk in their records management programs and 43 percent were at moderate risk. Overall, only 21 percent of federal agencies and components responding were at low risk. For electronic records, 39 percent were at high risk, and for e-mail, 48 percent were at high risk. The archivist referred to these results as "alarming" and "worrisome"; in a subsequent oversight hearing, the director of NARA's Modern Records Program testified that the findings were "troubling" and "unacceptable."

- **Risk No. 4:** NARA thus faces the risk that if its efforts to get agencies to submit schedules for outstanding agency systems continue to be successful, it will be unprepared to deal with the workload. The jump in its backlog associated with the 2009 deadline for scheduling electronic systems suggests that this is a real concern. NARA has acknowledged that in light of the volume and complexity of electronic records increasing each year, keeping pace with the requirements to schedule all existing electronic records is a continuing challenge for both NARA and agencies. However, it has not assessed the risk that it may be unable to keep up with schedules submitted, nor has it developed plans to mitigate that risk. Unless it does so, the risk increases that the backlog may increasingly hinder agencies' records management—for example, they may be required to retain records unnecessarily that they would otherwise be authorized to dispose of, and they may be delayed in transferring permanent records to NARA.

**Best Practices for Risk Management**

In response to the risk factors reported by the GAO, the following recommendations were made to NARA:

- *In Key Management Areas, NARA Has Policies and Procedures That Are Consistent with Its Strategic Planning, Although Gaps Remain.* NARA's policies and procedures for key aspects of governance, human capital, and collaboration are generally aligned with its strategic planning, but selected areas have gaps. With regard to governance policies and procedures, NARA has defined and delegated areas of authority and responsibility that are generally aligned with its strategic plan, but it is not managing risk at the enterprise level. In addition, it has developed a strategic human capital plan that is consistent with our human capital strategic framework, but its implementation of the plan has been delayed, so that the agency is not yet managing human capital strategically. To its credit, NARA is taking advantage of numerous collaboration opportunities, which are generally aligned with the goals and strategies in its strategic plan. If NARA addresses the identified gaps in governance and human capital, it will be better positioned to achieve its goals.

• *NARA Has Policies and Procedures Defining Key Aspects of Governance, But It Lacks an Enterprise Risk Management Capability.* GAO previously described governance as the process of providing leadership, direction, and accountability in fulfilling an organization's mission, meeting objectives, and establishing clear lines of responsibility for results. Enterprise-wide risk assessment and management is a key part of governance.

• *NARA Does Not Manage Enterprise Risk on a Continuous Basis.* Enterprise-wide risks are those that would threaten an organization's ability to carry out its mission, such as an act of terrorism, loss or compromise of critical information (such as classified or personally identifiable information), or a natural disaster. Without an effective program of risk assessment and internal control, management may have less assurance that it is using organizational resources effectively and efficiently, or that agency assets and operations are protected. As our previous work has shown, and as called for by the Standards for Internal Control in the Federal Government, agencies should continuously and systematically monitor their internal and external environments to anticipate future challenges and avoid potential crises.

GAO advises that decisions for enterprise-wide risk management should be made in the context of an organization's strategic plan, and organizations should have risk planning documents that address risk-related issues that are central to the organization's mission. According to NARA program officials in 2010, NARA performs risk management for the ERA project, its major system investment. The agency manages ERA's risks using an agency-level risk review board, a program-level risk review board, and a technical risk review team. In addition, officials stated that the ERA program office produces monthly reports that include top identified risks and specify associated mitigation strategies. Risk status is communicated to senior NARA management and OMB on a monthly basis and to Congress on a quarterly basis. The project uses an automated tool to track and manage risk. However, although NARA has identified important risks facing the agency, it currently has no dedicated active function to manage these risks at the enterprise level. Some risks of which NARA is aware include:

- Technological change causing record formats to become obsolete and unreadable

- Failure of the ERA project

- Effects of climate change or natural disasters (such as on continuity of operation, preservation requirements, locations of facilities, and energy use)

According to NARA officials, the organization had a risk review board, which existed for about two years, but it became inactive. This occurred because the board's discussion of risk tended to focus on either project and program risks or highly generic risks. NARA officials told us that the agency has also relied on a work group of senior executives, the Lifecycle Guidance Team, to address enterprise-wide risks. However, as currently established, the Lifecycle Guidance Team does not explicitly focus on enterprise risk management. The members of this team, chaired by the deputy archivist, are members of NARA's senior staff. However, although the team is at an appropriate level of seniority to address enterprise risk management, this function is not part of its charter. According to the charter, the group focuses on ensuring that NARA's records life cycle initiatives are effectively coordinated, integrated, and implemented agency-wide, and it provides leadership and oversight to initiatives to advance the agency's mission and strategic goals and improve records, information, and knowledge management government-wide. Among the initiatives it is reviewing or has reviewed are systems in operation or in development, for which project risks have been discussed. However, these risks are not enterprise risks.

According to NARA officials, the development of a new process and system for internal control has recently been proposed. The process and system, to be based on a similar system at the Library of Congress, are intended to automate internal controls and would include assessment and categorization of risk on the functional level. According to the officials, such an implementation would benefit NARA's risk management and internal control capabilities. This proposal has been reviewed by senior management, but it is still in the first stages of planning and does not yet include a clear picture of which divisions will be responsible for dealing with strategic risks. At the time of this report, agency officials also acknowledged that NARA has neither completed a time frame for implementation nor established an estimated finish date.

Unless NARA begins to manage its enterprise risks on a continuous basis, there is a greater likelihood that serious threats to NARA may not be addressed.

## Performance Audit Conclusions

NARA had taken steps to expand its oversight activities and improve their effectiveness. Although it cannot by itself ensure that agencies are managing records appropriately (agencies control and are responsible for their own records), NARA can use its oversight activities to help determine where records management improvements are most needed and improve its ability to influence agencies to give more priority to records management programs. This will require that it continue to build and improve its oversight activities, including studies, surveys, inspections, and reporting. As NARA continues to refine its approach to oversight, it will be important for it to consider how to validate self-assessment data (for example, by doing follow-up interviews) and how to strategically plan inspections to maximize their value as oversight tools, by, for example, defining key practices and inspecting these at multiple sites. Further, it will also be important going forward for NARA to assess the risk that its capacity to process and approve schedules may not be sufficient to meet the demand.

As an agency with a broad mission, NARA faces numerous challenges, for which its strengths in seeking collaborative opportunities should be helpful. Further, NARA's organizational responsibilities are generally aligned with its strategic plan, and it has developed a human capital strategic plan that, if implemented effectively, would give NARA the capability to strategically manage its human capital, as called for in our strategic human capital framework. However, there are opportunities for improvement. For a few specific strategies, NARA has not yet established clear lines and assignments of responsibility. In addition, the lack of adequate enterprise-wide risk management leaves the agency vulnerable to a variety of risks that may not be foreseen or mitigated. And until NARA has implemented the capability to manage its human capital strategically, the risk remains that it will not have the staff with the skills needed to meet present and future mission needs.

## Recommendations for Executive Action

To help NARA improve its management and oversight capabilities, GAO recommended that the archivist of the United States take the following six actions:

- To help ensure that its future assessments of the status of government-wide and agency records management are accurate, develop additional means to validate the self-reported data in its surveys.

- To ensure that its inspections program helps provide a comprehensive view of federal records management and greater impetus for agency improvement, develop a plan, with milestones, that provides for systematically and strategically targeting inspections to maximize their value as oversight tools.

- To help ensure that it can manage the backlog in the scheduling process, assess the risk that it will be unable to keep up with schedules submitted and develop plans to mitigate that risk, if indicated.

- To ensure that its organization and governance reflect its strategic goals and strategies, ensure that all the specific strategies in its strategic plan have clear lines and assignments of responsibility.

- To ensure that NARA's senior staff and decision makers can appropriately and quickly assess threats and vulnerabilities stemming from enterprise risks, develop and assign responsibility and resources for an enterprise-wide risk management capability that allows it to monitor its internal and external environments continuously and systematically.

- To ensure that it has the appropriate skills and staff to meet present and future needs, give priority to completing its skills, needs, and gap analyses and developing a plan to fill those gaps.

## chapter THREE

# Managing and Communicating Risk

In a 2014 survey of public sector risk professionals, 56 percent of respondents indicated that *the scope of the ERM effort within their organization cuts across the entire organization.*[1] This response is consistent with the COSO definition of ERM, which emphasizes the broad-based application of risk management throughout an organization. Through ERM, risk management is not treated as a compliance issue but rather creates an environment in which the proactive identification and management of risk is communicated at all levels of the organization.

The context in which risk is communicated depends on how risk management functions are structured at an organization. A common approach is to manage and communicate risk along business lines. For example, this type of approach is reflected in the annual reports of some private sector firms, such as the Adidas Group. As part of their summary report, Adidas outlined the Group's most important risks and opportunities and summarized them into four main categories: strategic, operational, legal and compliance, and financial. The federal government is another sector that engages in the business line approach to managing and communicating risk. Government agencies as a whole have replicative organizational structures. So risk is usually managed based on the organizational structure. Most agencies manage risk across the common business lines, which include but are not limited to human resource management, facility management, IT management, and grants management. Others have also added strategic and operational risk to the mix. With some exceptions, agencies may manage risk according to a program rather than a business line, such as the Department of Education, which established their ERM program for their Federal Student Aid Program.

A great concern for any organization is ensuring that they capture the key risks that could adversely impact them. While there is no guarantee that all risk can be comprehended, having a system that helps raise an organization to meet this goal is optimal. But an even greater goal is being able to understand how different risks interrelate. Having an organizational risk management structure that does not inhibit this level of fluidity in risk communication and management is of utmost importance. A tool that can help craft that type of environment is a risk taxonomy.

According to the Treasury Board of Canada Secretariat, a risk taxonomy is a "comprehensive, common and stable set of risk categories that is used within an organization. By providing a comprehensive set of risk categories, it encourages those involved in risk identification to consider all types of risks that could affect the organization's objectives. A common set of risk categories facilitates the aggregation of risks from across the organization and provides a stable set of risk categories. This also helps to facilitate a comparative analysis of an organization's risks over time."[2]

Once established, "the organization should encourage those involved in risk identification to use the risk taxonomy to categorize identified risks. Using the risk taxonomy in risk identification helps to ensure that all types of risks have been considered."[3]

Table 3.1 presents the Treasury Board of Canada Secretariat list of "potential risk categories and a brief description of the types of risks, both threats and opportunities, which could fall under each category. [Agencies may use] these categories in identifying and aggregating their risks and may adapt the categories to their own needs."

Managing risk by business line does not suggest that ERM is not being practiced at an organization. If done properly, even the not-so-obvious risk can be identified through this structure as long as ERM is practiced.

Another school of thought for managing and communicating risk is in contrast to the business line approach. Described as "thought-provoking," this new framework, developed by Robert Kaplan and Anette Mikes, "allows executives to tell which risks can be managed through a rules-based model and which required [an] alternative approach. Their research identifies just three

## Table 3.1
## Risk Taxonomy

| | |
|---|---|
| Business processes | Threats and opportunities associated with business process design or implementation. |
| Capital infrastructure | Threats and opportunities associated with an organization's capital infrastructure, including hard assets (e.g., buildings, vessels, scientific equipment, fleet) but excluding IT. |
| Communications | Threats and opportunities associated with an organization's approach and culture of communication, consultation, transparency, and information sharing, both within and outside the organization. |
| Conflict of interest | Threats and opportunities associated with perceived or potential conflicts between private and public interests. |
| Financial management | Threats and opportunities associated with the structures and processes of an organization to ensure sound management of financial resources and its compliance with financial management policies and standards. |
| Governance and strategic direction | Threats and opportunities associated with an organization's approach to leadership, decision making, and management capacity. |
| Human resources management | Threats and opportunities associated with staff/management turnover; employment/ work culture; recruitment, retention, and staffing processes and practices; succession planning and talent management; and employee development, training, and capacity building. |
| Information management | Threats and opportunities associated with an organization's capacity and sustainability of information management procedures and practices. |
| Information technology | Threats and opportunities associated with an organization's capacity and sustainability of information technology, both the infrastructure and utilization of technological applications. |
| Knowledge management | Threats and opportunities associated with an organization's collection and management of knowledge, including intellectual property, organizational or operational information and records, and scientific data. |

(continued)

**Table 3.1**

**Risk Taxonomy (*Continued*)**

| | |
|---|---|
| Legal | Threats and opportunities associated with an organization's management of its legislative, advisory, and litigation activities, including the development and renewal of, and compliance with, laws, regulations, international treaties/agreements, and policies. |
| Organizational transformation and change management | Threats and opportunities associated with significant structural or behavioral change within an organization related to mandate, operating context, leadership, and strategic direction. |
| Policy development and implementation | Threats and opportunities associated with an organization's design, implementation, and compliance with the government-wide policy suite as well as its own internal policies and procedures. |
| Privacy/information stewardship | Threats and opportunities associated with an organization's protection of intellectual property and personal information. |
| Program design and delivery | Threats and opportunities associated with an organization's design and delivery of specific programs, which may impact the organization's overall objectives. |
| Project management | Threats and opportunities associated with an organization's process and practice of developing and managing major projects in support of its overall mandate, as well as risks associated with specific projects that may require ongoing management. |
| Political | Threats and opportunities associated with the political climate and operating context of an organization. |
| Reputational | Threats and opportunities associated with an organization's reputation and credibility with its partners, stakeholders, and the public. |
| Resource management | Threats and opportunities associated with the availability and level of resources of an organization to deliver on its mandate, as well as the organization's management of these resources. |
| Stakeholders and partnerships | Threats and opportunities associated with an organization's partners and stakeholder demographics, characteristics, and activities. |
| Values and ethics | Threats and opportunities associated with an organization's culture and capacity to adhere to the spirit and intent of the Values and Ethics Code for the Public Service. |

*Source:* Treasury Board of Canada Secretariat (www.tbs-sct.gc.ca).

categories of risk."[4] (The following series of quoted extracts are from this source, unless otherwise noted.)

- *Preventable.* These are internal risks, arising from within the organization, that are controllable and ought to be eliminated or avoided. These include illegal, unethical, or inappropriate actions, as well as breakdowns in operational processes. In the federal government, these are typically covered by internal control schemes. These kinds of risks are best controlled through active prevention: monitoring operational processes and guiding people's behaviors and decisions toward desired norms.

- *Strategic.* These differ from preventable risks because they are not necessarily undesirable. For example, developing a satellite-based air traffic control system may be seen as taking a strategic risk over the proven, ground-based radar-controlled air traffic control system. Strategy risks cannot be managed through a rules-based control system [or as a compliance issue]. Instead, you need a risk-management system designed to reduce the probability that the assumed risks actually materialize and to improve the company's ability to manage or contain the risk events should they occur.

- *External risks.* Organizations cannot prevent external risks from happening. So mangers need to forecast what these risks might be and develop ways to lessen their impact. They cannot be avoided, only managed. The model for addressing external risks is the use of open and explicit risk discussions.

According to Kaplan and Mikes, "each approach [within their framework] requires quite different structures and roles for a risk-management function. One way to implement this integrative approach is to anchor risk discussions in strategic planning functions; this function already serves as integrative in most large organizations and points to positive action rather than constraints. It is about turning the conversation from risk management that 'focuses on the negative' to a risk strategy that aligns with the 'can do' culture most leadership teams try to foster when implementing strategy."

Within the framework of ERM, both approaches can facilitate a discussion about varying types of risk in relation to each other and how they interact. This action will help inform leadership of key risks when identifying strategic goals. The underlying question is whether one approach is more effective than the other. Overall, culture still plays a major role in whether an organization practices risk avoidance or risk management when it comes to managing and communicating risk. However, once these risks are articulated, agencies should "then move to a more formal process of risk assessment to address those risks."

## GLOSSARY OF RISK MANAGEMENT TERMS

*Source:* GAO Risk Management Framework (GAO, 2005) and the draft ISO 31000 International Standard dated November 2009.* Reprinted with permission. IBM Center for the Business of Government, "Managing Risk in Government: An Introduction to Enterprise Risk Management," 2010.

Consequence: The expected worst case or reasonable worst case impact. This loss or damage may be long or short term in nature.

Monitoring and evaluation: A continuous repetitive assessment process to keep a risk management process current and relevant. It includes, among other activities, external peer review, testing, and validation.

Opportunity cost: The value of opportunities foregone.

Risk: An event that has a potentially negative impact and the possibility that such an event will occur and adversely affect an entity's assets, activities, and operations.

Risk appetite: Amount and type of risk that an organization is prepared to pursue, retain, or take.

Risk assessment: The process of qualitatively or quantitatively determining the probability of an adverse event and the severity of its impact.

Risk identification: The process of finding, recognizing, and describing risks.

Risk management: A continuous process of managing—through a series of mitigating actions that permeate an entity's activities—the likelihood of an adverse event and its negative impact. Risk management addresses risk before mitigating action, as well as the risk that remains after countermeasures have been taken.

Risk management framework:* A set of components that provide the foundations and organizational arrangements for designing, implementing, monitoring, reviewing, and continually improving risk management throughout the organization.

Risk owner: A person or entity with the accountability and authority to manage the risk.

Risk profile: A description of any set of risks. (The set of risks can contain those that relate to the whole organization, part of the organization, or as otherwise defined.)

Residual risk: The risk remaining after risk treatment. Residual risk can contain unidentified risks and can also be known as "retained risk."

Risk treatment: Process to modify risk. Risk treatment can involve: (1) avoiding the risk by deciding not to start or continue with the activity that gives rise to the risk, (2) taking or increasing risk in order to pursue an opportunity, (3) removing the risk source, (4) changing the likelihood, (5) changing the consequences, (6) sharing the risk, (7) retaining the risk.

Stakeholder: A person or organization that can affect, be affected by, or perceive themselves to be affected by a decision or activity.

## WRITING RISK STATEMENTS

One of the most challenging but critical elements in an organization's risk management process is the ability to articulate and present risk information clearly and meaningfully. Without clear risk statements, it is difficult to perform effective risk assessments. Furthermore, unclear risk statements can lead to a misrepresentation of an organization's specific risk. This can lead to greater vulnerabilities. Therefore, risks need to be well stated. Writing risk statements is a standard practice in risk management processes; differences may be more a matter of style and semantics than of substance. For instance, some organizations prefer to express risk statements in IF/THEN format, showing cause and effect as well. That is to say, IF "X" happens, THEN "Y" is the result/impact.

Using the potential HR risk listed in Table 1.2. in Chapter One, the risk statement using an IF/THEN format may be written as follows:

> **IF** leadership gaps are not filled, **THEN** the agency strategic objectives will not be properly managed leading to missed performance goals.

Regardless of these minor variations, the fact remains that "a good risk statement should be concise and readily understood across an organization, as its precision can influence the development of effective risk responses, choices of action plans and the quality of decision making pertaining to the risk. It is important to develop risk statements that accurately identify and convey threats and opportunities in a way that is tailored to each organization."[5]

## DEVELOPING A RISK STATEMENT

When developing risk statements, the Canadian government considers both threats and opportunities. For example, a risk statement for a threat involves at least two elements: the event itself and the potential negative impact of such an event if left unmanaged:

> Risk statement (threat): If (event) occurs, the consequences could result in (negative impact).

> Example: The segregation of reporting practices for regional and headquarters inspection activities may leave an oversight gap in compliance, which may allow unregulated materials to enter the country illegally.[6]

Likewise, opportunity statements provide an accurate picture of an event that has a positive impact. It is important to note that opportunity statements can be challenging and difficult to craft. Because impacts are typically felt in more than one area or function across an organization, or by multiple stakeholders, opportunities can arise from various situations and approaches. A suggested method for developing a risk statement for an opportunity also involves at least two elements: the event itself and the potential positive impact of such an event if managed appropriately:

> Risk statement (opportunity): If (event) occurs, the consequences could result in (positive impact).

> Example: In the event of further operational realignment, there is an opportunity to partner with portfolio agencies to achieve efficiencies in delivering support services.[7]

The Canadian Risk Management Framework emphasizes the following key factors when establishing risk statements:

- Risk events and their impacts, both positive and negative, should be relevant to the mandate and other objectives of the organization. Risk statements that are too general become vague and can lead to the presentation of risk information that is unclear and potentially misleading. As a result, organizations are encouraged to develop clear and concise risk statements, whether specific or broad in content, that are relevant to the mandate and business of the organization.

- A specific risk statement is a targeted description of a threat or opportunity that includes important details, including the potential impact within an organization that may or may not be common or shared with other organizations and stakeholders. Specific risk statements may change more frequently because they focus on a precise and targeted event. Specific risk statements are often easier to manage, as the precise nature of the risk is transparent to decision makers.

- A broader risk statement articulates a risk using language that may reflect common threats or opportunities and the potential impact that could apply broadly throughout the organization. Broader risk statements may provide stability because they could be less likely to change over time and tend to be more horizontal in nature. This may be beneficial when working with information that is sensitive and where specific details cannot be shared.[8]

"Regardless of the structure chosen, organizations are encouraged to develop well–articulated risk statements, i.e., those that are clear, meaningful and concise, and that can present useful and relevant information to senior management to help support risk-informed decision making."[9]

## INVENTORY OF RISK STATEMENTS

Exhibit 3.1 presents an inventory of risk statements based on the Canadian government's risk taxonomy.

## Exhibit 3.1
## Inventory of Risk Statements

**Business Processes**

Threats and opportunities associated with business process design or implementation:

- The department may not have a business process in place to adequately manage key programs, which may lead to weakened results.
- Current departmental processes to track, analyze and report on key grants and contributions programs may not support effective risk management and other accountability requirements, leading to weakened performance results.
- The organization could restructure the departmental business processes based on other jurisdictions' best practices to support more effective risk management and other accountability requirements, leading to improved performance results.

**Capital Infrastructure**

Threats and opportunities associated with an organization's capital infrastructure, including hard assets (e.g., buildings, vessels, scientific equipment, fleets) but excluding information technology (IT):

- Some elements of the organization's real property portfolio are aging and will require ongoing maintenance and life-cycle investment that cannot be delivered as planned. This may result in the department not achieving its key performance targets.
- The organization may not be able to meet the planned requirements for up-to-date laboratory facilities to support scientific activities, leading to a possible compromise or delay in regulatory approvals.
- The organization could explore changes to its current accommodations approach as a result of lacking available office space within the current building, which may result in innovative accommodation solutions for employees.

**Communications**

Threats and opportunities associated with an organization's approach and culture of communication, consultation, transparency, and information sharing, both within and outside the organization:

- The organization may lack capacity to meet public expectations for information on a timely basis. This may result in a loss of confidence in the organization.

- The department may not be able to meet the public's expectations for timely access to complete and accurate information in times of crisis, leading to possible health and safety risks and a loss of confidence in the organization.
- The department could develop and implement social media practices to better meet public expectations for timely access to complete and accurate information in times of crisis.

## Conflict of Interest

Threats and opportunities associated with perceived or potential conflicts of interest:

- Members of the Advisory Committee may have conflicting interests or may object to certain reforms, which may result in an increased advantage or disadvantage to certain stakeholders.
- Departmental officials may be offered gifts or hospitality from local vendors with whom they have a high volume of business. Accepting such gifts or hospitality may result in a conflict of interest between the department and the vendor community, compromising the public's confidence in the department's ability to carry out its mandate fairly and objectively.

## Financial Management

Threats and opportunities associated with the structures and processes of an organization to ensure sound management of financial resources and its compliance with financial management policies and standards:

- The organization may conduct insufficient monitoring of partners, recipients or projects to ensure that the funds are used for intended purposes and to achieve stated outcomes, resulting in fraudulent actions.
- A lack of internal controls over financial reporting may result in lapsed funds in the fourth quarter, preventing the organization from making critical capital investments.
- To alleviate reporting burden for partners and recipients, while maintaining effective internal control over funds, the organization could modernize and improve risk-based approaches within the organization's grants and contribution processes.

## Governance and Strategic Direction

Threats and opportunities associated with an organization's approach to leadership, decision making, and management capacity:

- The organizational governance structure may not be able to provide sufficient and appropriate oversight on a timely basis to support effective decision making.

*(continued)*

# Exhibit 3.1
## Inventory of Risk Statements (*Continued*)

- The segregation of reporting practices for regional and headquarters inspection activities could leave an oversight gap in compliance promotion, which may allow unregulated materials to enter the country illegally.

### Human Resources Management

Threats and opportunities associated with staff and management turnover; the employment/work culture; recruitment, retention, and staffing processes and practices; succession planning and talent management; and employee development, training, and capacity building:

- The organization may be unable to sustain a workforce that has the appropriate competencies, resulting in inadequate support to deliver and manage programs and services.
- Due to retirements and a shortage of qualified senior scientists, the department may be unable to attract and retain senior scientific talent. This may result in an inability to deliver the department's science and technology agenda.
- Given the large number of retiring qualified senior scientists, some retiring employees could mentor junior scientists and seek alternative work arrangements that could help stagger retirement dates and lessen the impact of senior staff turnover.

### Knowledge Management

Threats and opportunities associated with an organization's knowledge assets, including people, data, and information:

- The department's "silo" approach to managing renewal may result in a loss of information that weakens corporate culture.
- The department may lack capacity to integrate a systematic approach to identify, capture, preserve, and share information among new recruits and retirees, which may result in a loss of focus and business intelligence, compromising value for clients.

### Information Management

Threats and opportunities associated with the capacity and sustainability of information management procedures and practices:

- The current tools to manage information may make records unobtainable, resulting in delayed responses to official requests.
- Significant delays in retrieving records as a result of current tools for data storage and retrieval practices may leave the department unable to

adequately respond to Access to Information requests and e-discovery exercises.

- Improving records management processes and tools through investing in new technologies and liaising with organizations identified as having best practices may lead to more effective management and response to official requests.

## Information Technology

Threats and opportunities associated with the capacity and sustainability of IT systems and practices, including infrastructure and use of technological applications:

- The agency's IT systems may not support the need for key staff to work remotely, leading to process inefficiencies.
- The organization's remote access servers and enabling software may become increasingly outdated and expensive to operate and cannot be easily updated to respond to changing operational needs of inspectors. This may result in decreased productivity and an inability to meet new regulatory compliance requirements.

## Legal Considerations

Threats and opportunities associated with an organization's management of its legislative, advisory, and litigation activities, including the development and renewal of, and compliance with, laws, regulations, international treaties, agreements, and policies:

- A delayed response to legal proceedings may affect the department's ability to work with key stakeholders.
- Failing to respond in a timely manner to an "x" court ruling could impact industry in the "y" sector (and consumers in "z" markets).

## Change Management

Threats and opportunities associated with significant structural or behavioral change within an organization related to mandate, operating context, leadership, and strategic direction:

- The organization's transformation agenda may not be well understood or communicated to employees, resulting in lost opportunities for engagement.
- The organization's transformation agenda may lack a tailored communications plan and implementation strategy, which may prevent employees from fully participating in renewal activities.

*(continued)*

# Exhibit 3.1
## Inventory of Risk Statements (*Continued*)

- Significant change and business transformation may inspire staff to rethink how they deliver on priorities relating to policy and programs.

### Policy Development and Implementation

Threats and opportunities associated with an organization's design, implementation, and compliance with the government-wide policy suite as well as its own internal policies and procedures:

- The department's policy approach to cost recovery may not be aligned with key stakeholder concerns, leading to inefficiencies and consumer frustration.
- The department's use of cost recovery in its policy approach to international cargo may place it at odds with current European Union practices, leading to a significant competitive disadvantage for domestic industry.
- Effectively addressing gaps and inefficiencies in trade policy and regulation may result by addressing the organization's policy approach to cost recovery.

### Privacy and Information Stewardship

Threats and opportunities associated with an organization's protection of intellectual property and personal information:

- The security of departmental networks and records could be seriously compromised if new standards are not implemented.
- Departmental IT and records management processes may not fully protect citizen information holdings and could result in mismanagement of personal information by the organization, leading to personal injury and significant legal exposure to the Crown.

### Program Design and Delivery

Threats and opportunities associated with an organization's design and delivery of specific programs, which may impact the organization's overall objectives:

- Organizational restructuring and realignment of programs design and delivery could result in partnering with portfolio agencies to achieve efficiencies in delivering support services.
- The design of the "x" program delivered through the "y" branch could become misaligned with changes to emerging standards and best practices, leading to marginal benefit to stakeholders and weakened value for money.

## Project Management

Threats and opportunities associated with an organization's process and practice of developing and managing major projects in support of its overall mandate, as well as risks associated with specific projects that may require ongoing management:

- Without the implementation of a project management and communications approach, the organization may not effectively develop and successfully deliver several key projects in support of the organization's priorities.
- Without the implementation of recognized project management standards and a supporting communications strategy, the organization may not effectively develop and successfully deliver the Pluto and Mars projects in support of the organization's priority to explore neighboring planets.

## Political Considerations

Threats and opportunities associated with the political climate and operating context of an organization:

- The organization may be unable to table new legislation given the parliamentary focus on red-tape reduction initiatives.
- The department may not have enough time to table new legislation in advance of a fall election.

## Reputational Considerations

Threats and opportunities associated with an organization's reputation and credibility with its partners, stakeholders, and the Canadian public:

- Fraudulent behavior may result in a loss of reputation for the department and the Government of Canada.
- Fraudulent behavior associated with misappropriations of funds and the misuse of public assets may result in a loss of reputation for the department and the Government of Canada.

## Resource Management

Threats and opportunities associated with the availability and level of resources of an organization to deliver on its mandate, as well as the organization's management of these resources:

- The organization could leverage resources from the private sector (telecom, finance) to further advance the objectives of the Information Technology Security Strategy.

*(continued)*

## Exhibit 3.1
## Inventory of Risk Statements (*Continued*)

- The forecasted reductions in departmental budget allocations may affect current regulatory responsibilities, which may expose the department to possible noncompliance with international treaties to which Canada is a signatory.

### Stakeholders and Partnerships

Threats and opportunities associated with an organization's partners and stakeholder demographics, characteristics, and activities:

- The organization could enhance its emergency management capacity and improve its ability to work with external partners to prepare for and provide leadership and coordination in the management of public health events on behalf of the federal government.
- The department's partners in delivering health services and equipment to stakeholders in the north may no longer be capable of meeting their obligations because of unpredictable fluctuations in weather. This may affect the health and safety of stakeholders.

### Values and Ethics

Threats and opportunities associated with an organization's culture and capacity to adhere to the spirit and intent of the Values and Ethics Code for the Public Sector:

- Staff and management may not be fully aware of the department's Values and Ethics Code, which may result in misconduct.
- A real or perceived breach of the organization's values and ethics could occur, given the nature of the organization's mandate and the lack of awareness among staff and management. This may negatively impact innovation and front-line decision making.

*Source:* www.tbs-sct.gc.ca.

## RISK ASSESSMENT TECHNIQUES

Risk Assessment is a common component of any risk management framework. It can be found in several of the well-known frameworks, including COSO ERM, the GAO Risk Management Framework, and the international risk management framework, ISO 31000. Without engagement through risk assessment, the process for managing risk would be incomplete and anemic. Risk assessment adds the extra benefit of "understanding the risk and its potential impact upon objectives, [providing] information for decision makers, and [contributing] to the understanding of risk."[10]

Risk assessment is defined as "that part of risk management which provides a structured process that identifies how objectives may be affected, and analyzes the risk in term of consequences and their probabilities before deciding on whether further treatment is required."[11] The process strives to answer the following questions:

- What can happen and why (by risk identification)?
- What are the consequences?
- What is the probability of their future occurrence?
- Are there any factors that mitigate the consequence of the risk or that reduce the probability of the risk?
- Is the level of risk tolerable or acceptable and does it require further treatment?[12]

Risk assessment is also a key component of the GAO Risk Management Framework. In this framework, "Risk assessment addresses the identification and evaluation of potential risks to an agency's ability to achieve goals and objectives so that management can design and implement responses to prevent or mitigate identified risks." GAO points out that an agency's risk management program should:

- Identify potential events which may adversely affect the agency . . . and evaluate the events based on the likelihood of occurrence and impact.
- Require continuous identification and evaluation of potential risks since governmental, economic, industry, legislative, and operating conditions continually change.

Because the identification, likelihood of occurrence, and impact of risk are the products of risk assessment, risk managers need tools and techniques to help describe the uncertainty to organizations. In 2009, the American National Standards Institute (ANSI) adopted a set of "Risk Assessment Techniques" (Standard Z690.3) to aid in this process. Published by the American Society of Safety Engineers (ASSE), the standard "provides guidance on selection and application of systematic techniques for risk assessment."[13] As mentioned in earlier chapters, most organizations manage and identify risk to some extent. Organizations are astute in identifying what "might happen or what situations might exist that might affect the achievement of its objectives . . ."[14] Risk assessment provides "an improved understanding of identified risks that could affect achievement of objectives, and the adequacy and effectiveness of controls already in place."[15] An example of common risks that are managed by employees in a specific federal job series is displayed in Table 1.2 in Chapter One.

The Risk Assessment Techniques Standard lists thirty types of tools and techniques used for risk assessment. The complexity of the techniques ranges from low to high. Some of the common techniques of low to moderate complexity used in agency ERM programs include checklists, structured interviews and brainstorming, cost-benefit analysis, root-cause analysis, and cause-and-effect analysis. Highly complex techniques include cause/consequence analysis and hazard and operability studies.

## Assessing Key Risks

After utilizing the process for writing clear and concise risk statements and applying the techniques for conducting risk assessments, the organization is positioned to provide an "overview of the risks to which senior management should devote most of their attention and gives staff, external partners and advisors a clear 'snapshot' of the organization's key risks."[16] At this juncture,

- Top risks should be listed according to their residual risk exposure.

- Risks should be labeled or named and accompanied by a risk description.

- Each department and agency should identify the key risks to their organization in the context of their strategic objectives and outcomes; key risks are those that have the greatest potential to impact the achievement of the organization's objectives and outcomes.

- Key risks can be listed alone or alongside a risk matrix.

## Key Risk Matrix

The Risk Matrix is a tool that illustrates the ranking of risks based on an assessment of their likelihood and impact. The size of the matrix will depend on the organization's preference; some organizations use a 3 × 3 matrix, others use a 5 × 5 matrix.[17] For example, IT investments in government exceeding a certain dollar threshold must report their status of risk on a 3 × 3 matrix designed by the U.S. Office of Management and Budget (OMB). This may differ from a matrix used to assess risk to programs that finds a 5 × 5. Thus, "organizations are encouraged to select a matrix size according to their needs and translate between matrices if required. Given that the matrix demonstrates visually how each risk is ranked in accordance with likelihood and impact criteria, and where risks stand in relation to other risks, it is considered essential."[18]

## Mapping Risks to Strategic Outcomes

Organizations should provide a statement that describes what the impact, result, or effect would be if a key risk is not mitigated, including the consequences to an organization's strategic outcomes. Mapping risks to strategic outcomes is essential, as it provides additional insight for managers to understand which outcomes are susceptible to which risks.[19] This reinforces and supports the management of risks to strategic objectives as part of GPRAMA.

Here are some helpful tips from the Treasury Board of Canada Secretariat:

- Identify which strategic outcomes are exposed to which risks.

- Explain the significance of the analysis.

- Use [identified strategic outcomes] to anchor the mapping.

- The format of this information may vary depending on the organization. Diagrams may be used, a narrative may be used, or some combination of both.

- The format of the content may reflect the complexity of the organization and the sophistication of the analysis. There is no expectation that all organizations must present their analysis in a similar manner.[20]

In the state of Washington ERM practices, the scores for identified risks are plotted on a graph that measures likelihood on one axis and impact on the other axis (see Exhibit 3.2). Most risk maps use color to show priority, with red in the area where the highest scores fall. It is common to see different words used to describe the map, scores, and categories, like "Frequency/Severity" or "Likelihood/Consequence." Use words that work best for your group.[21]

**Exhibit 3.2**
**State of Washington Risk Map**

| RISK MAP | 1 Very Little | 2 Minor | 3 Major | 4 Critical | 5 Fatal |
|---|---|---|---|---|---|
| 5 Almost Always | | | | | |
| 4 Frequent | | | | | |
| 3 Often | | | | | |
| 2 Once or Twice | | | | | |
| 1 Hardly Ever | | | | | |

Once the most important risks are identified, the next task is to develop a plan to mitigate or "treat" the risks. In ERM, you can:

- Avoid (usually by discontinuing the activity)
- Accept and monitor (this should include setting a threshold to begin treatment)
- Reduce the likelihood
- Reduce the impact
- Transfer (generally through insurance or a contract)

Identifying risks is important to the ERM process, but the purpose of ERM is to increase the chances of meeting critical goals. Identifying risk is just the beginning. "It is important to do the hard work of the treatment plan."[22]

# Risk Management Frameworks and Standards

As federal managers move toward strengthening risk management processes at their agencies, a risk framework or standard will be needed to help navigate the complexities of risk integration within the organization. Part of the process involves selecting a risk management framework and/or standard that works best for their organization. ERM implementers will discover, through massive searches of resources, that there are several frameworks and standards available for their consideration. However, before a selection is made, managers must understand the differences between a standard and a framework.

Depending on the context in which standards are discussed, they can be defined as "an established norm or requirement, usually a formal document that establishes criteria, methods, processes and practices under the jurisdiction of an international, regional, or national standards body."[1] However, according to federal government policy, the term "standard," or "technical standard" includes all of the following:

1. Common and repeated use of rules, conditions, guidelines, or characteristics for products or related processes and production methods, and related management systems practices.

2. The definition of terms; classification of components; delineation of procedures; specification of dimensions, materials, performance, designs, or operations; measurement of quality and quantity in describing materials, processes, products, systems, services, or practices; test methods and sampling procedures; or descriptions of fit and measurements of size or strength.

3. The term "standard" does not include professional standards of personal conduct or institutional codes of ethics.

Industry experts note that "standards are usually conceptual with little guidance on practical application, though guidance on how to implement a standard can be developed. When standards are developed by standards organizations, the input is usually solicited from a diverse community and the standard is voluntary to use. However, if a government adopts a standard it can become mandatory to use. Auditors are the most frequent users of standards to assess organizational internal controls against."[2]

## WHY VOLUNTARY STANDARDS? A LOOK AT OMB CIRCULAR A-119

The federal government encourages federal participation in voluntary consensus standard development and use. According to the Office of Management and Budget (OMB) Circular A-119, "Federal Participation in the Development and Use of Voluntary Consensus Standards and in Conformity Assessment Activities," all federal agencies must use voluntary consensus standards in lieu of government-unique standards. Revised in 1998, OMB Circular A-119 establishes policies on federal use and development of voluntary consensus standards and on conformity assessment activities. Public Law 104–113, the "National Technology Transfer and Advancement Act of 1995," codified existing policies in A-119, established reporting requirements, and authorized the National Institute of Standards and Technology to coordinate conformity assessment activities of the agencies. This directive is specific to the use of voluntary standards in procurement and regulatory activities, except where inconsistent with law or otherwise impractical.

However, there are instances when standards can be used for other agency activities not related to procurement and regulations, such as management operations. Circular A-119 makes concessions for this circumstance, stating that "all Federal agencies and departments shall use technical standards that are developed or adopted by voluntary consensus standards bodies, using such technical standards as a means to carry out policy objectives or activities determined by the agencies and departments." That is to say, if ERM implementers find it difficult to determine which risk management framework to use, OMB A-119 can help narrow that decision, placing precedence on the use of standards over general risk management frameworks or guidelines.

The advantage of using recognized standards is the assurance that the content and concepts have been vetted and benchmarked for decision making and that "they rely on a management system rather than a program to allow adoption within all levels of an organization."[3] In either case, awareness of what the options are, in addition to their purpose, strengths, and weaknesses, will make the framework selection process simpler. Exhibit 4.1 presents a few common frameworks and standards that can be adopted by agencies in a full or modified version.

## Exhibit 4.1.
## Comparison of Standards and Frameworks

| Similarities Among the Standards | Differences Among the Standards |
| --- | --- |
| All standards and frameworks are similar in the following ways:<br><br>• Adoption of an enterprise approach, with executive-level sponsorship and defined accountabilities<br><br>• Structured process steps, oversight and reporting of the identified risks<br><br>• Understanding and accountability for defining risk appetite and acceptable tolerance boundaries<br><br>• Formal documentation of risks in risk assessment activities<br><br>• Establishment and communication of risk management process goals and activities<br><br>• Monitored treatment plans | ISO 31000: 2009<br><br>The primary difference for ISO 31000 is the shift from event to the effect that risk and risk management have on an organization's objectives. Trying to predict events can be difficult and challenging. Objectives, on the other hand, typically are clearer and more precisely articulated. What ISO 31000 does is put the emphasis squarely on risk management as a strategic discipline for making risk-adjusted decisions, rather than a compliance-based function. The ISO is currently working on a technical report that provides guidance for the implementation of ISO 31000. |

*(continued)*

## Exhibit 4.1.
## Comparison of Standards and Frameworks (*Continued*)

| Similarities Among the Standards | Differences Among the Standards |
| --- | --- |
| | **GAO Risk Management Framework: 2005** |
| | The framework has been developed so that individual phases of the approach, such as risk assessment, do not become ends in themselves, but provide a full cycle of related activities, from strategic planning through implementation and monitoring. However, without an existing implementation guide, this framework is often viewed as a tool used for auditing and compliance purposes, as seen in various GAO reports with a focus on risk management issues at agencies. |
| | **OCEG Red Book 2.0: 2009** |
| | The major difference for the OCEG approach is the formal integration of the governance, risk, and compliance processes, ideally supported by a common technology platform. In this framework, risk is given a limited role focused on identification and measurement. The primary directive for risk, though not exclusively, is to measure the likelihood of an event that has an adverse effect on objectives. |
| | **COSO: 2004** |
| | COSO, more than any other framework, places a greater degree of responsibility on the board, requiring that the board not only support ERM but also have direct involvement in the ERM process. COSO also has an Application Techniques document, which provides a variety of real-world processes, exercises, and tools that can be implemented by an organization to fulfill the ERM components. |

| Similarities Among the Standards | Differences Among the Standards |
|---|---|
| | **FERMA: 2002** |
| | The FERMA standard was not designed to create a prescriptive process for enterprise risk management. Instead, the standard describes necessary component parts of an ERM framework. These components represent [best practices] against which organizations can measure themselves. In this process, organizations can leverage an awareness of the upside and downside of risk in order to bring value to the organization as well as to all stakeholders. The upside and downside of risks are viewed in the context of both the activity and the various stakeholders who can be affected. |
| **BS 31100: 2008** | |
| The similarities between the British Standard BS 31100 and ISO 31000 are significant. Organizations located in the UK who have used the HM Treasury's Orange Book, *Management of Risk: Guidance for Practitioners* (published by the Office of Government Commerce) may find its familiarity meaningful. | |

*Source:* Reprinted with permission and adaptations from RIMS.

## GAO RISK MANAGEMENT FRAMEWORK

The GAO Risk Management Framework[4] was developed using several resources, including the Government Performance and Results Act (GPRA) of 1993; the Government Auditing Standards, 2003 Revision; GAO's Standards for Internal Control in the Federal Government (November 1999); guidance from the Office of Management and Budget (OMB); the work of the President's Commission on Risk Management; white papers; and the ERM approach of the COSO. The framework was field tested on several GAO reviews and is considered a starting point in a field that is evolving; the entire cycle of risk management activities should be viewed as a goal.

The framework has been developed so that individual phases of the approach, such as risk assessment, do not become ends in themselves, but provide a full cycle of related activities, from strategic planning through implementation and monitoring. The process is dynamic, and although the various phases appear linear, new information can be entered at any phase. The GAO framework can be used to inform agency officials and decision makers of the basic components of a risk management system or can be used as a stand-alone guide. It is designed to be flexible, in that the approach may be applied at various organizational levels ranging from that of a department of a multiagency organization down to that of a specific project or program. Because there is no one uniformly accepted approach to risk management, terms and activities may differ across organizations.[5]

The phases contained in the GAO framework (see Figure 4.1) are:

*Strategic goals, objectives, and constraints:* Addresses what the strategic goals are attempting to achieve and the steps needed to attain those results.

*Risk assessment:* Addresses identification of key elements of potential risks so that countermeasures can be selected and implemented to prevent or mitigate their effects.

*Alternatives evaluation:* Addresses the evaluation of alternative countermeasures to reduce risk that are being considered, with their associated costs.

*Management selection:* Addresses where resources and investments will be directed for alternatives evaluation and other management criteria, such as availability of funds.

*Implementation and monitoring:* Addresses how countermeasures will be applied and the mechanism to keep security measures updated.

The U.S. Government Accountability Office (GAO) is an independent, nonpartisan agency that works for Congress. Often called the "congressional watchdog," GAO investigates how the federal government spends taxpayer dollars. The head of GAO, the comptroller general of the United States, is appointed to a fifteen-year term by the president from a slate of candidates Congress proposes. The GAO mission is to support the Congress in meeting its constitutional responsibilities and to help improve the performance and

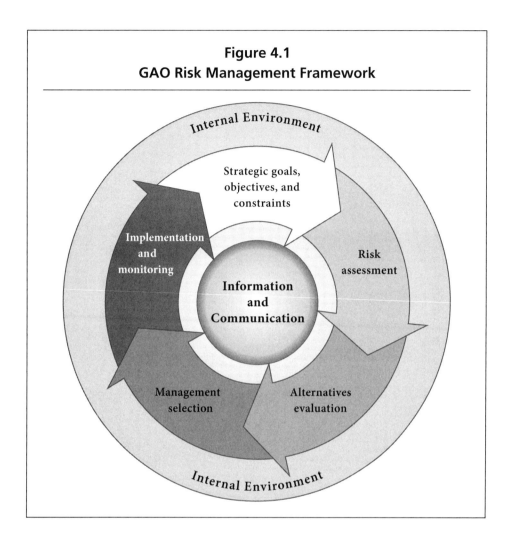

**Figure 4.1**
**GAO Risk Management Framework**

Internal Environment

Strategic goals, objectives, and constraints

Implementation and monitoring

Risk assessment

Information and Communication

Management selection

Alternatives evaluation

Internal Environment

ensure the accountability of the federal government for the benefit of the American people.[6] Because of GAO's position, agencies consider engagements and recommendations made by GAO a top priority.

When designing and implementing ERM, the GAO Risk Management Framework is the first framework that agencies should consider. Although GAO does not require that agencies adopt their Risk Management Framework, the agency frequently uses its framework in risk management–oriented engagements that it conducts. Usually, GAO findings from studies completed on agencies regarding an area of vulnerability or risk are compared against the elements of the GAO Risk Management Framework.

## Table 4.1
## GAO Risk Management Framework Matrix

| Risk Management Component | Description | Key Elements | Check (X) |
|---|---|---|---|
| Strategic goals, objectives, and constraints | | An agency's risk management program should: | |
| | | Require mission-based strategic goals and objectives, which are clearly articulated and measurable, to be set as a pre-condition for effective risk management. Without clearly identified strategic goals and objectives, an agency cannot effectively identify and address potential risks to its mission, prioritize risk, or identify criteria against which to measure performance. | |
| | | Require agencies to identify constraints (such as legislative requirements or resources) that may limit effective risk management. | |
| Risk assessment | Addresses the identification and evaluation of potential risks to an agency's ability to achieve goals and objectives so that management can design and implement responses to prevent or mitigate identified risks. | An agency's risk management program should: | |
| | | Identify potential events that may adversely affect the agency—called risks—and evaluate the events based on likelihood of occurrence and impact. | |
| | | Require continuous identification and evaluation of potential risks, as governmental, economic, industry, legislative, and operating conditions continually change. | |

| | | |
|---|---|---|
| Alternatives evaluation | Addresses the identification and evaluation of alternative ways in which the agency can act to alter either the likelihood of occurrence or the impact of a potential risk. | An agency's risk management program should:<br><br>Identify alternative ways the agency can respond to prevent or mitigate an identified risk.<br><br>Evaluate the identified alternatives to consider the effect on likelihood of occurrence and impact of a potential risk.<br><br>Evaluate the identified alternatives to consider the costs and benefits. |
| Management selection | Addresses the selection of a response to mitigate an identified risk, based on the alternatives evaluated and management priorities, such as management's attitude toward risk and how limited resources will be targeted. | An agency's risk management program should:<br><br>Require management to select and document an alternative, such as revising or creating a policy or procedure, for addressing an identified risk.<br><br>Require management to document the rationale for selecting the alternative. |
| Implementation and monitoring | Addresses how risk responses will be applied and assessed to improve efficiency and effectiveness. Addresses how the risk management program will be assessed to determine whether changes are needed to improve efficiency and effectiveness. | An agency's risk management program should:<br><br>Implement management's selected alternative to address risk.<br><br>Periodically assess management's selected alternative to address risk.<br><br>Periodically assess the efficiency and effectiveness of the entire risk management program. |

(continued)

## Table 4.1
## GAO Risk Management Framework Matrix (*Continued*)

| Risk Management Component | Description | Key Elements | Check (X) |
|---|---|---|---|
| Internal environment | Addresses how management will establish and maintain a positive environment that sets the tone throughout the agency and is the foundation upon which all other components of risk management operate. | An agency's risk management program should: | |
| | | Include an agency's risk management philosophy to help position the agency so that it can effectively recognize and manage risk. | |
| | | Require oversight by a high-level senior body within the agency. | |
| | | Incorporate the importance of integrity and ethical values to increase the effectiveness of the risk management program. | |
| | | Hold managers accountable for their assigned duties in the risk management program. | |
| | | Require management to organize its risk structure to provide a framework for the agency to plan, execute, control, and monitor risk activities. | |
| | | Require management to initially train its personnel to help ensure that they have the necessary knowledge and skills to perform their assigned tasks. | |
| | | Ensure that management maintains the competence of the agency's personnel by providing for continuous training to update personnel on risk management practices and techniques. | |
| Information and communication | Addresses the need to identify and communicate pertinent information in a form and time frame that allow personnel to carry out their risk management responsibilities. | An agency's risk management program should: | |
| | | Require pertinent information to be collected from and disseminated to relevant internal stakeholders in a form and time frame consistent with the agency's risk management needs. | |

*Source:* Adapted from the GAO Risk Management Framework (GAO-09–687).

If other optional frameworks are more appropriate for agency use, agencies should ensure that the principles of the GAO Risk Management Framework are addressed. This may not be a difficult decision to make, as most frameworks are now pretty consistent across the board and share similar themes. When starting or assessing an agency ERM program or initiative, implementers should consider elements outlined in the GAO Risk Management Framework matrix (see Table 4.1).

## ISO 31000: INTERNATIONAL RISK MANAGEMENT STANDARD

The International Organization for Standardization (ISO) is a worldwide federation of national standards bodies. A new standard issued by this organization, ISO 31000, provides a universal risk management framework for use across various entities, sectors, and organizations (see Figure 4.2). Although all organizations

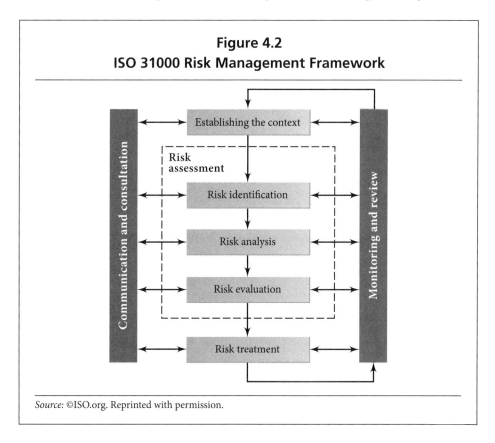

**Figure 4.2**
**ISO 31000 Risk Management Framework**

*Source:* ©ISO.org. Reprinted with permission.

manage risk to some degree, ISO 31000 establishes a number of principles considered essential to make risk management effective. Published in November 2009, ISO 31000 is the first international standard on the practice of risk management. The standard applies to any type or size of organization in any country.[7]

The standard has been widely adopted as the norm for risk management practices, but it is not intended to be a compliance-oriented standard. Although global adoption of ISO 31000 has been robust, implementation of the standard is strictly voluntary. However, the U.S. Technical Advisory Group (US TAG), which reviewed and commented on the standard before its final publication, approved ISO 31000:2009 as the standard for the practice of risk management in the United States. The American National Standards Institute (ANSI) has adopted the standard for use in the United States.

ISO 31000 recommends that organizations develop, implement, and continuously improve a framework whose purpose is to integrate the process for managing risk into the organization's overall governance, strategy and planning, management, reporting processes, policies, values, and culture. "For traditional risk managers in the U.S., it is important to remember that this new standard is intended to build upon what you already do well and expand your view about risk,"[8] notes Dorothy Gjerdrum, chair of the U.S. Technical Advisory Group for ISO 31000.

According to Gjerdrum, the United States, up to this point, has been creative and forward thinking about risk finance and risk transfer techniques, but not as forward thinking about identifying a broad range of risks (beyond insurable risk, beyond hazard identification, beyond emergency planning or disaster preparedness) or addressing cumulative or crossover risks (such as IT or pandemic planning).

In contrast to other standards, "a real strength of this new approach is the identification of risk owners and the necessary widespread education about risk—both inside and outside your organization. It increases accountability and strengthens communication. The link to business objectives (at all levels) strengthens both the relevance and the importance of risk management. Ultimately, it will make risk management central to the success of an organization, and an intimate part of key processes such as planning, management and governance."[9]

Although the practice of risk management has been developed over time and in many sectors in order to meet diverse needs, the adoption of consistent processes within a comprehensive framework can help to ensure that risk is managed effectively, efficiently, and coherently across an organization. The generic risk management approach described in ISO 31000 provides principles and guidelines for managing any form of risk in a systematic, transparent, and credible manner and within any scope and context. This international standard has the potential to meet the needs of a wide range of stakeholders, including:

- Those responsible for developing risk management policy in their organization
- Those accountable for ensuring that risk is effectively managed within the organization as a whole or within a specific area, project, or activity
- Those who need to evaluate an organization's effectiveness in managing risks
- Developers of standards, guides, procedures, and codes of practice that—in whole or in part—set out how risk is to be managed in the specific context of the documents

Similar to the COSO and GAO frameworks, the ISO 31000 standard provides a holistic view of risk management, with familiar terms and processes. However, as a generic standard, it will have a much broader appeal and application across multiple industries, including the government.

ISO 31000 offers a risk management architecture that describes the relationship between risk management principles, a risk management framework, and risk management process. According to ISO 31000, "for risk management to be effective, an organization should at all levels comply with several principles" (see Figure 4.2). The principles cover vast themes and can serve as a foundation for shaping an organization's risk philosophy. Common among the integration activities around ERM is the effectiveness of the management framework. Without a framework, it would be difficult to manage risks effectively. "The framework ensures that information about risk is derived from the risk management process [and] is adequately reported and used as a basis for decision making and accountability at all relevant organizational levels."[10] An important element of the framework is not "to prescribe a management system, but rather to assist the organization to integrate risk management into its overall management system."[11] The risk management process is "a systematic application" of a series of elements, such as "management policies, procedures and practices to the activities of communicating, consulting, establishing the context, and identifying, analyzing, evaluating, treating and monitoring and reviewing risk."[12]

In addition to ISO 31000, there are two other useful documents addressing risk management and risk assessment being adopted as American National Standards:[13]

- ISO Guide 73:2009, Risk Management Vocabulary
- IEC/ISO 31010:2009, Risk Management Risk Assessment Techniques

## COSO ERM INTEGRATED FRAMEWORK

The COSO ERM framework is a landmark document issued in September 2004, which provides a set of standards that elevated risk management to a higher level in the business arena. COSO provides a three-dimensional model that ERM encompasses (see Figure 4.3.) On the right face of the cube in the figure are

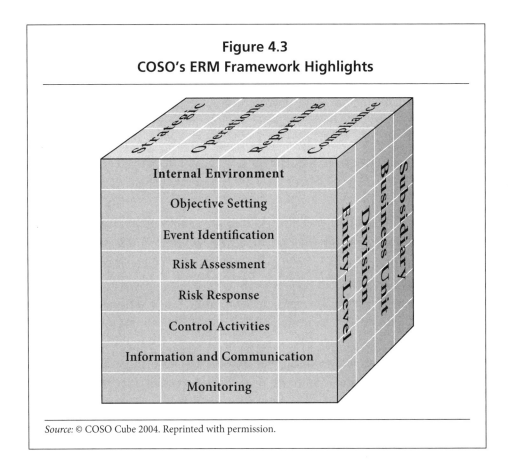

**Figure 4.3**
**COSO's ERM Framework Highlights**

*Source:* © COSO Cube 2004. Reprinted with permission.

Subsidiary, Business Unit, Division, and Entity-Level, representing the need for all levels of the organization to be a part of the ERM program. Across the top of the cube are four categories of the organization's objectives. The organization's operations and activities can fit into one category or multiple or all categories. On the front face of the cube are the ERM interrelated components, which are derived from the way management operates the enterprise and are integrated in the management process. These ERM components need to be present and effective to ensure that the organization can operate and have the optimum outcome. If there are weaknesses in any of the components, then the likelihood of an event occurring that might prevent the organization from meeting its objectives increases; if the ERM components are effective and integrated into the organization's processes, then the organization can expect successful outcomes and can take greater risks.

The three dimensions of the COSO ERM framework can be categorized as organizational objectives, management operations, and an entity's units. Organizational objectives are important because "risk is only present where it impacts an organization's objectives." This dimension says that "ERM is about four main considerations that mean an enterprise views risk at a strategic level, within operations, with full consideration of corporate reporting and obligations and also the field of compliance with laws, regulations, and procedures."[14]

Management operations provides a risk cycle for starting the process. It comprises eight interrelated components derived from the way management runs an enterprise and is integrated with the management process. ERM is not a serial process, in which one component only affects the next. Rather, "it is a multidirectional, iterative process in which almost any component can and does influence another."[15]

In the past, the COSO ERM framework has been the primary source for federal managers seeking to understand the key components of a risk management system. However, many public sector managers found the framework difficult to implement because it didn't speak to the language of government, such as "providing effective programs and services" rather than "improving profit margins"—the focus of the private sector companies.[16] In the last few years, additional frameworks and standards have emerged that closely relate to the business operations of public sector organizations.

## OCEG RED BOOK 2.0: 2009

According to a RIMS 2011 report,

> The Open Compliance and Ethics Group (OCEG) describes itself as "a nonprofit think tank that helps organizations drive principled performance by providing standards, tools and resources that enhance corporate culture and integrate governance, risk management, compliance, internal control and ethics processes."[17]
>
> In integrating and aligning governance, risk management, and compliance (GRC) efforts, OCEG describe its "framework for principles performance" in two parts: the Red Book, which contains the overview and principles of the GRC capability model, and the Burgundy Book, which contains "procedures and assessment criteria to facilitate management and evaluation of a GRC system." It focuses on the application of GRC methods "by which [the enterprise] establishes and stays within the boundaries it will observe while driving toward its [financial and nonfinancial objectives]." The approach is comprehensive and somewhat prescriptive in identifying accountabilities, as well as the parts of the organization and processes needed to be included in the GRC model. It assumes certain universal outcomes:

- Achievement of business objectives
- Enhancement of the organizational culture
- Increase in stakeholder confidence
- Preparation and protection of the organization
- Prevention, detection, and reduction of adversity
- Motivation and inspiration of desired conduct
- Improvement in responsiveness and efficiency
- Optimization of economic and social value[18]

## FERMA: 2002

An excerpt focusing on this standard from the United Kingdom provides the following description of FERMA:[19]

FERMA is a risk management standard adopted by the Federation of European Risk Management Associations. It was created by a team comprised of the members of the major United Kingdom–based risk management organizations: the Institute of Risk Management (IRM), the Association of Insurance and Risk Managers (AIRMIC) and ALARM, the National Forum for Risk Management in the Public Sector. The standard sets out a strategic process, starting with an organization's overall objectives and aspirations, through to the identification, evaluation and mitigation of risk, and finally the transfer of some of that risk to an insurer [see Figure 4.4].

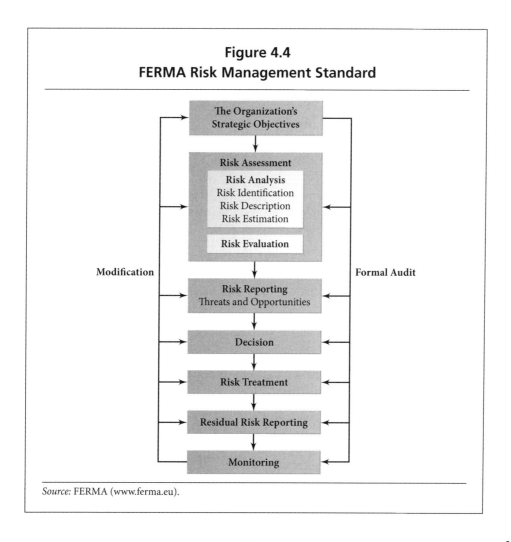

**Figure 4.4**
**FERMA Risk Management Standard**

*Source:* FERMA (www.ferma.eu).

FERMA: 2002 adopts the definition of risk as the combination of "the probability of an event and its consequences." The standard is careful to emphasize the view that in any risk-related circumstance there are "opportunities for benefit (upside) or threats to success (downside)." Management of these opportunities and threats is described as a key part of any organization's strategic planning. Risk management is described as the methodical process of identifying all risks to achieving objectives and then applying risk treatments that add "maximum" sustainable value to the organization.[20] Because the process of risk management is embedded in management systems, it must be integrated as part of the organization's culture. This includes assigning responsibility for managing risks as a part of the job description of managers and employees to promote operational efficiency at all levels.

## BS 31100: 2008

Another standard developed in the United Kingdom is the British Standard 31100. Developed by the British Standards Institution (BSI), BS 31100 is described as:

> A general risk management standard that provides a basis for understanding, developing, implementing and maintaining proportionate and effective risk management throughout an organization, in order to enhance the organization's likelihood of achieving its objectives. BS 31100 contains a set of basic risk management principles which are applicable to any organization, but the way they are implemented will vary according to an organization's nature, including size and complexity, and context. The British Standard describes how risk management embodies a framework and process that enable any organization to proactively manage uncertainty in a systematic manner at all levels within the organization, from strategic to operational perspectives. BS 31100 is intended for use by anyone with responsibility for any of the following:

- Ensuring an organization achieves its objectives
- Ensuring risks are proactively managed in specific areas or activities

- Overseeing risk management in an organization

- Providing assurance on the effectiveness of an organization's risk management

- Reporting to stakeholders through disclosures in annual financial statements, corporate governance reports and corporate social responsibility reports[21]

## AN EXPANDED VIEW OF ISO 31000

In the 2014 ERM Core Competency Survey for Public Sector Risk Professionals, 45 percent of the 103 respondents had a higher level of awareness of ISO 31000 in comparison to 39 percent who were aware of the COSO ERM framework. When asked which of the standards they preferred to use for ERM implementation, 46 percent identified ISO 31000 compared to 18 percent who identified the COSO ERM framework. This feedback suggests that there are key perceptions and variables driving the popularity of ISO 31000 over other standards and frameworks.

## A GLOBAL UPDATE ON ISO 31000

*Source:* G31000.org.

**Which foreign national governments have adopted ISO 31000?**

Up to forty countries have adopted ISO 31000 as their national risk management standard, including in the United States under the label ANSI/ASSE/ISO 31000. Based on informal information collected by G31000, here is the list of countries [as of November 2012]: Argentina, Australia, Austria, Belarus, Bulgaria, Brazil, Canada, Chile, China, Czech Republic, Denmark, Estonia, Finland, France, Germany, India, Iran, Israel, Italy, Japan, Malaysia, Mexico, Netherlands, New Zealand, Norway, Poland, Portugal, Romania, Russia, Singapore, Slovak Republic, Slovenia, South Africa, Spain, Sweden, Switzerland, Thailand, Turkey, United Kingdom, Uruguay, and the United States (see Figure 4.5).

Moreover, it has been translated into twenty-three languages: Bulgarian, Czech, Dutch, English, Estonian, Farsi, Finnish, French, German,

Hebrew, Italian, Japanese, Norwegian, Polish, Portuguese, Romanian, Russian, Slovak, Slovenian, Spanish, Swedish, Thai, and Turkish.

## Why is ISO 31000 preferred by other national governments over other frameworks, such as COSO ERM?*

In 2004, the Committee of Sponsoring Organizations of the Treadway Commission (COSO), a joint initiative of five private sector organizations established in the United States, expanded the Internal Control–Integrated Framework with the publication of COSO Enterprise Risk Management–Integrated Framework (COSO ERM), proposing a broader subject of enterprise risk management. At that time, the project, led by PricewaterhouseCoopers, was highly welcomed by the private and the public sector, as the first global ERM reference.

Since the official publication of the ISO 31000:2009 *Risk Management— Principles and Guidelines* on November 15, 2009, many organizations, including the public sector, have realized that they need a proactive management tool based on risk-based decision making, while realizing that COSO is more a mitigation tool, providing assurance on the effectiveness of controls.

As part of management and the decision-making process used internally at all levels of the organization, ISO 31000 promotes an ERM structure based on the responsibility of the top management and the accountability of managers for their decisions. On the other hand, the overall intention of ERM, according to COSO ERM, is to provide reasonable assurance of achieving objectives based on risk appetite, controls, reporting, and compliance with laws and regulations. Since the 2008 financial crisis, most organizations have realized that they need to go beyond controls and compliance toward uncertainty and performance management, as suggested in ISO 31000.

*The five COSO supporting organizations—namely, the American Accounting Association (AAA), the American Institute of Certified Public Accountants (AICPA), Financial Executives International (FEI), the Association of Accountants and Financial Professionals in Business (IMA), and the Institute of Internal Auditors (IIA).

# Figure 4.5
## World Map of ISO 31000

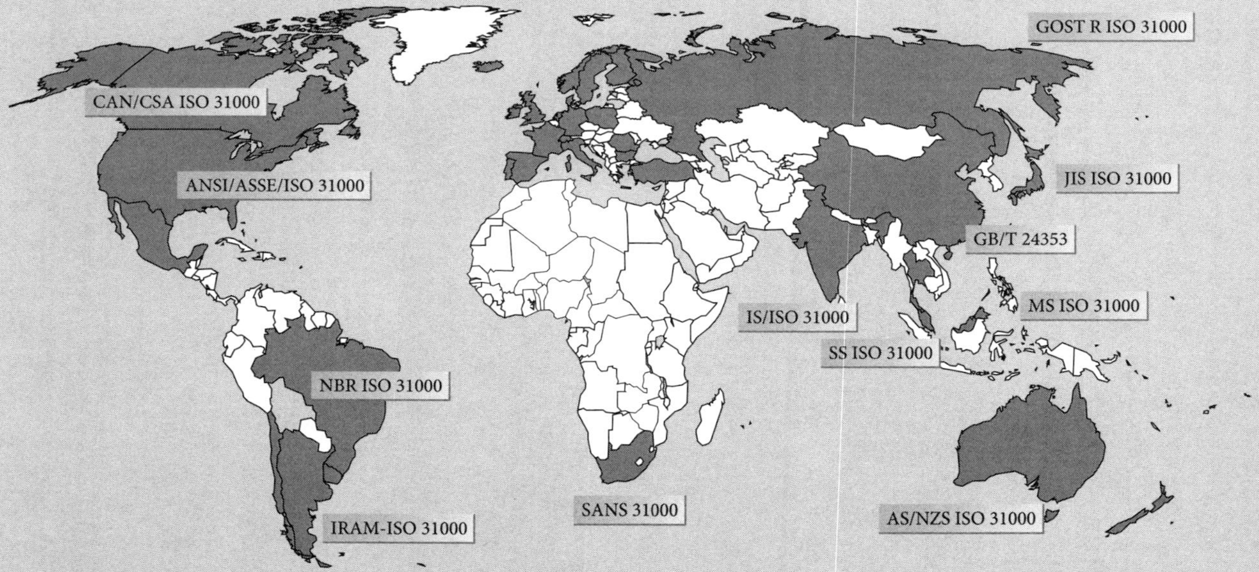

GOST R ISO 31000

JIS ISO 31000

GB/T 24353

MS ISO 31000

SS ISO 31000

IS/ISO 31000

AS/NZS ISO 31000

SANS 31000

CAN/CSA ISO 31000

ANSI/ASSE/ISO 31000

NBR ISO 31000

IRAM-ISO 31000

### Which foreign national government is considered the most progressive in adopting ISO 31000?

The ISO 31000 standard is based on the standard AS/NZS4360 representing twenty years of experience of risk management standardization in Australia and New Zealand. Risk management has been embedded consistently with all other standards, policies, and guidelines issued by public authorities.

The second leader in ERM is the public sector in Canada, which has a highly centralized common and shared services organization called PWGSC, dealing with procurement, real estate, telecommunications, and IT services to all government departments. Since 1997, all standards, policies, and guidelines issued by public authorities refer to CAN/CSA-Q850–97: *Risk Management: Guideline for Decision-Makers*, a reference specifically dedicated to the public sector.

Finally, it is important to recognize the advancement of South Africa in corporate governance, which has been a strong base underlying the remarkable progress made in the adoption of ISO 31000 in the public sector and the Western Cape government in particular.

### Has any foreign or national government been able to measure the impact of ISO 31000 implementation on government performance?

It is important to understand that the ISO 31000 risk management standard is the result of the experience, input, and in-depth exchange of knowledge among up to sixty countries, under the leadership of Australia, New Zealand, Canada, Switzerland, France, and the UK.

When risk management is aligned with organizational objectives at all levels and managers are making risk-balanced decisions under the guidance of a structured framework and process, risk management is associated with uncertainty and performance rather than mitigation, controls, and compliance.

The performance of national and local governments is recognized at the international level by organizations like the UNECE or OECD making recommendations based on best practices and success stories among their members. We could argue that the countries having been the least affected by the global financial crisis are Australia, New Zealand, Canada, Singapore, and Switzerland, and a high level of excellence by local governments such as Victoria in Australia or Cape Town in South Africa. This performance can only be achieved by sound policies, standards, and procedures where risk management is helping managers to make decisions under uncertainty, which represents the philosophy under ISO 31000.

**What are the advantages of ISO 31000 adoption and implementation in national governments?**

The advantages are:

- Ensuring compatibility. A common reference structure and process to ensure compatibility of different risk management frameworks, guidelines, standards, policies, and so on.

- Reduce exposure of public, private or community enterprises, associations, or groups to a wide range of known and emerging risks of organizations and the establishment of public, corporate, and solidarity funding for social, environmental, and economic risks—whether it's business as usual or an economic crisis, a natural disaster or any other form of public service disruption.

- Increase the likelihood to achieve objectives. The public, private or community enterprises and associations of all types and sizes face internal and external factors and influences that make it uncertain whether and when they will achieve their objectives.

- Structure authority, resources, and competences of national and local governments in order to mitigate negative consequences and make financial provisions for the effect of uncertainty on their objectives.

- Increase protection of the public from global crises, especially the impact of weak, volatile financial markets.

- Better governance. The challenge facing many public and private organizations is that they regularly demonstrate low levels of risk management and governance in general, but often lack sufficient awareness of the risks to which they are exposed.

- Enhance education and knowledge. Organizations require awareness, education, and skills regarding risk management in order to facilitate their social and economic integration and development and their well-being; this may also help to limit social public spending, and it is equally important for the development of sound, efficient, and competitive enterprises in global markets.

- Improve awareness. Governments and relevant public and private institutions in national and local governments and economies are expected to advocate the benefits of international guidance aimed at improving awareness and education on risk management issues.

- International exposure. The implementation of the UNECE Risk Recommendations will have to take into account, depending on national specificities, the differing needs for awareness and education in management of risks.

- Better regulatory and supervisory management. Local initiatives have already been undertaken by many national and local governments, by stakeholders involved in the awareness and education process who are putting a risk management regulatory and supervisory framework into place.

**What is the future of ISO 31000 in the foreign national government operations?**

As markets become more competitive, it is anticipated that the ISO 31000 standard adoption will become even more widespread across various industries.

# Risk and Performance Management

chapter
FIVE

T he approaches to risk and performance in the private and the government sectors have more similarities than differences. Both sectors aim to achieve maximum performance while safeguarding assets and exploiting opportunity. Managers and executives of organizations in these sectors seek to return value to internal and external stakeholders, engaging in transparency through reporting mechanisms (such as annual reports or annual performance plans), and to ensure that organizational missions are linked to strategy, objectives, and performance goals, and that metrics are established to track progress (see Exhibit 5.4 later in this chapter).

Private organizations drive results through a return-driven strategy (RDS), whereas governments do so through a mission-driven strategy (MDS). CEOs of corporations have described a return-driven strategy as "a clear and concise way of looking at the key issues that drive profitable businesses."[1] They added that "the value of Return Driven Strategy is that it provides a framework and a language for communicating and understanding how our business strategy will drive profitability and growth and how best to execute it."[2] A mission-driven strategy, on the other hand, asks "Are we doing the right things for the right reasons?" and "Are we focusing on the right initiatives and objectives that best serve the organization?"[3] In government, we might add, the agencies also focus on initiatives and objectives that best serve internal and external stakeholders such as taxpayers and Congress. Both the private and the government sector carry out their strategies through frameworks that help

151

facilitate and structure a deeper understanding of the organization's strategy. The government's framework is outlined in the Government Performance Results Act (GPRA 1993) and GPRA Modernization Act of 2010 (GPRAMA). Though risk is referred to as an inherent part of strategy design, there is no specific risk management framework referenced as a tool for navigating the detailed linkages between risk and the strategic process. Agencies can determine which frameworks (COSO ERM or ISO 31000) are best suited to facilitate the strategic planning process.

Private sector organizations have optional frameworks to choose from; one that is offered is the Strategic Risk Management Framework developed by Frigo and Anderson.[4] The components of this framework correspond to risk areas that impact a firm's business strategy, profitability, and growth.

Long term, as strategic risk management matures in both sectors, government agencies and companies should be in a better position to see the correlation between good risk management practice and organizational value. The private sector has already begun to investigate this promising performance metric. A survey report by Ernst & Young (EY), based on 576 interviews with companies around the world and a review of more than 2,750 analyst and company reports, notes: "Companies that succeed in turning risk into results will create competitive advantage."[5] Furthermore, "E&Y's research suggests that companies with more mature risk management practices also generated the highest growth in revenue."[6] On the opposite end of the spectrum, poor risk management can lead to a negative effect on performance. After the Target data breach in December 2013, which compromised personal or payment information for as many as 110 million people, Target reported that "the widespread theft . . . had a significant impact on the company in the fourth quarter, slicing profit more than 40 percent from the same period the year before."[7] The company reported net earnings of $520 million in the fourth quarter of 2013, down 46 percent from the same period the year before, when earnings were $961 million. Earnings per share were 81 cents in the quarter, down from $1.47 the year before. It was determined that "these costs may have a material adverse effect on Target's results of operations."[8]

For government, how to design such a metric is still open to discussion, though the GPRAMA pushes agencies to take a hard look at program outcomes. One idea that could be further looked into is showing a correlation between the impact of reputation risk on the agency and the annual government "Best Places to Work" survey conducted by the Partnership for Public Service. Agencies could assess whether a recent reputation risk that materialized had an impact on their ranking and index score in the survey. Consequently, agencies could also see if there is a correlation between positive program outcomes and an increase in human capital assets, such as successful recruitments for mission-critical jobs.

These are a few novel ideas that can help jumpstart the risk-and-performance correlation, but a system for valuating good risk management to successful program outcomes may be some time in the making. Ideally, government practitioners will continue to track and benchmark developments in the private industry in this area and identify opportunities to adapt such practices into an approach suitable for the agency performance environment.

## RISK AND PERFORMANCE: GOVERNMENT

The U.S. federal government is the world's largest and most complex entity, and its budget outlays have exceeded $3.5 trillion in the past several years. "These outlays are used to fund a broad range of programs and operations such as food safety, providing homeland security, monitoring incidence of infectious diseases, or improving response to natural disasters."[9] However, long-term projections of growing federal deficits will lead to significant performance and management challenges that the federal government needs to confront if it is to sustain the quality and level of services, programs, and operations that taxpayers have come to expect. There are five specific areas where government faces challenges:

1. Adopting a more coordinated and crosscutting approach to achieving meaningful results.

2. Addressing weaknesses in major management functions.

3. Ensuring that performance information is both useful and used in decision making.

4. Instilling sustained leadership commitment and accountability for achieving results.

5. Engaging Congress in identifying management and performance issues to address.[10]

Over the years, many initiatives to improve government performance have been introduced, including Executive Order 13450 (in 2007) for improving government performance, which set up the role of the Performance Improvement Officer, the Program Assessment Rating Tool (PART) 2002, President's Management Agenda (2001), and the National Performance Review/National Partnership for Reinventing Government (1993–2000). Yet lawmakers see the timely issuance of the Government Performance and Results Act (GPRA) Modernization Act of 2010 (GPRAMA) as the best resource to help address the aforementioned challenges. The original GPRA legislation, first enacted in 1993, was the government's response to the results-based management and strategic planning activities practiced in the private sector. Though a promising practice in the private sector, it was extremely unlikely that strategic planning could be instituted in the federal environment without a structure, clarity, and consistency. Hence the motivation for passing GPRA was to address these hurdles. Before the implementation of strategic planning and performance measurement practices was considered, Congress recognized that federal managers were at a great disadvantage in comparison to their counterparts in other industries, finding that

- Waste and inefficiency in federal programs undermined the confidence of the American people in the government and reduced the federal government's ability to address adequately vital public needs.
- Federal managers are seriously disadvantaged in their efforts to improve program efficiency and effectiveness, because of insufficient articulation of program goals.
- Congressional policymaking, spending decisions, and program oversight are seriously handicapped by insufficient attention to program performance and results.

Thus GPRA aimed not only to ensure an acceptable level of public confidence in its public servants, but also to hold federal agencies accountable to citizens for program performance, results, service quality, customer satisfaction, fiscal responsibility, and overall improvement of internal federal government management (see Exhibit 5.1).

# Exhibit 5.1
## Overview of the GPRA Modernization Act of 2010

On January 4, 2011, President Obama signed the GPRA Modernization Act of 2010. The Act modernized the Federal Government's performance management framework, retaining and amplifying some aspects of the Government Performance and Results Act of 1993 (GPRA 1993) while also addressing some of its weaknesses. GPRA 1993 established strategic planning, performance planning and performance reporting for agencies to communicate progress in achieving their missions. The GPRA Modernization Act established some important changes to existing requirements. It builds on lessons agencies have learned in setting goals and reporting performance, but places a heightened emphasis on priority setting, cross-organizational collaboration to achieve shared goals, and the use and analysis of goals and measurement to improve outcomes. The GPRA Modernization Act serves as a foundation for engaging leaders in performance improvement and creating a culture where data and empirical evidence play a greater role in policy, budget and management decisions.

The purposes of the GPRA Modernization Act are to:

- Improve the confidence of the American people in the capability of the Federal Government, by systematically holding Federal agencies accountable for achieving program results;
- Improve program performance by requiring agencies to set goals, measure performance against those goals and report publicly on progress;
- Improve Federal program effectiveness and public accountability by promoting a focus on results, service quality and customer satisfaction;
- Help Federal managers improve service delivery, by requiring that they plan for meeting program goals and by providing them with information about program results and service quality;
- Improve congressional decision making by providing more information on achieving statutory objectives and on the relative effectiveness and efficiency of Federal programs and spending;
- Improve internal management of the Federal Government; and
- Improve usefulness of performance and program information by modernizing public reporting.

Source: Office of Management and Budget, "Overview of the Federal Performance Framework," http://www.whitehouse.gov/sites/default/files/omb/assets/a11_current_year/s200.pdf.

# Table 5.1
## Advantages of GPRA Implementation

| | |
|---|---|
| Adopting a more coordinated and crosscutting approach to achieving meaningful results | GPRA could help inform reexamination or restructuring efforts and lead to more efficient and economical service delivery in overlapping program areas by identifying the various agencies and federal activities—including spending programs, regulations, and tax expenditures—that contribute to crosscutting outcomes. |
| Addressing weaknesses in major management functions | Agencies need more effective management capabilities to better implement their programs and policies. GPRAMA requires long-term goals to improve management functions in five key areas: financial, human capital, information technology, procurement and acquisition, and real property. |
| Ensuring performance information is both useful and used in decision making | Agencies need to consider the differing needs of various stakeholders, including Congress, to ensure that performance information will be both useful and used. For performance information to be useful, it must be complete, accurate, valid, timely and easy to use. Decision makers often do not have the quality performance information they need to improve results. To help address this need, GPRAMA requires (1) disclosure of information about accuracy and validity, (2) data on crosscutting areas, and (3) quarterly reporting on priority goals on a publicly available website. |
| Instilling sustained leadership commitment and accountability for achieving results | A successful element of management improvement initiatives is the demonstrated commitment of top leaders. GPRAMA assigns responsibilities to a Chief Operating Officer and Performance Improvement Officer in each agency to improve agency management and performance. |
| Engaging Congress in identifying management and performance issues to address | Performance improvement initiatives must be useful to Congress for its decision making; garnering congressional buy-in on what to measure and how to present this information is critical. GPRAMA significantly enhances requirements for agencies to consult with Congress. |

*Source:* Government Accounting Office, GAO-11–466T.[11]

Part of the consistency element needed to ensure implementation success resulted in the establishment of five agency GPRAMA requirements: (1) submission of strategic plans on a four-year cycle, (2) submission of an annual performance plan, (3) completion of an annual performance report, (4) conduct of quarterly performance reviews on priorities, and (5) conduct of annual strategic reviews.

In moving forward, the GAO reported that "the GPRA Modernization Act can offer opportunities to help make tough choices in setting priorities as well as reforming programs and management practices to better link resources to results." The bottom line is that many, if not all "federal programs and activities need to be reexamined; program structures that are outdated, overlapping or fragmented must be reformed or restructured, and weaknesses in management capacity" must be corrected. To that end, lawmakers foresee the following ways that GPRA, if carefully implemented, can help address the five challenges shown in Table 5.1.

In May 2013, the Obama administration completed a major milestone in the performance initiative with the release of the initial Federal Program Inventory. The Federal Program Inventory is a list of programs run by federal agencies; it provides Congress and the public with a clearer picture of the programs that exist across the federal government. The Performance.gov website notes that "development of the Federal Program Inventory is an important additional step that will help bring together information from multiple sources, including the budget information presented in the President's Budget and agency performance goals." As an initial focal point of the performance initiative, the Obama administration waged an aggressive campaign to eliminate duplication and waste. In five budgets, President Obama identified, on average, more than 170 cuts, consolidations, and savings, totaling about $25 billion each year. For example, the 2015 President's Budget includes proposals to streamline science, technology, engineering, and math (STEM) programs; training and employment services; and the Preventive Health and Health Services Block Grant (PHHSBG).[12]

## MANAGING RISK TO PERFORMANCE

The GPRA Modernization Act "requires agencies to set long-term goals and objectives as well as specific, near-term performance goals. Agency leaders, at all levels of the organization, are accountable for choosing goals and indicators wisely, and for setting ambitious, yet realistic targets"[13] (see Figure 5.1).

# Figure 5.1
## Illustration of Goal Relationships

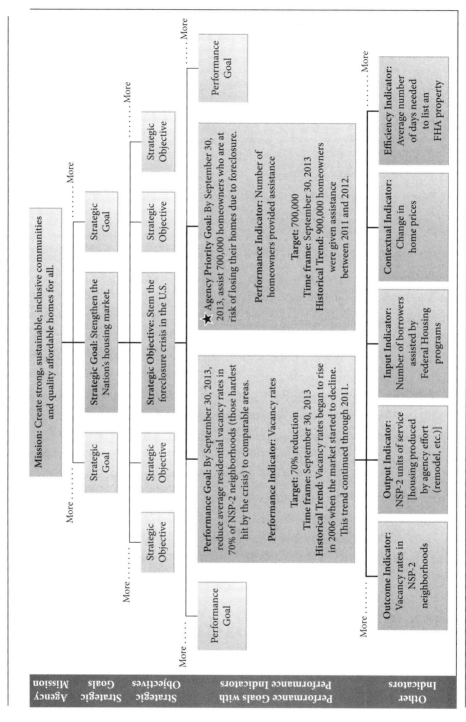

| Agency Mission | Strategic Goals | Strategic Objectives | Performance Goals with Performance Indicators | Other Indicators |
|---|---|---|---|---|

**Mission:** Create strong, sustainable, inclusive communities and quality affordable homes for all.

**Strategic Goal:** Strengthen the Nation's housing market.

**Strategic Objective:** Stem the foreclosure crisis in the U.S.

★ **Agency Priority Goal:** By September 30, 2013, assist 700,000 homeowners who are at risk of losing their homes due to foreclosure.

**Performance Indicator:** Number of homeowners provided assistance

**Target:** 700,000
**Time frame:** September 30, 2013
**Historical Trend:** 900,000 homeowners were given assistance between 2011 and 2012.

**Performance Goal:** By September 30, 2013, reduce average residential vacancy rates in 70% of NSP-2 neighborhoods (those hardest hit by the crisis) to comparable areas.

**Performance Indicator:** Vacancy rates

**Target:** 70% reduction
**Time frame:** September 30, 2013
**Historical Trend:** Vacancy rates began to rise in 2006 when the market started to decline. This trend continued through 2011.

**Outcome Indicator:** Vacancy rates in NSP-2 neighborhoods

**Output Indicator:** NSP-2 units of service [housing produced by agency effort (remodel, etc.)]

**Input Indicator:** Number of borrowers assisted by Federal Housing programs

**Contextual Indicator:** Change in home prices

**Efficiency Indicator:** Average number of days needed to list an FHA property

*Source:* Office of Management and Budget, "Overview of the Federal Performance Framework," http://www.whitehouse.gov/sites/default/files/omb/assets/a11_current_year/s200.pdf.

GPRAMA also emphasizes that

> Wise selection of goals and indicators should reflect careful analysis
> of the characteristics of the problems and opportunities an agency
> seeks to influence to advance its mission, factors affecting those
> outcomes, agency capacity and priorities. To successfully deliver
> services to the public in a cost-effective way, agencies must establish
> a performance culture where both leaders and staff constantly
> ask and try to answer, questions that help them find, sustain, and
> spread promising practices and policies. Agencies are expected
> to set ambitious goals in a limited number of areas that encourage
> innovation and adoption of evidence-based strategies that push
> them to achieve significant performance improvements beyond
> current levels.[14]

The Federal Performance Framework notes that "OMB generally expects
agencies to make great progress on all of their ambitious goals and achieve most
of them, but at the same time will work with an agency that consistently meets
a very high percentage of its ambitious goals to assure it is setting sufficiently
ambitious goals," and furthermore, that OMB "will also work with agencies to
develop performance improvement plans to support progress on the more
challenging goals and objectives. Agencies are accountable for constantly
striving to achieve meaningful progress and find lower-cost ways to achieve
positive results."[15]

The implementation of the performance framework would not be complete
without an often overlooked core component—that is, the management of
risk to strategic objectives. Although risk management is a key to meeting
performance commitments, GPRAMA does not provide a description of risk
in an expanded context. Rather, it defers to short, indirect references to the
terminology when setting agency priority goal reviews; government-wide, crosscutting priority goal reviews; and consolidated information on government
websites. But the lack of references does not diminish the significant role that
risk and risk management play in the process. For example, strategic objectives,
as defined in the performance framework, reflect the outcome or management
impact the agency is trying to achieve. It is the bridge between strategic goals
(a statement of aim or purpose) and performance goal (a statement of the level
of performance accomplished within a time frame). Without clear strategic

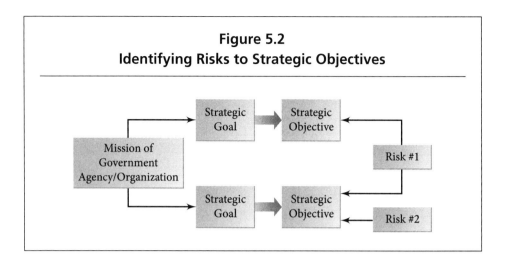

**Figure 5.2**
**Identifying Risks to Strategic Objectives**

objectives, agencies can miss targets and understate their contributions, and thus risk being perceived by stakeholders as ineffective or underachieving. Although avoiding vague strategic objectives is key to performance planning, understanding and managing the risks to achieving objectives overall is just as important (see Figure 5.2).

Early identification of risks to the achievement of strategic objectives, as well as the trade-offs and gains for accepting, avoiding, or transferring risk, will help determine if performance goals are realistic and attainable. Depending on how uncertainty is characterized (by way of quantification and measurement techniques), the consideration of risk then becomes the litmus test in progress toward achievement. To some extent, it provides a level of reasonable, but not absolute, assurance that the organization will achieve what it has set out to do.

## AN EXPANDED VIEW OF STRATEGIC RISK MANAGEMENT

Seasoned executives are all well aware that they must focus risk management on creating as well as protecting value. They also understand that they need to clearly link strategy and risk management and be able to identify and manage risk in a highly uncertain environment. This newfound revelation was just one of many lessons learned by organizations during the global financial crisis. However, as the acceptance of ERM expands in organizations and more management teams become familiar with its concepts, a recurring question regarding the differences or similarities of strategic risk management and ERM has become front and center. Revisiting the COSO, RIMS, or IIA definition of ERM, we see an explicit link between strategic risk management and ERM. To reemphasize COSO's definition, ERM "is a process, affected by an entity's board of directors, management and other personnel, applied in *strategy setting* and across the enterprise"—thus making the connection that ERM is directly related to "strategy setting."

Furthermore, COSO defines strategic objectives as "high-level goals, aligned with and supporting an [organization's] mission."[16] This definition echoes, to some extent, similar themes outlined in the GPRA Performance Management Framework for government agencies. As with GPRA, the strategic objectives referenced in COSO's ERM integrated framework "are the core of an organization's strategy." Further insights emerging from collaborative research in the area of strategic risk management suggests that "both internal and external events and scenarios that can inhibit an organization's ability to achieve its strategic objectives are strategic risks, which are the focus of strategic risk management (SRM). Accordingly, SRM is a critical part of an organization's overall ERM process. It isn't separate from ERM but is a critical element of it, and one that has been becoming more important."[17] In recent literature reviews, SRM is being touted as the new core competency for directors and management teams of organizations. It is believed by some that a focused application of SRM principles at a micro level can further develop an organization's ERM capabilities and processes. The basis for such an assumption stems from the increased pressure that directors and executives are seeing from shareholders, regulators, and rating agencies. These vested partners have expectations that organization leaders understand risk; are managing the organization's risks, including strategic risks; and are embracing transparency in the risk management process[18]—and all of this, "coupled with the catastrophic losses incurred by some organizations has fueled the current emphasis on strategic risk management."[19]

Leading thought leaders of SRM offer the following definition of strategic risk management for organizations: "Strategic Risk Management is a process for identifying, assessing and managing risks and uncertainties, affected by internal and external events or scenarios, that could inhibit an organization's ability to achieve its strategy and strategic objectives with the ultimate goal of creating and protecting shareholder and stakeholder value. It is a primary component and necessary foundation of Enterprise Risk Management."[20]

The definition is based on six principles, which also incorporate ERM (see Exhibit 5.2). Of course, the principles and definition of SRM are adaptable to the organization and depend on the existing level of maturity of the ERM. For organizations already mature in ERM, the inclusion of SRM as a core competency on a grander scale will be a refinement and evolution. For those organizations just starting out with ERM, using SRM as the kickoff point would be a move in the right direction. A checklist of key SRM activities can serve as a road map for practicing the new core competency (see Exhibit 5.3). The checklist reinforces the role of the board and the need to engage them as part of successful ERM and SRM implementation. Risk assessment, which is a common component of any risk management framework, is integrated, and the context in which risks are managed must also be considered. Other critical steps to SRM include establishing a built-in frequency for periodic updating and reporting, as well as embedding risk monitoring into other core processes such as budgeting, business performance monitoring, scorecards, and performance measurement systems.[21] Exhibit 5.4 provides definitions of some key performance terms.

---

### Exhibit 5.2
### Six Principles of Strategic Risk Management

1. It's a process for identifying, assessing, and managing both internal and external events and risks that could impede the achievement of strategy and strategic objectives.

2. The ultimate goal is creating and protecting shareholder and stakeholder value.

3. It's a primary component and necessary foundation of the organization's overall enterprise risk management process.

4. As a component of ERM, it is by definition effected by boards of directors, management, and others.

5. It requires a strategic view of risk and consideration of how external and internal events or scenarios will affect the ability of the organization to achieve its objectives.

6. It's a continual process that should be embedded in a strategy setting, strategy execution, and strategy management.

---

*Source*: Excerpt from the Strategic Finance 2011 article "What Is Strategic Risk Management?" © 2011 Strategic Finance. Reprinted by permission.

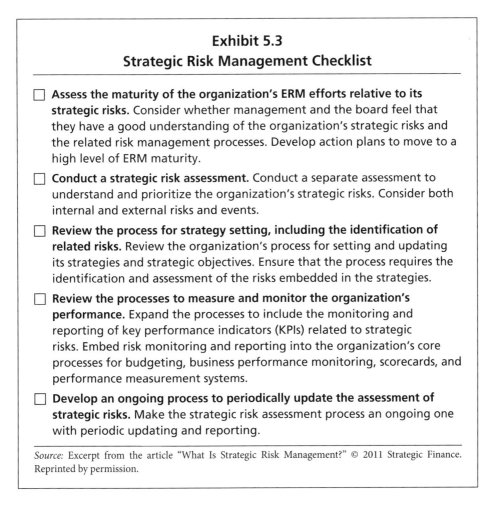

**Exhibit 5.3**
**Strategic Risk Management Checklist**

☐ **Assess the maturity of the organization's ERM efforts relative to its strategic risks.** Consider whether management and the board feel that they have a good understanding of the organization's strategic risks and the related risk management processes. Develop action plans to move to a high level of ERM maturity.

☐ **Conduct a strategic risk assessment.** Conduct a separate assessment to understand and prioritize the organization's strategic risks. Consider both internal and external risks and events.

☐ **Review the process for strategy setting, including the identification of related risks.** Review the organization's process for setting and updating its strategies and strategic objectives. Ensure that the process requires the identification and assessment of the risks embedded in the strategies.

☐ **Review the processes to measure and monitor the organization's performance.** Expand the processes to include the monitoring and reporting of key performance indicators (KPIs) related to strategic risks. Embed risk monitoring and reporting into the organization's core processes for budgeting, business performance monitoring, scorecards, and performance measurement systems.

☐ **Develop an ongoing process to periodically update the assessment of strategic risks.** Make the strategic risk assessment process an ongoing one with periodic updating and reporting.

*Source:* Excerpt from the article "What Is Strategic Risk Management?" © 2011 Strategic Finance. Reprinted by permission.

As the government moves forward in managing risks to strategy to improve the performance and results of its programs, the key challenge that GPRAMA implementers will face will require much action. More specifically, implementers "need to ensure that the law's many procedural requirements do not overwhelm federal agencies to the extent that agency leaders focus on compliance rather than on improving performance."[22] However, public management experts see the law as "a catalyst for creating a culture that thrives on outstanding performance." In response to the spirit of GPRAMA, experts also note that "the systems, processes, and procedures that commonly accompany any performance management system are intended to help frame it. They do not produce performance . . ."

Rather, the "appeal to the motivation that public servants have to help others through their work is the secret to effective performance in government."[23]

*Bring strategic risk management to life:* The following excerpt (Exhibit 5.5) is a first-person account on the challenges of applying strategic risk management to a major government agency.

---

## Exhibit 5.4
## Glossary of Key Performance Terms

**Annual Performance Plan (APP).** Under the GPRA Modernization Act, an agency's Annual Performance Plan defines the level of performance to be achieved during the year in which the plan is submitted and the next fiscal year.

**Annual Performance Report (APR).** A report on the agency performance that provides information on the agency's progress achieving the goals and objectives described in the agency's Strategic Plan and Annual Performance Plan, including progress on the Agency Priority Goals.

**Outcome.** The desired results of a program.

**Performance Goal.** A statement of the level of performance to be accomplished within a time frame, expressed as a tangible, measurable objective or as a quantitative standard, value, or rate.

**Performance.gov.** Web-based system that includes performance information about the Executive Branch, and is the government-wide performance website required under the GPRA Modernization Act of 2010.

**Performance Improvement Council (PIC).** The PIC consists of Performance Improvement Officers from the 24 CFO Act agencies and other agencies and is chaired by the Chief Performance Officer and Deputy Director for Management at OMB or the Associate Director for Performance and Personnel Management as the designee. The purpose of the Council is to develop recommendations relating to performance management policies, requirements, and criteria for analysis of program performance.

**Performance Indicator.** The indicator for a performance goal or within an Agency Priority Goal statement that will be used to track progress toward a goal or target within a time frame.

**Performance Management.** Use of goals, measurement, evaluation, analysis, and data-driven reviews to improve results of programs and the effectiveness and efficiency of agency operations.

**Strategic Goal.** A statement of aim or purpose that is included in a Strategic Plan. Strategic goals articulate clear statements of what the

---

agency wants to achieve to advance its mission and address relevant national problems, needs, challenges and opportunities.

**Strategic Objective.** Strategic objectives reflect the outcome or management impact the agency is trying to achieve and generally include the agency's role. Each objective is tracked through a suite of performance goals and other indicators.

**Strategic Plan.** The Strategic Plan presents the long-term objectives an agency hopes to accomplish, set at the beginning of each new term of an Administration. It describes general and longer-term goals the agency aims to achieve, what actions the agency will take to realize those goals and how the agency will deal with the challenges likely to be barriers to achieving the desired result.

**Strategic Review.** An agency's management process (or set of processes) used to assess progress on its strategic objectives.

**Target**. Quantifiable or otherwise measurable characteristic that tells how well or at what level an agency or one of its components aspires to perform.

---

*Source:* "Overview of the Federal Performance Framework," http://www.whitehouse.gov/sites/default/files/omb/assets/a11_current_year/s200.pdf.

---

## Exhibit 5.5
## The Challenge of Applying Strategic Risk Management to Homeland Security

The concept of strategic risk management is not new. Businesses are constantly assessing the risks they face and taking steps to adjust to changing circumstances—whether it be selling or purchasing new assets, taking on or reducing debt, or increasing or reducing their workforce. On a micro level, families are risk managers as well. We are constantly assessing risks that we face and responding. We purchase insurance to shift certain risks to others. We take steps like fixing an old roof or getting more exercise to mitigate risks to our property or personal health. Certain risk we choose to accept—like the risk of driving to work or allowing an old tall tree to remain right next to our home. The range of choices we make in our lives are, in a sense, a form of strategic risk management.

Application of strategic risk management to the concept of homeland security, however, is relatively new and a poorly understood topic . . . it

*(continued)*

# Exhibit 5.5
## The Challenge of Applying Strategic Risk
## Management to Homeland Security (*Continued*)

was natural to turn to the field of risk science, which has been developing for decades to guide risk reduction efforts in health, the environment, transportation safety, and a variety of other areas. While there is no agreed-upon definition for the term "risk," in its new publication, *DHS Risk Lexicon*, the [Department of Homeland Security's] extended definition of risk is "potential for an adverse outcome assessed as a function of threats, vulnerabilities, and consequences associated with an incident, event, or occurrence."

By developing tools to make mathematical calculations of these factors, risk science can provide a means of assessing the risk reduction value of a given policy, program, or budgetary investment. Even in fields where risk science is well developed, such as environmental protection, results of risk analysis are still only tools that inform decision making and cannot dictate policy results or replace the need for judgment. Political dialogue in the years immediately following 9/11—where it appeared that every identification of a potential gap in our security led to proposals for a new program and new spending—made it clear that the government should not promise and could not deliver absolute security from terrorism. Eventually, this reality began to be reflected in the rhetoric of our political leaders, who began to speak in terms of reducing and managing risk.

In April 2002, Tom Ridge noted that "as a free and open and welcoming society, we will always be at risk. We can never totally eliminate it—but we are working every day and using every resource at our disposal to reduce it." In 2005, this concept was adopted as the official doctrine of the Department of Homeland Security by then-Secretary Michael Chertoff, who stated, "We need to adopt a risk-based approach in both our operations and our philosophy.... Risk management must guide our decision making as we examine how we can best organize to prevent, respond, and recover from attack."

"Risk management" is defined by DHS as the process by which society attempts to reduce risk "to an acceptable level at an acceptable cost." Identifying risk management as a core principle guiding DHS activities made a great deal of sense. Yet, putting this concept into practice in the homeland security domain has proven to be a daunting task. From the earliest days after creation of the department, many placed faith in the idea that we could develop a formula or matrix that could answer the questions such as, "How much should we be spending to keep us safe?" or "Should we be spending more money on chemical detectors on subways or new anthrax vaccine?"

*Source:* David H. Schanzer and Joe Eyerman, "Improving Strategic Risk Management at the Department of Homeland Security," in *Managing Risk in Government: An Introduction to Enterprise Risk Management.* Reprinted with permission. IBM Center for the Business of Government.

## RISK AND PERFORMANCE: PRIVATE SECTOR

In the private sector, risk management is a widely accepted practice designed to control risks that could lead to a business failure if not properly managed. For companies, profit maximization is the end result. This "Results-Driven Strategy"[24] is and has been a mainstay of business success for years. However, as the environment for conducting business becomes more volatile and risk becomes more dynamic, regulators and lawmakers have begun to take precautions to ensure that companies that help drive the economy are stable and remain viable. This includes ensuring the soundness of our nation's financial institutions that support these business enterprises.

From 2008 to 2013 there were a total of 489 bank failures.[25] The effect of the recession, inflation, and fluctuating unemployment has had an apparent impact on companies and has made thriving in the open market for some companies very difficult. As a case in point, in 2014, financial experts predicted that several brand names in America will go out of business unless there is a significant change of events. This prediction was based on the following major criteria:

- Declining sales and losses
- Disclosures by the parent of the brand that it might go out of business
- Rising costs that are unlikely to be recouped through higher prices
- Companies that are sold
- Companies that go into bankruptcy
- Companies that have lost the great majority of their customers
- Operations with withering market share[26]

These combined conditions have continued to push the significance of risk management front and center in the private sector. For example, the "U.S. Securities and Exchange Commission (SEC) now requires that proxy statements that public companies file include disclosure of risk-based compensation policies, the role of the board of directors in risk oversight, and the nature of communications between executives and the board on risk issues."[27] In addition, "the National Association of Corporate Directors' Blue Ribbon Report on Risk Governance urges boards to assess risk in strategy, closely monitor risks in culture and incentives, and consider risks to the firm's business."[28]

## Exhibit 5.6
## "At Risk" Brands as Reported by 24/7 Wall St.

**J.C. Penney Co. Inc. (NYSE: JCP)** has been in trouble for some time. Those who still believe in its future as an independent retailer point to the company's ability to get a loan of $2.25 billion from Goldman Sachs and other investors, secured primarily by real estate and leases.

**Nook.** Barnes & Noble Inc.'s (NYSE: BKS) e-reader was destined to struggle from the start. It was launched in October 2009, roughly two years after Amazon.com's Kindle, which was, and has remained, the market leader. Both products were hit by competition from Apple's iPad before the e-reader business even hit its stride. Tablet adoption is forecast to grow 30% next year, while e-readers are expected to drop 27%.

**Volvo.** In the United States, Volvo was never a giant manufacturer with a large number of models or ultra-high-end brands. In its most recent report, the company reported a net loss of roughly $118 million through the first half of the year. Through the first 10 months of the year, U.S. sales are down by 6.7%. The company's models compete directly with mid-luxury offerings from every large auto company, including giants General Motors and Toyota.

**WNBA.** The champion and protector of the Women's National Basketball Association, David Stern, will retire in February 2014. He has been the all-powerful commissioner of the NBA for three decades. It is hard to imagine how the WNBA could have survived without his support, and that will soon be gone. The league was founded in 1996, and currently has 12 teams. Six teams have disappeared since the league's beginning, and three have relocated.

*Source:* 24/7 Wall St., May 23, 2013, http://247wallst.com.

Another key example of this thrust to the forefront is the Standard & Poor's (S&P) decision to focus, for the first time, on enterprise risk management for nonfinancial companies. This move set a new direction in company credit ratings and "is a recognition that the numbers alone don't tell the whole story of company stability and creditworthiness."[29] It further reemphasizes that "when risk and uncertainty beset some of the most respected names in the business world, the importance of a strong credit rating has never been clearer."[30] When comparing the use of ERM as part of the credit review process for financial companies with nonfinancial companies, the financial sector has demonstrated discipline in the requirements for an ERM structure since

2005. These companies are acutely aware that during times of uncertainty, "investors demand the assurance and transparency of a highly rated company." They are also aware that a substandard evaluation in ERM structure "can lead to a disadvantage in the competition for investor dollars."[31] The results of this requirement have been fruitful thus far. In their annual reports to shareholders, companies now include an expanded summary about risk and opportunity as well as statements of risk (see Table 5.2).

## Table 5.2
## Adidas Group 2012 Corporate Risk Assessment

|  | Likelihood | Potential Impact |
| --- | --- | --- |
| *Strategic Risks* |  |  |
| Consumer demand risks | Possible | Significant |
| Operational Risks |  |  |
| Own-retail risks | Possible | Major |
| Supplier risks | Unlikely |  |
| Inventory risks | Possible | Significant |
| Personnel risks | Unlikely | Significant |
| IT risks |  | Major |
| Product innovation and development risks | Likely | Moderate |
| Risks related to rising input costs | Likely | Moderate |
| *Financial Risks* |  |  |
| Credit risk |  | Major |
| Interest rate risks | Probable |  |
| Currency risks | Probable |  |
| *Legal and Compliance Risks* |  |  |
| Legal risks | Possible | Major |
| Social and environmental risks | Possible | Major |
| Product quality risks | Possible | Significant |
| Risks related to product counterfeiting and imitation | Unlikely | Significant |

*Source:* Edited from the Adidas Group 2012 Annual Report. http://www.adidas-group.com/media/filer_public/2013/07/31/gb_2012_en.pdf.

For example, the Adidas Group employs more than 46,000 people in over 160 countries, and it produces more than 650 million product units every year (all figures relate to 2012). Adidas has the following Risk and Opportunity Management Principles:

> The Adidas Group is regularly confronted with risks and opportunities which have the potential to negatively or positively impact the assets, liabilities, financial position and profit and loss of the Group, or intangible assets such as brand image. We define *risk* as the potential occurrence of an external or internal event [or series of events] that may negatively impact our ability to achieve the Group's business objectives or financial goals. *Opportunity* is defined as the potential occurrence of an external or internal event [or series of events] that can positively impact the Group's business objectives or financial goals.[32]

However, extending the ERM rating for nonfinancial companies is a new path for S&P. An assessment by S&P revealed that ERM as a function in nonfinancial companies is still a work in progress. According to a 2010 "Frequently Asked Questions" publication, S&P began to widen the scope of their analysis to a limited number of nonfinancial companies' management. The goal was to enhance S&P's review of managers' ability to identify, monitor, and manage key risks and to specifically look at "how a firm's culture (communications, structures, incentives, and risk appetite) affects the quality of its decisions and at the role risk considerations play when making strategic decisions."[33] S&P has made it clear that management assessments have always been a part of their rating process and that "ERM reviews are simply extensions of the management assessments." Therefore, including the ERM reviews does not represent any changes to their overall standard ratings process.

## STANDARD & POOR'S ERM ANALYSIS

A nonfinancial company's ERM is scored from "most to least credit supportive." The scale has the following ranges: (1) very strong, (2) strong, (3) adequate with strong risk controls, (4) adequate, and (5) weak, based on the assessments of five subfactors, which are classified as positive, neutral, or negative.[34]

When S&P conducts an ERM analysis for nonfinancial companies (such as insurers), it evaluates the following five subfactors, here augmented with select descriptions of what positive scores are based on:

- *Risk management culture:* A positive score indicates that ERM is well entrenched in the organization, with a formal ERM framework, an independent and well-staffed ERM department, and active board participation.

- *Risk controls:* A positive score indicates that material risks are identified from all sources, and risk exposures with multiple metrics are frequently monitored.

- *Emerging risk management:* A positive score indicates that well-established processes are in place for identifying and monitoring emerging risks, analyzing their significance, and preparing for and/or potentially mitigating them.

- *Risk models:* A positive score indicates that risk models capture all material risks and risk interrelations in aggregating exposures.

- *Strategic risk management:* A positive score indicates that there is a track record of consistently using a risk versus reward decision-making framework to optimize risk-adjusted returns at an enterprise level.

Whether in the private sector or in the government environment, many continue to question the overall impact of ERM on firms and agencies. It is a valid question that is shared by private and public sector professionals, who in a sense face the same challenges and opportunities. A common question is whether private companies connect ERM development with their credit ratings. S&P's analyses revealed that the motivation for companies who implement ERM is not to influence credit ratings. Rather, "any positive credit rating action would stem from sustainability, improved cash flows, operating performance, or competitive advantages realized from successfully managing risk."[35] Consequently, "a negative rating action would result from unexpected large losses, chronic underperformance, or competitive disadvantages resulting from poor risk management."[36]

As for the future of ERM, S&P predicts that "ERM will not be a distinct discipline because it will become integrated with everyday practice."[37] Every senior executive's skill set will include risk management, though "risk management itself is ultimately the responsibility of all managers in an organization."[38]

# Building a Risk Culture

chapter
**SIX**

*The test in the real world is how competent the organization's risk management practices are, and the degree to which [an organization is] instilling risk management behaviors into its culture and management's decision-making [process]. In short, how mature is the company's enterprise risk management program and how thorough are its practices at all levels of the organization?*

—Risk & Insurance Management Society (RIMS), 2009

When one ponders how an organizational culture is changed, it is important to keep these few words in mind: "Culture change is hard, slow, and subject to frequent relapse."[1] The reality of this statement is designed not to discourage, but rather to equip one with the knowledge and awareness needed in the organizational quest to integrate ERM. In moving ERM forward, "culture provides an immediate, familiar outline of what you should pay attention to and the constraints within which you should steer your activities."[2] When challenges surrounding cultural change are respected and accepted, thought leaders and champions of ERM are better positioned to prepare and compensate for any setbacks that may occur. Part of that initial preparation involves understanding what culture is.

There are many theoretical descriptions of culture in the pages of many well-known and very prestigious textbooks, but the description most useful in the practical execution of ERM is one we know all too well—that is, "culture is what we do around here." In another sense, "culture is what we expect around here."[3] In a broader context, "cultures affect both what people expect from one another (these expectations are often called norms) and what people expect from their dealings with the external environment of customers, competitors, suppliers, shareholders, and so on. In either case expectations take the form of agreements about appropriate attitudes and behaviors."[4]

Every organization has culture. Culture will play a role in the successful design and implementation of ERM. The true success of ERM does not occur in the absence of culture. Nor does the success of ERM rely on whether a culture is considered positive or negative, flexible or inflexible. However, ERM success is influenced by *changes* in the culture. Because some level of cultural change is needed to launch ERM, one should "attempt culture change only when there is a specific problem to be solved and only when they can work with existing cultural strengths."[5]

Notable organizational culture expert Edgar Schein suggests the following approach to changing culture that ERM champions should take into consideration:

> Never start with the idea of changing culture. Always start with the issue the organization faces; only when those business issues are clear should you ask yourself whether the culture aids or hinders resolving the issues. Always think initially of the culture as your source of strength. It is the residue of your past successes. Even if some elements of the culture look dysfunctional, remember that they are probably only a few among a large set of others that continue to be strengths. If changes need to be made in how the organization is run, try to build on existing cultural strengths rather than attempting to change those elements that may be weaknesses.[6]

In government, the pattern for gaining ERM buy-in has been as a result of a major issue or issues that have occurred. In the governmental culture, issue management has been a springboard to the emergence of ERM in recent times. The hiring of CROs by several agencies on board or in the pipeline likely happens in direct response to an OIG or GAO review or recent event impacting that agency. This factual observation supports the notion that rather than viewing the cultural weaknesses of the organization that led to the event, the focus should shift to building on cultural strengths.

The Freddie Mac crisis of 2008 is a good reminder that the mere implementation of enterprise risk management activities is not enough to protect an organization from systemwide failures. Rather, it is imperative that organizations develop a culture of risk management in which a positive orientation toward the business discipline is embedded in the day-to-day operations of the organization. Essentially, "the key to successful enterprise risk management practices depends on the behavioral attributes of the organization at all levels."[7]

Citing the financial crisis at Citigroup, AIG, Freddie Mac, and Fannie Mae, the Risk & Insurance Management Society (RIMS) contends that of three possibilities, "the financial crisis resulted from a . . . *failure to embrace appropriate enterprise risk management behaviors*—or attributes—within these distressed organizations" and not so much "from a failure of risk management as a business discipline."[8]

When the United Nations conducted a benchmark framework review of ERM in its business systems in 2010, it discovered that the integration and adoption of ERM in its organizational culture was slow—a reflection of management behaviors toward ERM. They included a lack of collective understanding and commitment by senior management, lack of a formal implementation plan, uncertainty about how to implement and integrate ERM into organizational processes, lack of an appropriate governance structure, and the pressure of competing reform initiatives.[9]

Organizational culture "is the set of assumptions, beliefs, values and norms that are shared by an organization's members"—and are important to its success. The organizational culture gives an organizational identity to employees and is a source of stability and continuity for the organization. Cultures also attract attention and convey a vision.[10] Because organizational culture is a dynamic systems concept, each particular culture tends to attract and retain people who fit its values and beliefs.[11] As a subset of culture, how an organization manages risk then becomes subject to this dynamic system and therefore has far greater implications than first imagined.

Unfortunately, building a risk culture is considered rare in the public sector, though progress is being made by some agencies. A 2011 working paper by McKinsey & Company suggested that an initial first step to building a risk culture is the creation of a risk-training curriculum that addresses the organization's needs. According to the paper, "agencies should offer training that addresses tactical needs; such as courses on the proper use of risk-related tools and methodologies."[12] This training should also be tailored to senior management. While skill development is crucial, McKinsey estimates that a conscious effort by leadership is needed in three dimensions:

1. *Fostering understanding and conviction across the organization.* This involves the employees confirming that they know what is expected of them; they agree with it and they see it as meaningful;

2. *Role modeling.* This confirms that employees see superiors, peers, and subordinates behaving in the new way; and

3. *Establishing formal mechanisms for reinforcement.* This confirms that there are structures, processes, and systems in place that reinforce the change in behavior that an employee is asked to make.[13]

A study of corporate cultures at nine large companies suggests that despite the challenges, cultures can be changed through effective methodologies.[14] Building on Schein's idea that efforts to change culture should start with the issue the organization is facing, Newstrom and Davis share the effectiveness of various tools used to influence cultural change (Table 6.1).

## Table 6.1
## Methods for Influencing Cultural Change

| Culture-Change Methods | Level of Effectiveness |
| --- | --- |
| Communicate top management support | Very great |
| Train employees | Great to very great |
| Formulate value statements | Great |
| Reward behaviors | Moderate to great |
| Use stories and myths | Moderate |
| Publicly recognize heroes and heroines | Minimal to moderate |
| Use slogans | Minimal |
| Appoint a manager of culture | Minimal |

## RISK CULTURE SURVEY

A review of the literature suggests that assessing the risk culture in an organization is not limited to risk management activities but should take into account a variety of management functions and operations. This includes strategic planning, ethical values, training and awareness, and information flow. A combination of these elements ensures that a broad assessment of culture captures all the appropriate ERM behaviors as noted by RIMS. The *Sample Risk Culture Survey* (see Exhibit 6.1) consists of factor statements drawn from the GAO Internal Control Evaluation Tool and elements commonly considered during ERM implementation. The sample survey is intended to be a starting point and to assist in gauging the organization's environment for ERM readiness and socialization. This is important to assess in the early stages of implementation because of the impact culture can have on successful ERM. Experts suggest that because organizations need to take risks to achieve their objectives, a risk culture can make the organization "significantly better or worse at managing these risks."[15] The sample survey consists of thirty cultural factors and can be modified to fit the needs of an agency. Factors can be added or removed to reflect the scope of behaviors within a specific agency.

---

### Exhibit 6.1
### Sample Risk Culture Survey

| Cultural Factor | Agree | Disagree |
| --- | --- | --- |
| 1. Management fosters and encourages an agency culture that emphasizes the importance of integrity and ethical values. This might be achieved through oral communications in meetings, via one-on-one discussions, and by example in day-to-day activities. | | |
| 2. Management has an appropriate attitude toward risk taking, and proceeds with new ventures, missions, or operations only after carefully analyzing the risks involved and determining how they may be minimized or mitigated. | | |

*(continued)*

---

# Exhibit 6.1
## Sample Risk Culture Survey (*Continued*)

| Cultural Factor | Agree | Disagree |
| --- | --- | --- |
| 3. The agency has established entity-wide objectives that provide sufficiently broad statements and guidance about what the agency is supposed to achieve, yet are specific enough to relate directly to the agency. | | |
| 4. The agency has an integrated management strategy and risk assessment plan that considers the entity-wide objectives and relevant sources of risk from internal management factors and external sources and establishes a control structure to address those risks. | | |
| 5. Management has established overall entity-wide objectives in the form of mission, goals, and objectives, such as those defined in strategic and annual performance plans developed under the Government Performance and Results Act (GPRA). | | |
| 6. There is an appropriate risk awareness training program to meet the needs of all employees. | | |
| 7. Strategic plans address resource allocations and priorities. | | |
| 8. Risk identification and discussion occur in senior-level management conferences. | | |
| 9. All significant activities are adequately linked to the entity-wide objectives and strategic plans. | | |
| 10. The resources needed to meet the objectives have been identified. | | |
| 11. How risk is to be identified, ranked, analyzed, and mitigated is communicated to appropriate staff. | | |
| 12. Risk identification and discussion occur in senior-level management conferences. | | |
| 13. Risk identification takes place as a part of short-term and long-term forecasting and strategic planning. | | |

| Cultural Factor | Agree | Disagree |
|---|---|---|
| 14. In identifying risk, management assesses other factors that may contribute to or increase the risk to which the agency is exposed. | | |
| 15. After the risks to the agency have been identified, management undertakes a thorough and complete analysis of their possible effects. | | |
| 16. The agency has mechanisms in place to anticipate, identify, and react to risks presented by changes in governmental, economic, industry, regulatory, operating, or other conditions that can affect the achievement of entity-wide or activity-level goals and objectives. | | |
| 17. A determination is made on how best to manage or mitigate the risk and what specific actions should be taken. | | |
| 18. An ethical tone has been established at the top of the organization and has been communicated throughout the agency. | | |
| 19. Management takes quick and appropriate action as soon as there are any signs that a problem may exist. | | |
| 20. The organizational structure facilitates the flow of information throughout the agency. | | |
| 21. Key areas of authority and responsibility are defined and communicated throughout the organization. | | |
| 22. Mid-level managers can easily communicate with senior operating executives. | | |
| 23. Management has developed an approach for risk management and control based on how much risk can be prudently accepted. The approach is designed to keep risks within levels judged to be appropriate, and management takes responsibility for setting the tolerable risk level. | | |

(continued)

**Exhibit 6.1**
**Sample Risk Culture Survey (*Continued*)**

| Cultural Factor | Agree | Disagree |
| --- | --- | --- |
| 24. Responsibility for decision making is clearly linked to the assignment of authority, and individuals are held accountable accordingly. | | |
| 25. A clear and coherent shared vision of agency mission, goals, values, and strategies is explicitly identified in the strategic plan, annual performance plan, and other guiding documents, and that view has been clearly and consistently communicated to all employees. | | |
| 26. Management communicates frequently with internal oversight groups, such as senior management councils, and keeps them informed of performance, risks, major initiatives, and any other significant events. | | |
| 27. Risk management is viewed as a value-added resource and/or management tool. | | |
| 28. A common understanding and definition of risk is diffused throughout the organization. | | |
| 29. All employees are engaged in risk management, not just management. | | |
| 30. Management's strategy provides for routine feedback and monitoring of performance, risk, and control objectives. | | |

## chapter SEVEN

# ERM Maturity and Assessment

In the early stages of implementation at an organization, a great deal of support and cultivation is needed to ensure that ERM does not become a stagnate process but evolves over time. Many ERM implementers often communicate to stakeholders that ERM needs to evolve, and that integration will not happen overnight. Although this is true, the implementer should take care to include a missing component in ERM success—that is, the need to track and document that evolution. In a sense, ERM maturity is not too different from the process for reaching adulthood. Generally speaking, "maturity is the ability to respond to the environment in an appropriate manner."[1] In measuring maturity from adolescence to adulthood, psychologists have established "Marks of Maturity"[2] as guideposts to ensure that certain values and behaviors are instilled during various stages of development. In other words, to be considered an adult in society, an individual must possess a number of attributes and behaviors. Though maturity has different definitions across legal, social, religious, political, emotional, and intellectual contexts, the underlying concepts still apply.

In this chapter we discuss a number of different maturity models used by both private and public sector entities as well as describe the different types of variables taken into account when designing maturity models.

## ERM MATURITY MODELS

Maturity Model tools have been applied to many industries since being introduced within the software engineering arena in 1986. Over time the usage

**181**

of these models has expanded to reflect the needs of different organizations, from private companies to international governments (see Exhibit 7.1 later in this chapter). The underlying concept for measuring organizational maturity in a certain area has not changed, though the variables and terminology have been interchangeable. Following are examples of the differing approaches and designs developed over the last twenty-five years.

## SEI Capability Maturity Model for Software

Early on in the field of systems engineering, maturity was captured through a Capability Maturity Model (CMM). Historically, in November 1986, the Software Engineering Institute (SEI) began developing a process maturity framework that would assist organizations in improving their software process. This effort was initiated in response to a request to provide the federal government with a method for assessing the capability of their software contractors. After four years of experience with the software process maturity framework, the SEI evolved the software process maturity framework into a fully defined model. Using knowledge acquired from software process assessments and extensive feedback from both industry and government, the SEI produced an improved version of the process maturity framework called the Capability Maturity Model for Software (CMM).[3]

Over time, the original CMM was enhanced into what today is known as the Capability Maturity Model Integration (CMMI). CMMI is the successor to CMM. It is a more comprehensive framework, with an expanded application to all types of industries and not just software engineering. "It is [also] a process improvement approach that provides organizations with the essential elements of effective processes"[4]

The CMM framework comprises five levels of process maturity, each with specific characteristics and features.[5] A description of these levels is provided in Table 7.1.

Useful in benchmarking organizational performance, "a maturity model can be viewed as a set of structured levels that describe how well the behaviors, practices and processes of an organization can reliably and sustainably produce required outcomes."[6] Since the introduction of the SEI Capability Maturity Model, efforts to establish similar models in different industries have emerged, building on the CMM concepts.

## Table 7.1
## Five Levels of SEI Process Maturity

| | |
|---|---|
| Level 1: Initial | Chaotic, ad hoc, individual heroics—the starting point for use of a new or undocumented repeat process. |
| Level 2: Repeatable | The process is at least documented sufficiently such that repeating the same steps may be attempted. |
| Level 3: Defined | The process is defined/confirmed as a standard business process. |
| Level 4: Managed | The process is quantitatively managed in accordance with agreed-upon metrics. |
| Level 5: Optimizing | Process management includes deliberate process optimization/improvement. |

## RIMS Risk Maturity Model

Several frameworks and standards have been designed to help organizations institutionalize risk management as a business discipline. RIMS does not advocate a particular ERM framework and suggests that any one of them can work effectively. However, it does assume that, regardless of the standard, guideline, or framework used, "the key to successful ERM practice depends on the level of maturity the organization demonstrates in seven behavioral attributes":

- *Adoption of an ERM-based approach:* Gaining executive support in the corporate culture
- *Risk appetite management:* Establishing accountability in leadership and policies to guide decision making
- *Uncovering risks:* Performing risk assessments to document risks and opportunities
- *Business resiliency and sustainability:* Integrating ERM into operational planning and execution
- *ERM process management:* Integrating ERM into business processes
- *Root cause discipline:* Binding events to their process sources
- *Performance management:* Executing organizational vision, mission, and strategy through outcomes-based measurements[7]

The seven attributes are a part of the RIMS Risk Maturity Model (RMM) for ERM assessment. According to the RIMS website (RIMS.org), the RMM is a valuable tool for a business planning and risk mitigation approach to generate the requirements to improve risk management competency at an organization. Without an understanding of how effective a risk program is, it is difficult to plan for uncertainties or discover ways to strengthen an organization's risk mitigation strategy. The RMM provides standardized criteria by which organizations can benchmark risk management strategies in order to identify program maturity levels, strengths and weaknesses, and next steps in the evolution of an ERM program.

Similar to the SEI model, the RMM model consists of sixty-eight key readiness indicators that describe twenty-five competency drivers for seven attributes that create ERM's value and utility for an organization. The RMM maturity ladder is organized progressively, from "ad hoc" to "leadership," and depicts corresponding levels of risk management competency. The seven drivers for the systematic progression of levels are termed as "attributes." The model can help leadership teams define a road map to the successful adoption of ERM, which is designed to view risks across all areas of the business in order to identify strategic opportunities and reduce uncertainty. A unique feature of the model is its applicability regardless of the specialized frameworks and standards that your organization is using, whether it is the Australian/New Zealand Risk Standard, COSO ERM, COBIT, Standard & Poor's ERM, or Sarbanes-Oxley.

The RMM is a foundational tool used by executives and others "charged with risk management responsibilities to design sustainable ERM programs"[8] reflective of their organizations' strategies and short- and long-term business objectives. The RMM also allows companies to "assess their current practices against these validated risk competencies and create a road map to achieve whatever level they desire."[9] According to the RIMS State of ERM Report 2008, based on responses from 564 companies globally, the least mature attributes of organizations include risk appetite and risk tolerance, root cause discipline, and performance management.

## Aon Risk Maturity Index

The Aon Risk Maturity Index (RMI) is an innovative diagnostic tool that allows risk and finance leaders to efficiently self-assess their organization's risk management frameworks, receiving immediate feedback and suggestions for advancing their capabilities. The RMI objectively assesses observable practices and structures related to corporate governance, management decision-making processes, and risk management.[10]

Questions for the RMI align with ten characteristics of risk maturity:

- Board understanding and commitment to risk management
- Risk communication
- Risk identification
- Risk information and decision-making processes
- Risk analysis and quantification to understand risk and demonstrate value
- Executive-level risk management stewardship
- Risk culture: engagement and accountability
- Stakeholder participation in risk management
- Integrating risk management and Human capital processes
- Risk management focus on value creation[11]

Aon used data from over one hundred publicly traded companies around the world; "strong links between Risk Maturity Rating and stock price indicators were identified." Data showed that "organizations scoring at the top of the Risk Maturity Rating scale enjoy, on average, up to 50 percent lower stock price vitality than organizations scoring at the low end of the scale."[12]

The Aon RMI incorporates five levels of maturity, shown in Table 7.2.

Data collected from Aon's RMI indicated "a strong association between risk management and stable performance over time. Strong risk management also appeared to bolster financial performance and cushion organizations from negative external pressures. In a comparison of stock price returns during a period of challenging market conditions, only those organizations with higher Risk Maturity Ratings posted positive returns. Differences in average Risk Maturity Rating across industries indicate that some groups, such as the non-profit, education and public entity sectors, may lag their corporate counterparts in implementing advanced risk management practices"[13] (see Figure 7.1).

## State of Washington ERM Maturity

Washington's Enterprise Risk Management Maturity Model (ERMMM) was first developed in 2006.[14] The ERMMM was revised in 2008 to reflect the state

## Table 7.2
## Aon RMI Five Levels of Maturity

| | |
|---|---|
| Level 1: Initial/ Lacking | Component and associated activities are very limited in scope and may be implemented on an ad-hoc basis to address specific risks. |
| Level 2: Basic | Limited capabilities to identify, assess, manage, and monitor risks. |
| Level 3: Defined | Sufficient capabilities to identify, measure, manage, report, and monitor major risks; policies and techniques are defined and utilized across the organization. |
| Level 4: Operational | Consistent ability to identify, measure, manage, report, and monitor risks; consistent application of policies and techniques across the organization. |
| Level 5: Advanced | Well-developed ability to identify, measure, manage, and monitor risks across the organization; process is dynamic and able to adapt to changing risk and varying business cycles; explicit consideration of risk and risk management in management decisions. |

agencies' increased experience with ERM implementation. Annually, state agencies reassess their ERM programs using the Maturity Model. The model is an important tool for documenting risk management accomplishments, reviewing the ERM program and activities, and pinpointing areas that might need attention. It measures the progress of ERM implementation in five separate categories:

- *Fundamentals of Risk Management*—basic risk management functions at the agency
- *Executive Leadership*—how ERM information is provided to agency leadership
- *Integrating ERM*—how ERM is disseminated throughout the agency
- *Applying ERM*—how the agency uses ERM to analyze and manage its risk exposure
- *ERM Embedded*—how the agency uses ERM in its strategic operations

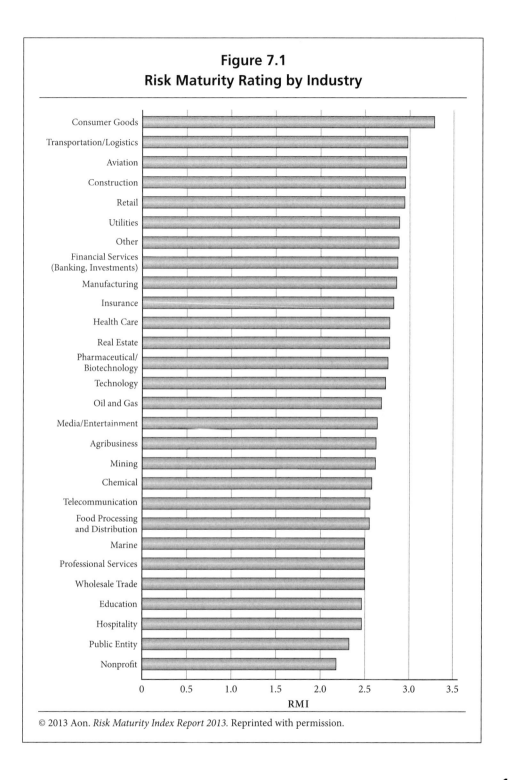

**Figure 7.1**
**Risk Maturity Rating by Industry**

© 2013 Aon. *Risk Maturity Index Report 2013.* Reprinted with permission.

In its 2011 report on ERM maturity, the state of Washington reported the following Maturity Model improvements:

- *Integrating ERM into Agency Culture.* Since 2008 the thirty-two large state agencies that completed the Maturity Model had improved in all components except for this area.

- *Fundamentals of Risk Management.* All thirty-two agencies had achieved more than 80 percent of the elements. The number of agencies completing 90 percent or more of the elements had steadily increased every year.

- *Executive Leadership.* The number of agencies that have completed at least 90 percent of the elements has steadily increased. Only three agencies had met less than 80 percent of the elements, and this group's numbers had steadily decreased.

- *Integration of ERM into Agency Culture.* Agencies had faced some challenges when seeking to enhance this area. Although the number of agencies with 90 percent or more of the elements had steadily increased, this group is a minority of the thirty-two agencies.

- *Applying ERM Principles.* The number of agencies that have completed at least 80 percent of the elements had steadily increased.

- *Embedding ERM into Agency Operations.* The number of agencies that have completed at least 90 percent of the elements had steadily increased. However, there had been no increase in nearly half of the agencies in this category.[15]

---

**Exhibit 7.1**
**Canada Treasury Board Risk Management**
**Capability Model: An Excerpt**

---

Organizations need to reflect on their integrated risk management approach. Comparing risk management approaches with those implemented in other departments and agencies may not provide insight or meaningful information due to the tailored approaches adopted by each individual organization. As a result, organizations may want to consider using a benchmarking tool to gauge their own capability in key areas of risk management.

## What does the Risk Management Capability Model do?

The Risk Management Capability Model is a diagnostic tool that allows organizations to benchmark their current risk management capability. This Model is part of the suite of guides and tools that accompany the Treasury Board (TB) Framework for the Management of Risk, including the *2010 Guide to Integrated Risk Management*.

The Risk Management Capability Model may be used to create a picture of an organization's current risk management approach, which can be used to inform a discussion on whether resources need to be allocated or diverted to fill gaps or improve capability in key areas of risk management excellence.

## How do Canadian agencies use the Risk Management Capability Model?

The levels of capability are designed as profiles against which organizations are encouraged to self-identify. The table format gives organizations flexibility in mapping their current capability against a number of key risk management areas of excellence. It is expected that organizations will have a spectrum of capabilities, based on their objectives, size and complexity of mandate. For example, "governance, leadership and accountability" may be developing, while "training" may be initiated.

Recognizing and addressing differing levels of capability in key areas may lead to a discussion on where an ideal state has been achieved and where focused attention may be required. Organizations should be asking themselves if they are operating at the right level for any given risk management activity. The Capability Model is not intended to be used in a linear fashion. It is not necessary, or suitable, for an organization to meet the highest tier in every area. In addition, capability levels in some areas may change over time depending on the organization's objectives and priorities.

## What is meant by "initiated," "developing" and "systematic"?

"Initiated," "developing" and "systematic" are terms used to describe an organization's capability in key areas of risk management excellence.

### Initiated

Is a term that applies to risk management activities that are still in the planning phase and therefore not in place yet or that have been recently

(*continued*)

## Exhibit 7.1
## Canada Treasury Board Risk Management
## Capability Model: An Excerpt (*Continued*)

introduced in parts of the organization. The term recognizes that while the concept of risk management has been adopted by a few key employees, an organizational approach has yet to be developed.

*Developing*

Is a term that applies to risk management activities that may be in place and are evolving. Developing risk management activities may not yet be consistently practiced across the organization. The term recognizes that efforts may be under way to advance some risk management activities in order to achieve a more systematic approach.

*Systematic*

Is a term that applies to risk management activities that are part of a broader planned and methodical approach to integrated risk management. The term recognizes the proactive and adaptive nature of a more complete and robust integrated risk management approach.

**Key considerations when using the Risk Management Capability Model**

- The Capability Model is a diagnostic tool meant to provide insight and act as a reference for discussion. The Model's purpose is to help organizations self-identify at what stage they are in terms of certain risk management activities and to promote discussion on advancing their approach.

- The five activities identified are meant to help senior management focus on key areas of risk management excellence. The three tiers are designed to express an attainable level of capability applicable to micro, small and large organizations.

- The most appropriate level of capability for an organization will depend on the nature of risks identified and managed, the complexity of the organization's mandate and the organization's size.

- Achieving "systematic" across the table may not be appropriate or suitable. Organizations should allocate efforts carefully based on their current and emerging priorities.

- An organization's capability in any given area of risk management activity may change over time.

*Source:* www.tbs-sct.gc.ca/tbs-sct/rm-gr/guides/rmcm-mcmgr-eng.asp.

## Table 7.3
## Treasury Board Risk Management Capability Model

| Areas of Risk Management Excellence | Capability | | |
|---|---|---|---|
| | Initiated | Developing | Systematic |
| Governance, leadership, and accountability | RM is identified as a result of necessity. RM governance activities may cease once the issue is managed. Tolerance for risk is concentrated at the individual level. | RM practice is encouraged but not always required or does not always occur. Some accountability for RM is identified on some projects, and governance mechanisms are beginning to include risk information. Some staff in parts of the organization are risk aware; remaining staff may regard RM as a process burden. | RM is identified as a priority for the organization. Roles, responsibilities, and accountabilities are clearly defined in all parts of the organization. Resources are dedicated and risk awareness is promoted. Senior management proactively communicates risk tolerance. |
| Priority setting and decision making | Risk information is informally noted and occasionally considered, depending on the issue management requirements. Decisions may be based on an inconsistent understanding of risk. | Risk information is periodically considered as part of operational and/or corporate processes. The organization is developing a consistent understanding of risk to support decision making. | Consistent and coherent risk information is integrated into operational and corporate processes. The Corporate Risk Profile or similar tool acts as a strategic framework for priority setting and decision-making activities, |

*(continued)*

## Table 7.3
## Treasury Board Risk Management
## Capability Model (*Continued*)

| Areas of Risk Management Excellence | Capability | | |
| --- | --- | --- | --- |
| | Initiated | Developing | Systematic |
| | | | including the seizing of opportunities to advance new policies and programs. |
| Monitoring, performance, and outcomes | Limited monitoring of risk responses may occur. | There is some evidence of monitoring of risk responses. | Monitoring of risk responses occurs on a routine basis with clear and measurable evidence of im-proved outcomes as a result of RM practice. |
| | The monitoring of RM practice occurs informally as a result of individual inquiry. | The organization may make adjustments to its RM approach as a result of occasional reviews. The reviews may not always be communicated across the organization. | Accountable parties routinely assess the performance of the organization's RM approach to incorporate improvements and lessons learned. The results of reviews are communicated across the organization. |
| | RM practice may need tailoring in order to reflect the size and mandate of the organization. | The organization is developing indicators to measure the performance of risk responses over time. | Performance indicators are embedded in key RM activities. |
| | | There is some evidence of im-proved outcomes as a result of RM practice. | |

| Capability | | | |
| --- | --- | --- | --- |
| **Areas of Risk Management Excellence** | **Initiated** | **Developing** | **Systematic** |
| Training and continuous learning | Training opportunities are available to staff based on individual interest and access to self-directed learning. | RM training is targeted to some staff within the organization, with limited learning resources available. | RM training is promoted to all staff within the organization and in personal learning plans, including plans for senior management. Informal networks are in place to support best practices and continuous learning. |
| Stakeholder engagement and communication | There is limited internal engagement and communication of cross-sectorial risks. The organization rarely engages its external stakeholders and partners on interdepartmental risks. | There is periodic engagement on cross-sectorial risks within the organization. The organization recognizes the need to engage its external partners and stakeholders on interdepartmental risks and is developing a risk communication plan or strategy. | There is proactive engagement on cross-sectorial risks within the organization. External partners and stakeholders are proactively consulted on interdepartmental risks. Risk communication is identified as part of the RM approach and enhances the organization's risk culture. |

## THE ROLE OF THE INTERNAL AUDITOR IN ERM

There have been recent debates about the role of the Inspector General (IG) in ERM and how it intersects with those who manage and champion ERM. For those who oversee ERM, it is important to have a clear understanding of these matters, as both communities play a positive role in managing agency performance. From the IG community perspective, the intent of the internal auditing function is not to "supplant the agency's responsibility to properly identify and control risks."[16] In fact, the IG community supports agencies having comprehensive enterprise risk management programs in place and taking responsibility for "accurately assessing and dealing with agency risks . . . although they do not have primary responsibility for ERM implementation."[17] Yet according to the Institute of Internal Auditors (IIA), internal auditors do play an important role in monitoring, examining, evaluating, and reporting on ERM.

More specifically, there are several ways in which internal auditors may add value to ERM:

- Reviewing critical control systems and risk management processes and responses for adequacy and effectiveness
- Providing advice in the design and improvement of control systems and risk-mitigation strategies
- Implementing a risk-based approach to planning and executing the internal audit process
- Ensuring that internal audit resources are directed at those areas most important to the organization
- Challenging the basis of management's risk assessments and evaluating the adequacy and effectiveness of risk-treatment strategies and the reliability of management's assurances
- Providing assurances on the completeness, accuracy, and appropriateness of management's classification and reporting of risks
- Facilitating ERM workshops[18]

Consequently, there are several roles internal auditors should not undertake in ERM. They include:

- Setting the risk appetite
- Imposing risk management processes

- Management assurance on risks

- Taking decisions on risk responses

- Implementing risk responses on management's behalf

- Accountability for risk management[19]

Another suggested role of the IG is to "accurately access the sufficiency of the agency's risk management program and to identify risks not recognized by the agency as appropriate."[20] To successfully do so, IGs will need a framework against which to assess the agency's ERM structure.

In a 2014 ERM Core Competency Survey, 32 percent of survey respondents indicated that risk management in their organization is mainly oriented toward auditing and compliance. In addition, 34 percent of the respondents also indicated that their organization has adopted or considered ISO 31000 when implementing ERM, compared to 22 percent who identified the COSO ERM framework. Either the ISO 31000 Standard or COSO ERM framework could serve as a backdrop for auditing an agency's ERM.

What follows is a synopsis of the executive summary of an audit conducted by Public Safety Canada using the Canadian government's *Framework on the Management of Risk* as the auditing assessment tool. The audit offers insight into possible focus areas for conducting an audit of ERM in U.S. government agencies. A complete copy of the full audit report can be accessed at: https://www.publicsafety .gc.ca/cnt/rsrcs/pblctns/dt-ntgrtd-rsk-mngmnt/dt-ntgrtd-rsk-mngmnt-eng.pdf.

*Benchmarking an ERM Audit.* In September 2013, Public Safety Canada conducted an internal audit of Integrated Risk Management (IRM) as part of their annual risk-based audit planning process. The Government of Canada's IRM was designed and implemented by the Treasury Board Secretariat in early 2000 and issued as the *Framework on the Management of Risk*. The Framework was then updated to align with the principles of ISO 31000, issued in 2009. The Framework provides "guidance to [Canadian agency] Deputy Heads on the implementation of effective risk management practices at all levels of their organization."[21] This was Public Safety Canada's first attempt as an agency to audit IRM. In 2010, Public Safety Canada approved an Integrated Risk Management Policy, and in 2013 it updated the Integrated Risk Management Framework, which was "designed to communicate Public Safety's risk management strategy to all levels of staff, and supply the means to build and maintain risk management capacity."[22]

# CASE STUDY: THE PUBLIC SAFETY CANADA AUDIT OF INTEGRATED RISK MANAGEMENT

The objective of the Public Safety Canada (PSC) audit[23] was to (1) provide reasonable assurance that the department's approach to integrated risk management was adequate and effective, and (2) ensure that a consistent approach was used and that risk information was appropriately integrated into decision making.

The audit covered the period from September 1, 2011, to December 31, 2012.

## Summary of Findings

The audit found a well-defined and appropriately communicated PS Integrated Risk Management Policy (IRM policy) and PS Integrated Risk Management Framework (IRM framework). Both documents had identifiable objectives, clear roles and responsibilities, and reporting time frames that were aligned with the TB Framework for the Management of Risk and TB Guide to Integrated Risk Management.

## Public Service Canada Audit Criteria: Lines of Inquiry

**Line of Inquiry 1: Policy and Direction**   The Department has a formally defined, communicated, and adequate policy and direction in relation to risk management.

**Line of Inquiry 2: Governance**   The Department has adequate and effective governance over Integrated Risk Management, which would include clear roles, responsibilities, and accountabilities, and oversight mechanism.

*Note*: This includes such things as:

- Tone at the top
- Accountabilities of SPB and other branches
- Oversight by DMC, monitoring
- Having a champion
- Approval authority over risk reports, including escalation

**Line of Inquiry 3: Business Processes and Tools**   Comprehensive risk management tools and processes exist, are communicated, and are applied in conformity with departmental policy and direction.

Risk management tools include methods for all aspects of the risk management life cycle, including:

- Risk identification
- Risk assessment
- Response—action planning (based on tolerance)
- Approval—of all aspects of the risk assessment, response, etc.
- Communication/escalation

**Line of Inquiry 4: Integration and Use of Risk for Decision Making** Risk information is systematically used to inform key decisions, in conformity with the departmental directions and requirements on risk management, including vertical and horizontal management information sharing.

## Audit Findings, Recommendations, and Management Responses

The following are the findings, recommendations, and management responses to the Canadian government's integrated risk management audit.

*Policies and Directives.* The audit expected to find a clear and appropriately communicated policy, directives, and/or guidelines relating to IRM. It was also expected that employees understand the following:

- The objectives of the policy
- Their roles, responsibilities, and accountabilities
- How often risks and opportunities should be identified and assessed
- How risks should be integrated into business-planning, decision-making, and operational processes
- How compliance to the policy is monitored to ensure a continuous learning cycle

The audit found a well-defined and appropriately communicated PS Integrated Risk Management Policy (IRM Policy), and subsequent to the audit examination period, a PS Integrated Risk Management Framework (IRM Framework) was approved by senior management. Both documents had identifiable objectives, clear roles and responsibilities, and reporting time frames that were aligned with the TB Framework for the Management of Risk and TB Guide to Integrated Risk Management.

The IRM Framework that existed at the time of the audit was, for all intents and purposes, similar to the recently approved version. It provides guidance on the key activities of a complete risk management life cycle. The audit also found that the guidance concentrated on how risks and opportunities should be identified, assessed, and, to some extent, integrated into planning instruments; however, neither one offered guidance on how to integrate risk management into decision-making or work processes. Although the existing guidelines are a good foundation, the TB Guide to Integrated Risk Management articulates a risk-informed approach to building risk management into existing governance and organizational structures, including business planning, decision-making, and operational processes.

The IRM Policy outlines the following processes to monitor the implementation of the policy:

- Departmental compliance with this policy may be assessed by internal audit, as part of its approved risk-based audit plan. Results of the internal audits will be reported to the deputy minister and the departmental audit committee.

- Select monitoring and reviews may also be requested by the chief risk officer to assess changes required to policies, directives, procedures, guidelines, and profiles in order to effectively manage risks, and/or to provide reports to the deputy minister, as required.

The previous and current version of the IRM Framework stipulates that in order to ensure that integrated risk management is implemented throughout the Department, the following three key mechanisms will be used:

- The Strategic Planning Division will promote the application of the IRM Policy in decision making and planning through the development of tools and mechanisms to facilitate the use of risk information in the Department.

- The TBS Management Accountability Framework (MAF) assessment will highlight best practices and areas of improvement.

- The Departmental Audit Committee's recommendations will be used by the Strategic Planning Division to improve IRM processes and ensure that they are responsive to departmental realities.

Although these monitoring mechanisms are positive and will provide some evidence of effectiveness, they remain periodic and at a high level. There was limited documentation or evidence to support the select monitoring and review of the implementation of the policy. There are no mechanisms that enable timely information on the state of implementation. The audit recognizes that the Strategic Policy Branch (SPB) has succeeded in putting in place many foundational elements with very few resources; however, a few select indicators would ensure that the momentum gained is not lost. An example of a possible indicator could be the tracking of the completion of Branch Risk Profiles (BRP).

*Operational Risk Management Tools.* The audit expected to find tools that would facilitate the full risk management life cycle. This would include tools that support the management of:

- Strategic-level risks and opportunities
- Individual specific risk applications, such as the management of grants and contributions
- Operational-level risks and opportunities

*Strategic Risk Management Tools.* The Corporate Risk Profile (CRP) is the departmental tool that captures the high-level strategic risks. Public Service has received strong MAF ratings for its CRP process. Additionally, there is positive evidence of the use of the CRP outputs in support of senior management decision making. On an annual basis, each branch is required to identify their risks and opportunities and bring this information forward for discussion and prioritization at horizontal departmental integration sessions. Each of the identified risks and opportunities is then assessed on the likelihood of occurrence and their impacts. The purpose of these integration sessions is to allow a "challenge" function and, more important, to ensure that the cross-cutting impacts of these risks and opportunities are appropriately identified and understood departmentally. Following these sessions, the top three risks and opportunities by program level of the Program Alignment Architecture (PAA) formed the CRP. Responsible directorates and mitigation plans were then identified for each strategic risk or opportunity.

## Identifying Strategic Risks

Generally, all interviewees indicated that branch meetings were held to identify potential risks related to their areas of responsibility in preparation for the CRP integration sessions. They also indicated that these risks were informed by other inputs, such as outputs from their specific use of risk management tools, stakeholder consultations, and interdepartmental committees. The audit found that the approaches to inform and assess the risks were not documented. Consequently, it was not possible to determine the completeness and sufficiency of this risk identification step and whether some operational and strategic risks were overlooked. The absence of documentation may also contribute to a misunderstanding and/or misinterpretation of the basis of these risks.

The audit noted that in some cases the input of risks for certain PAA level programs was limited in quantity; for example, one program identified only four high-level risks. Given the complexity and sensitivity of each program, the audit expected more detailed lists. The audit did not attempt to assess the sufficiency, validity, and relevancy of these risks. The limited number did raise concerns as to whether the Department has overlooked any risks and whether the process benefited from a robust horizontal "assessment and challenge."

## Assessing Strategic Risks

Interviewees indicated that the integration sessions were important in providing an opportunity for all participants to understand the departmental risk environment as well as the proposed mitigation plans and acceptable tolerances. Although there was no evidence to support the deliberation of these sessions, it was noted by participants that their ability to report back to their colleagues on a department-wide risk perspective contributed to a heightened risk awareness and knowledge.

The CRP presents the top three risks and opportunities for each program level of the PAA. As a result, it is possible that risks ranking lower than the top three in one specific program, but higher than the top three risks of other programs, will not be included in the CRP. Consequently, there is no mechanism in place to ensure that the Department's highest-ranking strategic risks are managed corporately and monitored by the most senior governance committees.

*Developing Risk Responses for Strategic Risks.* CRP risks and mitigation plans are developed in the fall as part of the regular departmental planning and reporting cycle. This information is then prepopulated by the Strategic Policy Branch into the Branch Business Plans (BBP) to ensure continuity. It is then expected that branches will appropriately update the mitigation plans into the respective directorate work plans. This exercise is positive in that it ensures that all CRP risks and mitigation plans are assigned to the appropriate branches.

To better understand the alignment of the risks and the associated mitigation plans, the auditors developed a link from the risks identified in the CRP to the risks identified in the business plans to the actions identified in the directorate work plans. The audit was able to trace the CRP outputs into the BBPs. As expected, the directorate work plans contained detailed actions that were intended to address the high-level CRP mitigation plans. However, it was not always clear whether:

- The mitigation plans identified responded to the original high-level CRP mitigation plans.

- The mitigation plans cascaded into the individual directorate work plans as appropriate.

- Changes to the mitigation plans were reassessed to ensure that they still sufficiently mitigated the risks.

There was also no evidence that DMC was made aware of or approved modifications to CRP mitigation plans. An example that highlighted the potential misalignment between the CRP mitigation plans and the directorate work plans was observed in one of the 2011–12 CRP risk statements: "That the Government Operations Centre (GOC) infrastructure may not support a coordinated response to an event affecting the national interest—space, security, survivability, and sustainability requirements." This risk statement and the related mitigation plans remained unchanged through 2013 to 2014. It was uncertain whether the CRP mitigation plans and the associated directorate work plans were either not addressed or not sufficient, or whether the Department chose to accept the risk without mitigating it.

## Specific-Use Risk Tools

As part of the audit, in the following program areas the specific use of risk management tools was examined:

- Public Safety Information Management System (PSIMS)—which captures risk information for individual recipients for departmental grants and contribution programs

- The All Hazards Risk Assessment (AHRA) tool—which, led by PS, in close partnership with Defense Research Development Canada–Centre for Security Science, supports all federal government institutions in fulfilling their legislative responsibility to conduct mandate-specific risk assessments as the basis for Emergency Management planning

- Critical Infrastructure tool—which was developed to support the goal of the National Strategy for Critical Infrastructure in partnership with federal, provincial, and territorial governments and critical infrastructure sectors for the purpose of improving information sharing and protection and sustaining a commitment to all-hazards risk management. This all-hazards approach considers natural hazards, accidental hazards, and intentional threats.

The audit found the development of these specific-use risk management tools to be a very positive step in fulfilling risk management and providing outputs to inform decision-making processes in support of these program areas.

It was indicated that these tools were in the early stages of implementation and therefore did not yet provide consistent and systematic outputs. The audit also noted that there was limited documented guidance to support how these tools were to be integrated into other risk-informed operations, such as:

- How interdependencies and information should be shared

- How outputs should be integrated into directorate, branch, and departmental risk management activities

- How these tools should support the complete risk management life cycle, including response and monitoring

Although the tools supported risk identification, assessment, and some aspects of response, none of the tools had defined approval, reporting, and monitoring mechanisms or processes.

*Operational Risk Management Tools.* Branch Risk Profiles (BRP), as identified in the PS Integrated Risk Management Framework, are intended to inform each branch's decision on plans, priorities, and resource allocation by capturing, assessing, and summarizing key risks that could most impact the achievement of branch objectives. Once finalized, the BRPs are used to drive discussions in the development of the CRP.

The audit found that BRPs were generally not completed or consistently maintained, nor did branches have any other consolidated risk document. In the instances in which branches had a documented BRP, its content was essentially the same as the CRP risks, with little additional information. Employees did not use any specific use or operational risk management tools to identify, assess, respond to, and monitor risks associated with policy development or research activities. Rather, the audit was told that these risks were identified through undocumented intuitive means or through stakeholder engagement and committees.

In the absence of a consolidated risk document, risk management is fragmented and disconnected, and consequently the department cannot easily be assured of the completeness and consistent interpretation of risk information and that all risks are appropriately considered throughout the planning and reporting stages. This may also impact the integrity of the planning process and may jeopardize the achievement of better performance.

## Governance

The audit expected to find governance structures that promote a risk-informed culture and management practices throughout the Department. It was also expected that departmental governance structures would monitor the management of risks and the implementation of the IRM policy and framework. The audit examined the following departmental committees:

- Departmental Management Committee
- Departmental Audit Committee
- Branch and Directorate Management Committees

**Departmental Management Committee (DMC).** The DMC terms of reference states that the committee's objectives are to review and approve policies, projects, plans, performance, and reports relating to a broad and diverse suite of corporate management programs and services for the Department, including risk management. Further, the IRM Policy requires that the DMC identify, assess, manage, and discuss corporate risks at least twice per year.

The audit found:

- In 2012–2013, DMC did not review the initial CRP update as it was approved bilaterally with the DM. The audit was informed that there were opportunities for all members to review and provide their input individually. However, members did not benefit from a collective discussion allowing for the understanding of the Department's risk tolerances.

- An update on the risks and their respective mitigation plans was presented during the mid-year review process. Interviewees noted that there was limited discussion, with only twenty minutes allotted on the agenda for the entire mid-year review of performance and risk; this is not conducive to a fulsome discussion. Further, the documentation supporting the mid-year discussion included only a "symbol" indicating risk status.. The audit expected a more deliberate discussion and consistent presentation of strategic risks and their mitigation by the senior management team.

- Finally, the audit noted that the onus was on individual presenters to the DMC to determine the criteria for the disclosure of risk information.

**The Departmental Audit Committee.**   The Departmental Audit Committee (DAC), which provides advice on such areas as risk management, was informed of risks and risk management processes on a regular basis throughout the audit period. DAC commended the progress made in the implementation of IRM. It was noted that this committee actively uses the outputs from the CRP to challenge departmental activities such as resource allocations. Advice from the committee members focused on the importance of not losing track of risks when moving on to the next issue and of the need to use risk information more strategically for such activities as linking resources to the areas of risk and priority.

**Branch   and   Directorate   Management   Committees.** Branch   and directorate management committees were identified as fundamental governance structures. However, none of these meetings had specific terms of reference or other agreed-upon processes defining what risk information should be presented or when it should be presented. Nor were any of the meeting discussions documented, which made it challenging for the audit to conclude whether these committees were providing any form of risk oversight. Compounded by the absence of BRPs and the lack of directorate risk information in the BBP, the audit could not conclude whether risk information was being used to inform decision making.

Without defined information requirements, documented discussions, and rigor in ensuring compliance and sufficient and appropriate risk information, including risk tolerances and mitigation status, risks may not be effectively reported and monitored. Organizations may be keeping information that prevents them from achieving objectives and the highest performance.

## Integration: Risk-Informed Decision Making and Culture

The audit expected to find risk-informed approaches to business planning, decision making, and operational processes. As stated in the PS IRM Framework, "The objective is to create an environment where all levels of the organization will instinctively look for risk and opportunities and take into account their impacts on departmental outcomes when making decisions at both the operational and the corporate levels."

**Departmental Level.** The audit found that senior managers have started to integrate risk information into key decision-making activities as risk has become more engrained. The inclusion of risk information has largely been done through the use of the CRP outputs and specific risk information presented to DMC. The audit noted the following examples:

• The Risk and Results Based Approach to Staffing, developed by the Human Resources Directorate, informs delegated managers on the risk tolerances of senior management for different types of staffing actions and categorizes them such that controls and reporting requirements are commensurate to the different levels of risks.

• During the development of the departmental priorities, SPB incorporated the CRP outputs into the planning process, ensuring the visibility of risks and opportunities and their alignment to each priority. The CRP outputs were further used in the development of the Report on Plans and Priorities. The integration of risks in this manner was a positive step in guiding the focus of the Department.

Even so, there continue to be gaps in regard to integrating risk information in decision making. For example, there was no systematic requirement for risk management information to be included in briefing notes, memos, status reports, or financial and nonfinancial performance reports.

The audit did note that the Strategic Planning Division, Strategic Policy Branch has started a Risk and Threat Assessment Community of Practice, which will provide a valuable means of tapping into departmental strengths and of sharing tools, information, and expertise both horizontally and vertically on an ongoing basis. This forum will provide an opportunity to learn and collaborate where possible and possibly reduce duplication of effort.

Departmentally, the audit found senior management generally supportive of risk management and that tolerances for certain risks were communicated to lower levels. Examples of the mechanisms used to establish a risk management

**Table 7.4**
**Public Service of Canada Key Risks Related to Integrated Risk Management**

| Risk Name | Description |
|---|---|
| 1. Culture | There is a risk that organizational culture and operating practices will not allow for or compel the optimal sharing of information and discussion of risk information. |
| 2. Business Process—Application of Tools | There is a risk that risk management tools will not be applied consistently or in an appropriately robust fashion. |
| 3. Inputs | There is a risk that individual risk management processes will not be informed by comprehensive inputs. |
| 4. Vertical Integration | There is a risk that the corporate risk profile and decisions resulting from it will not be appropriately informed by existing lower-level risk management processes and resulting risk information. |
| 5. Horizontal Integration | There is a risk that there will be insufficient sharing of risk information across branches and directorates. |
| 6. Functional Integration | There is a risk that managerial functions and decisions (such as priorities, resource allocation/reallocation, and program decisions) will not be properly informed by risk information. |
| 7. Response and Monitoring | There is a risk that risks will not be formally and appropriately responded to and monitored. |

environment included the official approval and communication of the IRM Policy and the completion and communication of the annual CRP.

However, as noted in previous audits, a culture of silos persists in some areas, which impedes broad and transparent departmental risk discussions. Without building the transparency and trust needed for a comprehensive risk understanding, departmental risk strategies and tolerances may not be clearly communicated, leading to suboptimal decisions and use of resources.

**Branch/Directorate Level.** As noted earlier, there were generally no BRPs and few operational risk management tools to facilitate risk awareness and understanding. Generally, at the branch and directorate level the use of risk was more intuitive. Risk management was less structured and often formalized only for the purpose of contributing to the required high-level CRP process or applied for a specific program need, such as the management of contribution recipients. A number of interviewees noted that the CRP outputs were of limited use and perceived it to be an administrative task with minimal added value. Therefore, in some cases it did not guide their decision-making activities. Generally, interviewees noted that information related to finances, HR capacity, and stakeholder concerns was the key source that informed decision making. Risks per se were not the focus of discussions. These indicators in and of themselves are not sufficient to enable robust integrated risk management. Although there were positive signals that some decisions were informed by risk, without a more structured and deliberate risk-informed approach, there is a risk that suboptimal decisions may be made.

### Preliminary Audit Risks

Based on these conditions and the risk factors that stem from them, Table 7.4 summarizes the key risks to which Public Service Canada is exposed in relation to Integrated Risk Management.

## chapter EIGHT

# ERM Core Competencies

In a risk culture, behavioral attributes are key and applicable not only for the overall culture but also at the individual level. RIMS emphasizes that in order to drive and sustain a risk management program and practice sound risk management, those responsible for leading risk activities in an organization need to develop a specific set of competencies and skills.

## ERM CORE COMPETENCY SURVEY

A survey of public sector risk professionals across federal, state, and local governments and nonprofit organizations (including universities) was conducted to help scan the environmental conditions under which ERM adoption was being implemented. The 2014 ERM Core Competency Survey for the Public Sector was designed to collect feedback from the leaders involved in the ERM process. The survey design was based on the Risk & Insurance Management Society's (RIMS) Risk Manager Core Competency Model and was modified to reflect the dynamics and operations of public sector organizations; therefore, not all skills are included in the survey responses.

The RIMS model reflects components of the best practices and best theoretical models preferred by the RIMS Fellow Advisory Council, the American Society for Training and Development, and basic business management texts. The RIMS model takes the best ideas from many models and modifies them to reflect the many different skills required for risk management.

The 2014 ERM Core Competency Survey consisted of twenty-three questions and was divided into two sections: (1) Demographics and (2) an Assessment of Conceptual, Technical, and Core Competency Skills for Risk Managers. There were 103 respondents to the survey.

## Conceptual, Technical, and Core Competency Skills

Respondents were asked to select the specific skills they would recommend for a successful risk management career. The skills were segmented into three areas:

- *Conceptual Skills.* This is the strategic layer, which requires the ability to understand all the organization's activities, how the pieces fit together, and how the organization can achieve its strategic goals. These skills include the ability to adopt a portfolio approach to ERM.

- *Technical Skills.* This is the operational layer, in which many of the traditional duties and specialized skills of risk managers come into play. Some skills

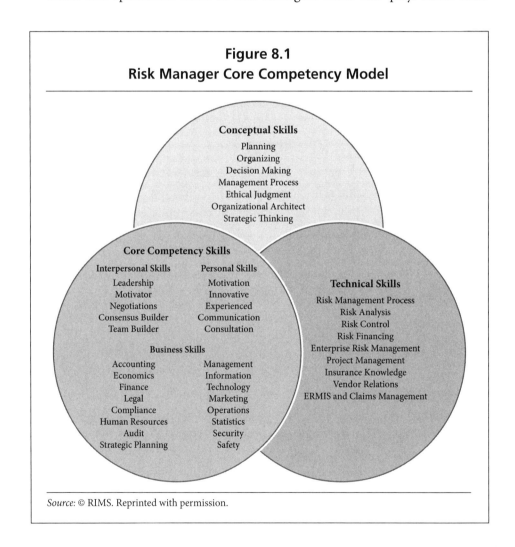

**Figure 8.1**
**Risk Manager Core Competency Model**

**Conceptual Skills**
Planning
Organizing
Decision Making
Management Process
Ethical Judgment
Organizational Architect
Strategic Thinking

**Core Competency Skills**

**Interpersonal Skills**
Leadership
Motivator
Negotiations
Consensus Builder
Team Builder

**Personal Skills**
Motivation
Innovative
Experienced
Communication
Consultation

**Business Skills**
Accounting
Economics
Finance
Legal
Compliance
Human Resources
Audit
Strategic Planning
Management
Information
Technology
Marketing
Operations
Statistics
Security
Safety

**Technical Skills**
Risk Management Process
Risk Analysis
Risk Control
Risk Financing
Enterprise Risk Management
Project Management
Insurance Knowledge
Vendor Relations
ERMIS and Claims Management

*Source:* © RIMS. Reprinted with permission.

may not be applicable; this depends on individual experience and the work environment.

- *Core Competency Skills.* The core competency skills are divided into three subcategories: interpersonal, personal, and business skills. The interpersonal and personal skills are sometimes considered "soft," but they are actually basic and essential business management skills. These form the basis on which all competent managers stand.

The skill sets are presented in Figure 8.1.

## SUMMARY OF SURVEY RESULTS

The 2014 ERM Core Competency Survey for the Public Sector was distributed to targeted members of several online communities: LinkedIn groups for the American Society for Public Administration, Budget Development in the Public Sector, and Public Sector Risk Management; and the FederalERM.org membership website.

There were a total of 103 respondents. A comparative analysis of feedback from state government respondents and from federal government respondents is provided in Tables 8.1 and 8.2.

### Survey Highlights

The following are highlights of key findings from the overall survey.

#### Demographics

- Of 103 respondents, the majority represented the federal government (61 percent), followed by 25 percent from state and local government.

- Sixty percent of respondents classified themselves as risk managers. Another 22 percent identified risk executive as their role in ERM activities.

- A little over 60 percent of the respondents said that their organizations had implemented enterprise risk management, compared to 37 percent of respondents whose organization had not.

- Just over 40 percent of respondents worked for small organizations of three thousand employees or fewer, compared to 25 percent of respondents whose organization comprised more than twenty-five thousand employees.

## Table 8.1
## ERM Components in Place in Organizations to Aid ERM Implementation

| ERM Components | State and Local Government Respondent Rank | Federal Government Respondent Rank |
|---|---|---|
| Risk Management Policy | 1 | 1 |
| Change Management Plan | 6 | 7 |
| Communications Plan | 2 | 5 |
| ERM Strategic Plan | 5 | 5 |
| Training and Education Plan | 2 | 3 |
| Identified Governance Structure | 5 | 2 |
| Written Endorsements from Senior Management | 4 | 4 |
| Interagency Collaborative Workgroups | 4 | 6 |
| IT and Database Systems; Dashboards | 3 | 6 |

## Table 8.2
## Top Three ERM Components in Place: State and Local Government versus Federal Government

| State and Local Government | Component Rank | Federal Government |
|---|---|---|
| Risk Management Policy | 1 | Risk Management Policy |
| Communications Plan and Training and Education Plan | 2 | Identified Governance Structure |
| IT and Database Systems; Dashboards | 3 | Training and Education Plan |

**Resources**

- Forty-two percent of respondents indicated that two to five employees are assigned to their organization's ERM effort. Twenty-four percent indicated that they were the only staff member assigned to their organization's ERM effort.

- A majority of respondents (64 percent) spend part of their time on ERM activities; 35 percent are assigned full-time to ERM activities.

- The majority of respondents (44 percent) did not have an ERM budget, and close to 20 percent did not know.

- Nearly 60 percent of respondents have more than ten years of risk management, internal controls, auditing, or financial management experience.

**ERM Practice**

- Nearly 38 percent of respondents said that "all decisions made in [their] organization take risk into account." A close 32 percent of respondents indicated that risk management "is mainly oriented towards auditing and compliance." Another 31 percent of respondents indicated that risk management is "mainly used in internal controls management."

- Nearly a third (32 percent) of respondents understood risk to be the "effect of uncertainty on objectives." A similar number, 31 percent, indicated that risk is a "combination of the probability of an event and its consequence." Twenty-one percent indicated that risk is "a chance of something happening that will have an impact on objectives."

- Forty-three percent of respondents indicated that they have a complete understanding of ISO 31000, compared to 39 percent of respondents who fully understood the COSO ERM Framework.

- Nearly 40 percent of respondents were not familiar with the GAO Risk Management Framework.

- Forty-five percent of respondents preferred to use ISO 31000 for ERM implementation. Just 18 percent indicated that they preferred to use the COSO ERM Framework.

- Less than 20 percent of respondents indicated they preferred to use the GAO Risk Management Framework to implement ERM.

- Just over a third (34 percent) of respondents indicated that their organization has adopted or considered ISO 31000 to implement ERM, compared to 22 percent who preferred the COSO ERM Framework. However, 31 percent indicated that they would use neither.

- A majority of respondents (72 percent) indicated that they have a risk management policy in place to aid in ERM implementation. Forty-nine percent indicated that they have an identified governance structure, and 45 percent have a training and education plan.

- A minority of respondents (17 percent) indicated that they use a change management plan.

## Skills for Career Success in Enterprise Risk Management

The majority of respondents to the ERM Core Competency Survey had more than ten years of experience in the area of risk management, internal controls, auditing, or financial management. Therefore, skill recommendations are based on the judgment of seasoned professionals who are familiar with what is needed to be successful in the area of enterprise risk management (see Table 8.3). Our

### Table 8.3
### Risk Management Training Rubric

**State and Local Government Workforce**

| Conceptual Skills | Technical Skills | Interpersonal Skills | Personal Skills | Business Skills |
|---|---|---|---|---|
| Strategic Thinking | Risk Management Process | Negotiation | Motivation | Strategic Planning |
| Ethical Judgment | Risk Analysis | Leadership | Communication | Safety |
| Organizational Architecture | Risk Control | Consensus Building | Consultation | Compliance |

**Federal Government Workforce**

| Conceptual Skills | Technical Skills | Interpersonal Skills | Personal Skills | Business Skills |
|---|---|---|---|---|
| Strategic Thinking | Risk Management Process | Team Building | Communication | Strategic Planning |
| Management Process | Risk Analysis | Consensus Building | Motivation | Management |
| Decision Making | Enterprise Risk Management | Motivation | Innovation | Change Management |

*Note:* Training rubric recommendations are based on feedback from state and local government survey respondents.

summary of the responses regarding recommended skill sets represents both state and local government and federal government respondent perspectives.

## Summary of Skill Recommendations—All Respondents

The next section provides an overall summary of skill recommendations based on feedback from both the state and federal government survey respondents.

**Core Competencies** *Conceptual Skills.* Eighty-seven percent of respondents indicated that *strategic thinking* is the top conceptual skill that they recommend for a risk professional; 83 percent indicated *ethical judgment* as the second-highest recommended skill. *Management process* rounded out the top three recommended areas, with 82 percent citing this skill.

*Technical Skills.* The majority of respondents (91 percent) indicated that understanding the *risk management process* is the top technical skill for a risk professional; 83`percent indicated *risk analysis* as the second most recommended skill. *Risk control* rounded out the top three recommended areas, with 80 percent citing this skill.

**Core Competency Skills** *Interpersonal Skills.* The majority of respondents (89 percent) indicated that *consensus building* is the top core competency interpersonal skill they would recommend for a risk professional. The second most recommended skill was *leadership* (88 percent), followed by *team building* (85 percent), rounding out the top three skills.

*Personal Skills.* The vast majority of respondents (95 percent) indicated that *communication* is the top core competency personal skill they would recommend for a risk professional. The second most recommended skill was *motivation* (94 percent), followed by *innovation* (90 percent), rounding out the top three skills.

*Business Skills.* Eighty-seven percent of respondents indicated that *strategic planning* is the top core competency business skill they would recommend for a risk professional. The second most recommended skill was a tie for *management* and *operations*, chosen by 81 percent of the respondents. *Change management* rounded out the top three skills, cited by 79 percent of the respondents. The least recommended business skills were *accounting* and *economics*.

## FEDERAL VERSUS STATE AND LOCAL GOVERNMENT VIEWS OF ERM

Do federal government risk professionals think differently about enterprise risk management than their state and local government counterparts? Is risk perceived in the federal sector in the same way it is in state and local government? Are the approaches to ERM the same in federal and state government environments? Does the level of commitment from leadership to ERM resources in state and local government vary as well?

The 2014 ERM Core Competency Survey provided insight to help answer these questions. A review of the survey responses from various sectors, such as state and local government, reveals similarities and differences in ERM design or implementation and helps to compare any risk management performance gaps.

The purpose of this analysis is to assess any contrasts and significant findings that could influence how ERM is perceived and practiced in both the federal and state governments.

### State and Local Government View of ERM—Survey Results

This section summarizes feedback received from state and local government survey respondents.

**Demographics**   A quarter of the 103 survey respondents to the 2014 ERM Core Competency Survey were from state and local government. The majority work for state and local government organizations with three thousand or fewer employees. When identifying their roles, the majority of these respondents considered themselves more a *risk manager* than a *risk owner*. Yet *risk owner* is the role the ISO 31000 identifies in its risk management principles and guidelines. There is no certainty that identifying as a risk manager rather than a risk owner has a significant impact on how risk is managed in an organization, but it may be worth exploring. The survey responses also suggest that having a risk owner in state and local government is not an indicator that the organization has implemented ERM. Hence, the majority worked for organizations that had *not* implemented ERM.

*Risk executive* was the other role the respondents identified themselves as filling, in contrast to the more popular *chief risk officer* title that is often used in industry.

**Resources**   Levels of investment in ERM vary by sectors. However, having two to five staff committed to ERM is standard, according to state and local survey respondents, though most work on ERM on a part-time basis. Spending half their time on ERM may be due to the lack of available program funds. Nearly 40 percent indicated that there was no program budget, and just as many were not sure. Respondents were not necessarily new to the profession, as nearly 70 percent indicated having more than ten years of experience in risk management, internal controls, auditing, or financial management.

**Cultural Views of Risk**   Culturally, nearly 45 percent of state and local respondents indicated that "all decisions made in their organization take risk into account"; 24 percent indicated that risk management is "mainly oriented towards insurance and is used in internal controls management." According to 52 percent of the state and local respondents, when risk is taken into account in all decisions, it is understood to be "the effect of uncertainty on objectives." There was little indication that risk is understood to be an "event that would have a negative impact on the organization."

**Risk Management Standards and Frameworks**   State and local government risk professionals indicated having a complete understanding of both ISO 31000 and the COSO ERM Framework, but more than 60 percent prefer to use ISO 31000 for ERM implementation over the COSO ERM Framework. A majority (53 percent) indicated that their organization has adopted or considered ISO 31000 to implement ERM. The scope of ERM is considered as "an effort that cuts across the entire organization." Data also suggested that using a hybrid risk management framework is seen as an option as well. Nearly 40 percent indicated that their organization had not considered or adopted either the COSO ERM Framework, ISO 31000 Standard, or GAO Risk Management Standard; rather, they opted for a hybrid approach that incorporates some variation of all three.

**Key Components of ERM**   Having a risk management policy is by far the most common component in place to aid ERM implementation in an organization. The majority (80 percent) of state and local respondents indicated that they have this factor, followed by the use of a communications plan and training and education plan, and an IT database system and dashboards. A change management plan was the least common component in place to aid in ERM implementation in state and local government.

### State and Local Government View of Skills for Career Success

Similar to the overall population of survey respondents, the majority of state and local risk professionals (69 percent) completing the ERM Core Competency Survey have more than ten years of experience in the area of risk management, internal controls, auditing, or financial management.

**Core Competencies** *Conceptual Skills.* Eighty-six percent of state and local respondents indicated that *strategic thinking* is the top conceptual skill that they recommend for a risk professional; 82 percent indicated *ethical judgment* as the second-highest recommended skill. However, unlike their federal government counterparts, 78 percent of state and local respondents cited *organizational architecture* as one of the top three recommended areas.

*Technical Skills.* The majority of state and local respondents (87 percent) indicated that understanding the *risk management process* is the top technical skill for a risk professional; 86 percent indicated *risk analysis* as the second most recommended skill. *Risk control* rounded out the top three recommended areas, with 82 percent citing this skill.

**Core Competency Skills** *Interpersonal Skills.* The majority of state and local respondents (95 percent) indicated that *negotiation* is the top core competency interpersonal skill they would recommend for a risk professional. The second most recommended skill was *leadership* (90 percent), followed by *consensus building* (85 percent), which rounded out the top three skills.

*Personal Skills.* The majority of state and local respondents (91 percent) indicated that *motivator* is the top core competency personal skill they would recommend for a risk professional. The second most recommended skills were equally important: *communication* and *consultation*, to round out the top three skills.

*Business Skills.* The majority of state and local respondents (82 percent) indicated *strategic planning* but also cited *safety* (82 percent) as the top core competency business skills they would recommend for a risk professional. However, in contrast to their federal government counterparts, *compliance* was cited by 79 percent of the respondents, rounding out the top three skills. Similar to federal government respondents, state and local risk professionals cited *accounting* and *economics* as the least recommended business skills.

## Federal Government View of ERM—Survey Results

The purpose of this analysis is to assess any contrasts and significant findings that could influence how ERM is perceived and practiced in the federal government.

**Demographics**   Again, a majority (63) of the 103 respondents to the 2014 ERM Core Competency Survey were from the federal government. The majority work for federal government organizations with three thousand or fewer employees. When identifying with roles, the majority of these respondents considered themselves a *risk manager* more than a *risk owner*. Yet *risk owner* is the role the ISO 31000 International Standard identifies in its risk management principles and guidelines. There is no certainty that identifying as a risk manager rather than a risk owner has a significant impact on how risk is managed in an organization, but it may be worth exploring. The survey responses also suggest that having identified *risk owners* in the federal government is not an indicator that the organization has implemented ERM. Hence, the majority worked for organizations that have implemented ERM. *Risk executive* was the other role the respondents identified themselves as filling, in contrast to the more popular *chief risk officer* title that is often used in industry.

**Resources**   Levels of investment in ERM vary by sectors. However, having two to five staff committed to ERM is standard, according to federal survey respondents, though most work on ERM on a part-time basis. Spending half their time on ERM may be due to the lack of program funds available. Nearly 50 percent indicated that there was no program budget. Respondents were not necessarily new to the profession, with 50 percent indicating they had more than ten years of experience in risk management, internal controls, auditing, or financial management.

**Cultural Views of Risk**   Culturally, nearly 40 percent indicated that risk management is "mainly used in internal controls management," while 38 percent indicated that risk is mainly oriented toward auditing/compliance. Just over 34 percent indicated that "all decisions made in [their] organization take risk into account." Unlike their state and local government counterparts, 42 percent of federal government respondents understand risk as a "combination of the probability of an event and its consequence," whereas 20 percent understand risk to be "the effect of uncertainty on objectives" or the "chance of something happening that will have an impact on objectives."

**Risk Management Standards and Frameworks** Forty-four percent of federal government risk professionals indicated having a complete understanding of the GAO Risk Management Framework. A quarter of federal respondents indicated that their organization has adopted or considered the GAO Risk Management Framework to implement ERM followed by 22 percent who cited the COSO ERM Framework. The concept of ERM is understood by federal risk professionals, as nearly 60 percent indicate that the scope of ERM is considered as "an effort that cuts across the entire organization."

**Key Components of ERM** Having a risk management policy is by far the most common component in place to aid in ERM implementation in an organization. The majority (68 percent) of federal government respondents indicated this was the case for their organization, followed by a recognition that an identified governance structure and a training and education plan are needed. Similar to their state and local government counterparts, they indicated that a change management plan was the least-common component in place to aid in ERM implementation.

### Federal Government View of Skills for Career Success

This section provides an overall summary of feedback from federal government survey respondents.

**Core Competencies** *Conceptual Skills.* Eighty-eight percent of federal government respondents indicated that *strategic thinking* is the top conceptual skill they recommend for a risk professional; 84 percent indicated both *management process* and *decision making* as the second-highest recommended skills.

*Technical Skills.* The majority of federal government respondents (92 percent) indicated that understanding the *risk management process* is the top technical skill for a risk professional; 80 percent indicated *risk analysis* as the second most recommended skill. *Enterprise risk management* rounded out the top three recommended areas, with 75 percent citing this skill.

### Core Competency Skills

*Interpersonal Skills.* Federal government respondents (87 percent) found the *team building, consensus building,* and *motivation* skills to be of equal importance, followed by *leadership* skills (85 percent).

*Personal Skills.* Unlike their state and local government counterparts, the majority of federal respondents (95 percent) indicated that *communication* is the top core competency personal skill they would recommend for a risk professional. The second most recommended skills are *motivation* and *innovation,* rounding out the top three skills.

*Business Skills.* Similar to their state and local government counterparts, the majority of federal government respondents (89 percent) indicated that *strategic planning* is the top core competency business skill they would recommend for a risk professional, followed by *management* and *change management* to round out the top three skills cited. Similar to state and local government respondents, federal risk professionals cited *accounting* and *economics* as the least recommended business skills, as well as *safety* and *security.*

## chapter NINE

# ERM Best Practices of Federal Agencies

## NINETY-DAY ACTION PLAN

- If you are new in the position of risk champion, ensure that the key stakeholders whose buy-in you need are clear about your objective. Often the ERM function is perceived as a shadow audit function and compliance exercise, rather than as a strategic management approach for improving organizational performance. The distinction needs to be made up front and socialized continuously.

- Identify the statutory authority or other comparable law that supports the need for ERM in your organization. The common authority used in federal government is OMB Circular A-123.

- Discover how the organization currently views and defines risk. Work with the highest level of leadership to pose the question, and meet one-on-one with these leaders to engage in a conversation about risk.

- Leverage any existing ERM/risk management activities taking place in the organization. You may find a few managers willing to champion your cause if they see ERM as a way to achieve similar objectives.

- If feasible, kick off a pilot project that gives existing organizational units an opportunity to expend resources (such as on your contractor). Offer a free training session or risk assessment exercise, and agree to deliver a tangible product that will help solve a problem as a result of their participation.

- Get top-level buy-in of ERM by producing a risk philosophy and principles document that can be used as a strategic communications tool. Having leadership's signature on a document that announces the agency's risk philosophy or statement of principles will help brand the ERM activities in the organization.

- Define the organizational gap. What will ERM offer the organization that isn't being done now?

- Join an interagency or other external professional group for ongoing support. Staying abreast of the most current practices and exchanging ideas with colleagues will help maintain the mental clarity needed to carry out the task at hand.

## SAMPLE IMPLEMENTATION PLAN

When implementing ERM, government leaders should keep in mind the following hands-on best practices identified by the agencies featured in this report:

### Getting Started

- Develop a risk management lexicon to ensure consistency of terminology across the organization.

- Establish a communications plan and stick with it.

- Don't underestimate the level of effort needed or shortchange the planning process.

- Customize ERM strategy, approach, and methodology based on your organization's specific requirements.

- Ensure support from senior leadership; this is critical to effectively identifying and addressing risks and opportunities.

- Train your employees.

### Organizing for ERM

- Establish a risk office or ERM organization. If this is not feasible, adopt an "everyone is a risk manager" philosophy.

- Have a dedicated risk champion with good communication skills.

- Ensure that the head of the ERM risk organization or the risk champion is a member of executive management.

- Establish and maintain executive-level support, ideally from the highest levels in the organization.

**Operating an ERM Program**

- Develop a policy that outlines the organization's expectations regarding the management of risks.

- Document the process and analysis so that it can be replicated.

- Provide specific examples of risks tailored to the organization, to aid in the learning process.

- Don't penalize risk identification—reward it. This is critical to changing the culture and effectively establishing an agency-wide ERM process.

- Engage those who manage risks, as well as areas with inherent risks, to develop analytical tools and recommendations. These stakeholders often know the consequences of effective and ineffective risk management, and they have the rigor in thinking and planning to address risks.

- Link risk training to business results, where possible.

- Seek diverse perspectives on issues, as these are critical to risk and opportunity management.

## WORDS OF WISDOM

- Establish short- and long-term strategic plans for ERM. ERM effectiveness is a matter of maturity. It takes time. Make sure stakeholders understand that ERM is a process that is strengthened over time.

- When considering ERM, agencies must establish a tone at the top in the organization. Without senior leadership support, it will be difficult to get buy-in throughout the organization, and ERM will be seen as yet another task and paper exercise rather than as a strategic management process.

- When adopting ERM, make sure the benefits are communicated to stakeholders. Beyond the need for compliance, demonstrate how ERM can enhance organizational performance, heighten awareness about risk management, improve workforce skill sets, and create a "safe place" for managers to discuss risk management outside of their comfort zones.

- Collaborate within and across other agencies. Don't work in a vacuum. Connect with agencies with similar operational functions or missions and benchmark risk management practices. Join organizations that both advocate ERM and provide resources for continuous learning in this subject matter.

• Don't reinvent the wheel. Use what you have. If there is an existing internal control framework in place, build on that. Strategize about how ERM can enhance or strengthen your existing internal control environment.

• Have experienced staff available to champion and carry out the vision of the ERM process. A knowledgeable workforce is the key to successful ERM implementation. If you cannot hire new staff, retrain the staff that you have.

• Communicate short wins immediately. Nothing reinforces success like results. Show stakeholders how ERM has led to successful identification and mitigation of risks, business opportunities, or cost savings.

## chapter TEN

# Conclusion

Some form of risk management exists in every organization. Government agencies are no exception. Managing risk in government is not a new practice in government; agencies have long implicitly or explicitly managed risks to missions. However, changes in operations and technology have contributed to a more dynamic risk environment. The nature of risk is evolving, and its dynamics originate from a continually changing variety of sources. Given these rapid environmental changes, much progress has been made in the area of risk management in government in a relatively short period. There are pockets within the government where risk is managed quite well, such as in specific functions, programs, and projects. But this approach to managing risks often presents a challenge, in that it often leads to ad hoc, unsystematic, and informal risk management practices. This can lead to a lack of understanding and consideration of the main enterprise-wide risk exposures affecting key organizational goals and objectives.

The adoption and practice of enterprise risk management (ERM) has expanded in both private and public industries over the years. And there are as many definitions of the term as there are organizations using it. Depending on the industry in which ERM is practiced, the term can take on different meanings. As noted in Chapter One, the Institute of Internal Auditors (IIA) defines ERM as "a structured, consistent and continuous process across the whole organization for identifying, assessing, deciding on responses to and reporting on opportunities and threats that affect the achievement of its objectives." Yet another professional society defines ERM as "a strategic business discipline that supports the achievement of an organization's objectives by addressing the full spectrum of its risks and managing the combined impact of those risks as an interrelated risk portfolio." The general idea is that ERM is a process that works well at all levels in an organization and is the common strand for collectively viewing, managing, and mitigating risk across an organization.

Unlike the nationwide policy that applies to all the Canadian provinces, there is currently no single, government-wide statutory mandate or policy requiring U.S. federal agencies to practice ERM. At best, many of the legislation and policy documents in place emphasize the need for and execution of risk management in general. Several sources, such as OMB Circular A-123, emphasize aspects of risk management, but it is specific to the financial management area. The lack of a specific directive from a leading government agency (OMB, GAO) may hinder the growth of ERM in government, though there is a continued effort in grassroots practices to promote the adoption of ERM from agency to agency. To some extent this is already taking place, as a majority of federal government risk professionals surveyed identified a risk management policy as the number one component in place in their organization to aid in ERM implementation.

As ERM continues to proliferate within agencies, adopting and instituting a risk management process will be critical to long-term success. Without the implementation of a risk management framework, agencies are at risk of launching ineffective ERM. A risk management framework and process is the basic foundation for building ERM success that is sustainable over time. There are several models to consider; each organization should choose the model that best suits its structure. The most widely used models are the GAO Risk Management Framework, the COSO ERM Integrated Framework, and the ISO 31000 Risk Management Standard.

Some standards and frameworks are preferred over others. In the 2014 ERM Core Competency Survey for the public sector, 53 percent of state and local government risk professionals indicated that their organization has adopted or considered ISO 31000 to implement ERM, whereas 25 percent of federal government risk professionals indicated that their organization has adopted or considered the GAO Risk Management Framework.

ERM has gained momentum in the private sector as a link to performance. Private sector professionals and organizations have begun to inquire into the link between an organization's performance and the integration of ERM. The primary question is whether there is empirical evidence that shows that a company with ERM outperforms a company without ERM. The move by ratings companies, such as Standards & Poor's, to include ERM in their rating assessments of companies has raised the importance of ERM to a new, heightened level. The federal government has begun a similar effort to link risk and performance. The revised OMB Circular A-11 promulgates the assessment of risk to strategic objectives. As agencies work toward perfecting the integration of risk management into the performance management framework, the effect on outcomes will become evident over time.

In fact, time will determine how well ERM is embedded in agencies. To monitor this progress, guideposts will be needed to assess an agency's level of ERM maturity. Several models have been designed to capture ERM maturity in private as well as public sector organizations. Agencies would do well to consider implementing a maturity tool early on in the ERM implementation to help move the initiative forward and to further link risk to performance.

The role of chief risk officer (CRO) has been emerging in the public sector. More agencies than ever are beginning to hire CROs. Industry experts have indicated that the CRO is a direct pathway for risk managers to excel in organizations, and the Department of Labor has identified the risk management specialist as a "bright outlook" occupation that is expected to grow rapidly in the next several years. A few of the top skills recommended for successful risk managers include strategic thinking, consensus building, strategic planning, and communication. All indicators point to ERM as a long-term discipline that many, if not all, organizations will be practicing in the coming years.

## NOTES

### PREFACE

1. Milakovich, M. E., and Gordon, G. J. *Public Administration in America.* Boston: Wadsworth, Cengage Learning, 2013.

2. "Distribution of Federal Civilian Employment by Branch." Sept. 2012. http://www.opm.gov/policy-data-oversight/data-analysis-documentation/federal-employment-reports/employment-trends-data/2012/september/graphic-presentation-of-federal-civilian-employment.

3. U.S. Office of Personnel Management. *Common Characteristics of the Government.* Washington, DC: OPM, 2013.

4. Reilly, S. "Retirement Wave Gaining Force." Feb. 2014. http://www.federaltimes.com/apps/pbcs.dll/article?AID=2014301300003.

5. Securities and Exchange Commission. *Sarbanes-Oxley Act of 2002.* Washington, DC: Government Printing Office, 2002. http://www.sec.gov/about/laws.shtml#sox2002.

6. American Recovery and Reinvestment Act. http://www.recovery.gov/arra/About/Pages/The_Act.aspx.

7. Securities and Exchange Commission, *Sarbanes-Oxley Act.*

8. Office of Personnel Management. 2013 Federal Employee Viewpoint Survey. http://www.opm.gov/news/releases/2013/11/opm-releases-2013-federal-employee-viewpoint-survey-governmentwide-results/.

9. Ibid.

10. Milakovich and Gordon, *Public Administration in America,* p. 11.

11. Ibid., p. xv.

12. Ibid.

13. Ibid.

14. Ibid., p. 11.

15. U.S. Government Accountability Office. "Debt Basics." http://gao.gov/special.pubs/longterm/debt/debtbasics.html.

16. U.S. Government Accountability Office. *The Federal Government's Long-Term Fiscal Outlook: Fall 2012 Update.* Report No. GAO-13–148SP. Washington, DC, 2012.

17. U.S. Government Accountability Office. *Budget Issues: Effects of Budget Uncertainty from Continuing Resolutions on Agency Operations.* Report No. GAO-13–464T. Washington, DC, 2013.

18. U.S. Government Accountability Office. "Homeland Security: Proposal for Cabinet Agency Has Merit, But Implementation Will Be Pivotal to Success." Report No. GAO-02–886-T. Washington, DC, 2005.

19. U.S. Government Accountability Office. High Risk List 2013. Washington, DC, 2013.

## INTRODUCTION

1. Association of Federal Enterprise Risk Management. http://www.AFERM.org.

2. Friel, B. "Learning It Your Way." http://www.govexec.com/magazine-analysis/magazine-analysis-management-matters/2010/07/learning-it-your-way/31860.

3. U.S. Department of Labor. http://www.onetcenter.org/online.html.

4. "CRO Emerging Trends." http://erm.ncsu.edu/library/article/cro-emerging-trends/#.UwV-iMKYbVI.

5. Mihm, J. C. "Wicked Issues, Hollow Government and the Vital Need for Risk Management." Presentation at the Federal Enterprise Risk Management Summit, Arlington, VA, Sept. 2011.

6. Ibid.

## CHAPTER ONE

1. Beasely, M. S., Branson, B. C., and Hancock, B. V. "Rising Expectations: Audit Committee Oversight of Enterprise Risk Management." *Journal of Accountancy*, 2008, 46–47.

2. Fox, C. "*A Guide to Starting an ERM Program*." May 2009. http://www .rmmag.org.

3. Committee on Sponsoring Organizations of the Treadway Commission. "Enterprise Risk Management—Integrated Framework: Executive Summary," 2004.

4. Ibid.

5. Institute of Internal Auditors. *Position Paper: The Role of Internal Auditing in Enterprise Risk Management.* January 2009.

6. Risk & Insurance Management Society. *RIMS Executive Report—The Risk Perspective: An Overview of Widely Used Risk Management Standards and Guidelines.* A Joint Report of RIMS Standards and Practice Committee and RIMS ERM Committee, 2011.

7. Pickett, S.K.H. *Enterprise Risk Management: A Manager's Journey.* Hoboken, NJ: Wiley, 2006.

8. Ibid.

9. Treasury Board of Canada Secretariat. *Integrated Risk Management Framework*, 2001.

10. Charette, R. "On the Lookout: If Government's Job Is to Protect the People, It Must Begin to Manage Risk—Before Disaster Strikes." *Government Executive*, 2009, 28–34.

11. Department of Housing and Urban Development (HUD). Press Release No. HUD 09–177. Sept. 18, 2009. http://www.hud.gov/news/index.cfm.

12. Ibid.

13. Committee on Sponsoring Organizations of the Treadway Commission, 2004.

14. Risk & Insurance Management Society. "The 2008 Financial Crisis: A Wake-up Call for Enterprise Risk Management." *Executive Report*, 2009.

15. Treasury Board of Canada Secretariat. *Integrated Risk Management Framework*. 2001.

16. Ibid.

17. Charette, "On the Lookout" (ch. 1, n. 10).

18. Beasely, Branson, and Hancock, "Rising Expectations."

19. Treasury Board of Canada Secretariat, Integrated Risk Management Framework.

20. Peter, M., Gjerdrum, D., and Peeling, K. "Eeny, Meeny, Miny, Moe—Catch a Standard by the Toe." Presentation at the RIMS Conference, Orlando, FL, 2009.

21. Ibid.

22. Executive Office of the President, Office of Management and Budget. The Federal Manager's Financial Integrity Act of 1982.

23. Ibid.

24. Ibid.

25. Association of Government Accountants (AGA). *Financial Management: Providing a Foundation for Transition*. Annual CFO Survey, July 2008.

26. Ibid.

27. Ibid.

28. Association of Government Accountants. *The New CFO Management Agenda*. Annual CFO Survey, Sept. 2013.

29. American Society of Safety Engineers. "Risk Management Principles and Guidelines: National Adoption of ISO 31000:2009." ANSI/ASSE Z690.2–2011.

30. Hardy, K. "ERM Core Competency Survey for Public Sector Risk Management Professionals." 2014.

31. Treasury Board of Canada Secretariat. *Integrated Risk Management Framework*.

32. Ibid.

33. Ibid.

34. U.S. Government Accountability Office. *Standards for Internal Control in Federal Government*. Report No. GAO-AIMD-00–21.3.1. Washington, DC: GPO, 1999.

35. Ibid.

36. Ibid., pp. 4–21.

37. U.S. Government Accountability Office. Internal Control Management Evaluation Tool. Report No. GAO-01–1008-G. Washington, DC, 2001.

38. Ibid., p. 5.

39. Ibid., p. 6.

40. U.S. Government Accountability Office. *Standards for Internal Control in Federal Government*. Report No. GAO-AIMD-00–21.3.1, pp. 69–70. Washington, DC, 1999.


## CHAPTER TWO

1. Charette, "On the Lookout" (ch. 1, n. 10).

2. U.S. Government Accountability Office. *Risk Management: Further Refinements Needed to Assess Risks and Prioritize Protective Measures at Ports and Other Critical Infrastructure*. Report No. GAO-06–91. Washington, DC, 2005.

3. Federal Drug Administration. Mission statement. http://www.FDA.gov.

4. U.S. Government Accountability Office, *Risk Management*.

5. Ibid.

6. Ginnie Mae. Mission statement. http://www.ginniemae.gov.

7. Ibid.

8. Buttimer, R. J. "Financial Risk Management in the Federal Government: Overview, Practice, and Recommendations." IBM Center for the Business of Government.

9. National Transportation Safety Board mission statement. http://www.NTSB.gov.

10. Charette, "On the Lookout" (ch. 1, n. 10).

11. United States Postal Service. Mission statement. http://www.usps.gov.

12. Garland, D. G. "Risk Recognition and Mitigation: Making CDC RiskSmart." Office of Executive Communication, PowerPoint presentation to the CDC leadership, 2008.

13. Garland, D. G. Interview with Karen Hardy, Centers for Disease Control and Prevention, December 29, 2008.

14. Eccles, R. G., Newquist, S. C., and Schatz, R. "Reputation and Its Risks." *Harvard Business Review OnPoint* (spring 2009): 97–108.

15. Ibid.

16. National Institutes of Health. Mission statement. http://www.nih.gov.

17. U.S. Government Accountability Office. *National Institutes of Health: Completion of a Comprehensive Risk Management Program Essential to Effective Oversight.* Report No. GAO-09–687. Washington, DC: GPO, 2009.

18. National Archives and Records Administration. Mission statement. http://www.nara.gov.

19. U.S. Government Accountability Office. *National Archives and Records Administration: Oversight and Management Improvements Initiated, But More Action Needed.* Report No. GAO-11–15. Washington, DC: GPO, 2010.

20. Ibid.

## CHAPTER THREE

1. Hardy, K. "ERM Core Competency Survey for Public Sector Risk Management Professionals," 2014.

2. Treasury Board of Canada Secretariat. "Guide to Risk Taxomonies." https://www.tbs-sct.gc.ca/tbs-sct/rm-gr/guides/grt-gtr01-eng.asp#toc2.

3. Ibid.

4. Chenok, D. J., Kamensky, J. M., Keegan, M. J., and Ben-Yehuda, G. *Special Report Series: Six Trends Driving Change in Government.* IBM Center for the Business of Government, 2013.

5. Treasury Board of Canada Secretariat. "Guide to Risk Statements." https://www.tbs-sct.gc.ca/tbs-sct/rm-gr/guides/rmg-gertb-eng.asp.

6. Ibid.

7. Ibid.

8. Ibid.

9. Ibid.

10. American Society of Safety Engineers. "Risk Assessment Techniques: National Adoption of IEC/ISO 31010:2009." ANSI/ASSE Z690.2–2011.

11. Ibid.

12. Ibid.

13. American Society of Safety Engineers, "Risk Assessment Techniques."

14. Ibid.

15. Ibid.

16. Treasury Board of Canada Secretariat. *Establishing a Corporate Risk Profile.* https://www.tbs-sct.gc.ca/tbs-sct/rm-gr/guides/gcrp-geprotb-eng.asp.

17. Ibid.

18. Ibid.

19. Ibid.

20. Ibid.

21. State of Washington. *Risk Management Basics.* Feb. 2010.

22. Ibid.

## CHAPTER FOUR

1. Risk & Insurance Management Society. *RIMS Executive Report* (ch. 1, n. 6).

2. Ibid.

3. Ibid.

4. U.S. Government Accountability Office. *Risk Management: Further Refinements Needed* (ch. 2, n. 2).

5. Ibid.

6. U.S. Government Accountability Office. Mission statement. http://www .gao.gov.

7. Gjerdrum, D. "An Overview of ISO 31000:2009—International Standard on the Practice of Risk Management." *PRMIA*, 2010.

8. Ibid.

9. Ibid.

10. American Society of Safety Engineers. "Risk Management Principles and Guidelines" (ch. 3, n. 10).

11. Ibid.

12. Ibid.

13. Ibid.

14. Pickett, *Enterprise Risk Management* (ch. 1, n. 7).

15. Committee on Sponsoring Organizations of the Treadway Commission. "Enterprise Risk Management—Integrated Framework: Executive Summary." 2004.

16. Ibid.

17. Risk & Insurance Management Society. *RIMS Executive Report* (ch. 1, n. 6).

18. Ibid.

19. Ibid.

20. Ibid.

21. Ibid.

## CHAPTER FIVE

1. "Return Driven Strategy: The Book." http://www.returndriven.com.

2. Ibid.

3. Ibid.

4. Frigo, M. L., and Anderson, R. J. "Strategic Risk Assessment: A First Step for Improving Risk Management and Governance." *Strategic Finance* (Dec. 2009): 26–33.

5. Ernst & Young Global Management. "Turning Risk into Results: How Leading Companies Use Risk Management to Fuel Better Performance." 2013.

6. Ibid.

7. Harris, E. A. "Data Breach Hurts Profit at Target." *New York Times*, Feb. 26, 2014. http://www.nytimes.com/2014/02/27/business/target-reports-on-fourth-quarter-earnings.html?_r=0.

8. Ibid.

9. U.S. Government Accountability Office. *Government Performance: GPRA Modernization Act Provides Opportunities to Help Address Fiscal, Performance, and Management Challenges.* Report No. GAO-11–466T. Washington, DC: GPO, 2011.

10. Ibid.

11. Ibid.

12. Federal Program Inventory Fact Sheet. http://www.Performance.gov.

13. Overview of the Federal Performance Framework. http//:www.whitehouse.gov/sites/default/files/omb/assets/a11_current_year/s200.pdf.

14. Ibid.

15. Ibid.

16. Committee on Sponsoring Organizations of the Treadway Commission. "Enterprise Risk Management—Integrated Framework: Executive Summary," 2004.

17. Frigo, M. L., and Anderson, R. J. "What Is Strategic Risk Management?" *Strategic Finance* (April 2011): 21–22, 61.

18. Ibid.

19. Ibid.

20. Ibid.

21. Ibid.

22. Chenok, Kamensky, Keegan, and Ben-Yehuda, *Special Report Series* (ch. 3, n. 4).

23. Ibid.

24. Frigo and Anderson, "What Is Strategic Risk Management?"

25. List of bank failures. http://www.fdic.gov.

26. Ibid.

27. "Credit FAQ: Standard & Poor's Looks Further into How Nonfinancial Companies Manage Risk." Standard & Poor's, June 2010.

28. Ibid.

29. "S&P's Fresh Look at Risk: A Company's Credit Rating Will Reflect Its Ability to Handle Risk." PriceWaterhouseCoopers, Dec. 2008.

30. Ibid.

31. Ibid.

32. Adidas Group. 2012 Annual Report. http://www.adidas.com.

33. "Credit FAQ: Standard & Poor's Looks Further into How Nonfinancial Companies Manage Risk." Standard & Poor's, June 2010.

34. "Credit FAQ: Enterprise Risk Management for Ratings of Nonfinancial Corporations." Standard & Poor's, June 2008.

35. Ibid.

36. Ibid.

37. Ibid.

38. Ibid.

## CHAPTER SIX

1. Weich, K. E., and Sutcliffe, K. M. *Managing the Unexpected*. San Francisco: Jossey-Bass, 2001.

2. Ibid.

3. Ibid.

4. Ibid.

5. Ibid.

6. Ibid.

7. Risk & Insurance Management Society. "The 2008 Financial Crisis: A Wake-up Call for Enterprise Risk Management." *Executive Report,* 2009.

8. Ibid.

9. Terzi, C., and Posta, I. "Review of Enterprise Risk Management in the United Nations System: Benchmarking Framework." Geneva: United Nations, 2010.

10. Newstrom, J. W., and Davis, K. *Organizational Behavior: Human Behavior at Work* (11th ed.). New York: McGraw-Hill Irwin, 2002, pp. 91, 96.

11. Ibid.

12. Braig, S., Gebre B., and Sellgren, A. "Strengthening Risk Management in the U.S. Public Sector." McKinsey & Company, Working Paper No. 28, May 2011.

13. Ibid.

14. Newstrom and Davis, *Organizational Behavior.*

15. Institute of Risk Management. *Risk Culture: Under the Microscope Guidance for Boards*, London, 2012, p. 6.

## CHAPTER SEVEN

1. "Maturity." http://en.wikipedia.org/wiki/maturity_(psychological).

2. "Marks of Maturity." PsychologyToday.com Blog. http://www.psychology today.com/blog/artificial-maturity/201211/the-marks-maturity.

3. "Capability Maturity Model for Software Technical Report." http://resources.sei.cmu.edu/library/asset-view.cfm?assetid=11955.

4. "What Is Capability Maturity Model Integration?" http://www.selectbs.com/process-maturity/what-is-capability-maturity-model-integration.

5. "Capability Maturity Model." http://en.wikipedia.org/wiki/Capability_Maturity_Model.

6. Ibid.

7. Risk & Insurance Management Society. "The 2008 Financial Crisis: A Wake-up Call for Enterprise Risk Management." *Executive Report*, 2009.

8. "Groundbreaking Study Validates Enterprise Risk Management Boost to Business Performance." Press release. New York: PR Newswire, Nov. 2008.

9. Ibid.

10. Risk & Insurance Management Society. "State of ERM Report: Executive Summary." *Executive Report,* 2008.

11. Aon Risk Solutions. "2013 Risk Maturity Index Report: Building a Robust Framework and Realizing Value from Risk Management." Apr. 2013.

12. Aon Risk Solutions, "2013 Risk Maturity Index Insight Report." Nov. 2013.

13. Ibid.

14. State of Washington, "Enterprise Risk Management Maturity Report 2011." Sept. 2011.

15. Ibid.

16. Moore, R., and Wagner, B. "The Role of the Office of Inspector General in Identifying Risks at a Government Agency." *Journal of Public Inquiry* (fall 2012–13): 2.

17. Ibid.

18. The Institute of Internal Auditors, "Perspectives on Enterprise Risk Management: A Holistic View of Risk," p. 9.

19. Ibid.

20. Ibid.

21. Public Safety Canada, "Internal Audit of Integrated Risk Management," September 2013.

22. Ibid., p. 1.

23. Public Safety Canada, "Internal Audit of Integrated Risk Management."

## Q1. What type of public sector organization do you work for or support?

| Answer Choices | Responses | |
| --- | --- | --- |
| Government (federal) | **61.17%** | 63 |
| Government (state or local) | **25.24%** | 26 |
| Nonprofit | **8.74%** | 9 |
| College or University | **4.85%** | 5 |
| **Total** | | **103** |

| # | Other (please specify) |
| --- | --- |
| 1 | Contractor |
| 2 | Advisor, consultant, trainer in ERM |
| 3 | Risk management and insurance broker |
| 4 | Private sector |
| 5 | Public broadcasting |
| 6 | Various short-term safety jobs at US naval stations |

## Q2. I am a:

| Answer Choices | Responses | |
|---|---|---|
| Government Employee | 66.99% | 69 |
| Government Contractor | 8.74% | 9 |
| College or University Employee | 2.91% | 3 |
| Nonprofit employee | 8.74% | 9 |
| Consultant | 12.62% | 13 |
| Total | | 103 |

| # | Other (please specify) |
|---|---|
| 1 | Public broadcasting employee |

## Q3. What role do you play in your organization's ERM activities?

| Answer Choices | Responses | |
|---|---|---|
| Risk Manager | 60.19% | 62 |
| Risk Owner | 7.77% | 8 |
| Risk Director | 16.50% | 17 |
| Risk Board Member | 4.85% | 5 |
| Risk Executive | 22.33% | 23 |

**Total Respondents: 103**

| # | Other (please specify) |
|---|---|
| 1 | ERM Program Manager |
| 2 | Sr. IT Audit Specialist |
| 3 | ERM Consultant |
| 4 | Program/Management Analyst |
| 5 | Risk Champion: responsible for day-to-day activities of the risk management program |
| 6 | Shadow practitioner |

| # | Other (please specify) |
|---|---|
| 7 | Manager Internal Control (MIC) Coordinator |
| 8 | Risk Management Officer |
| 9 | Risk Analyst at Agency HQ |
| 10 | Subject Matter Expert |
| 11 | Workers' Compensation Program Manager |
| 12 | Risk Analyst |
| 13 | Internal Control Manager (Internal Audit Manager) |
| 14 | IT Auditor |
| 15 | Risk Advisor |
| 16 | Internal consultant on program evaluation, risk, and other issues |
| 17 | Support to the CRO |
| 18 | Deputy Chief Risk Officer |
| 19 | Manage the daily activities associated [with] the oversight of Risk Management |
| 20 | Risk Management Program Staff |
| 21 | Oversee development of Integrated Risk Framework for my organization |
| 22 | Teach lessons on ERM activities to senior leaders in government |
| 23 | Safety Officer |
| 24 | Financial Specialist |
| 25 | Consultant |
| 26 | Head of internal audit |
| 27 | Internal Auditor |
| 28 | Identification and awareness of risk to Manager and Risk Owner |
| 29 | Contract safety professional |
| 30 | Risk advisor (to director, executive, and board levels) |
| 31 | Risk analysis consultant on projects |
| 32 | IT Auditor |
| 33 | Risk Management Liaison—oversee the Agency Program |
| 34 | Senior Risk Analyst (survey would not let me use "other" and move on) |
| 35 | Implementer |

### Q4. Has your organization implemented Enterprise Risk Management?

| Answer Choices | Responses | |
| --- | --- | --- |
| Yes | 62.14% | 64 |
| No | 37.86% | 39 |
| Total | | 103 |

### Q5. How many employees are in your organization?

| Answer Choices | Responses | |
| --- | --- | --- |
| 3,000 or less | 41.75% | 43 |
| 3,001 to 5,000 | 10.68% | 11 |
| 5,001 to 10,000 | 6.80% | 7 |
| 10,001 to 20,000 | 12.62% | 13 |
| 20,001 to 25,000 | 2.91% | 3 |
| Greater than 25,000 | 25.24% | 26 |
| Total | | 103 |

### Q6. How many staff members are assigned to your organization's ERM effort?

| Answer Choices | Responses | |
| --- | --- | --- |
| It's just me! | 24.27% | 25 |
| 2–5 | 42.72% | 44 |
| 6–10 | 12.62% | 13 |
| 11–25 | 7.77% | 8 |
| More than 25 | 12.62% | 13 |
| Total | | 103 |

## Q7. How much time do you spend on ERM activities?

| Answer Choices | Responses | |
|---|---|---|
| Assigned full-time to ERM | 35.92% | 37 |
| Spend part of my time on ERM | 64.08% | 66 |
| **Total** | | **103** |

## Q8. If there is a program budget for implementing ERM, how much is it?

| Answer Choices | Responses | |
|---|---|---|
| No program budget at this time | 44.66% | 46 |
| $100,000 or less | 10.68% | 11 |
| $101,000–$250,000 | 3.88% | 4 |
| $251,000–$350,000 | 2.91% | 3 |
| $351,000–$500,000 | 4.85% | 5 |
| $501,000–$999,999 | 4.85% | 5 |
| $1 million or more | 8.74% | 9 |
| Not sure | 19.42% | 20 |
| **Total** | | **103** |

## Q9. How many years of experience do you have in the area of Risk Management, Internal Controls, auditing, or financial management?

| Answer Choices | Responses | |
|---|---|---|
| None | 0.97% | 1 |
| 1 year or less | 0% | 0 |
| 2–5 years | 17.48% | 18 |
| 6–10 years | 22.33% | 23 |
| More than 10 years | 59.22% | 61 |
| **Total** | | **103** |

## Q10. How is risk management used within your organization?

| Answer Choices | Responses | |
|---|---|---|
| It is mainly oriented toward auditing/compliance. | 32.35% | 33 |
| It is mainly oriented toward insurance. | 9.80% | 10 |
| It is mainly oriented toward safety and security. | 18.63% | 19 |
| It is mainly used to report performance data internally and externally. | 17.65% | 18 |
| It is mainly used in internal controls management. | 31.37% | 32 |
| All decisions made in our organization take risk into account. | 37.25% | 38 |
| It is not used in our organization. | 5.88% | 6 |

**Total Respondents: 102**

## Q11. Which best reflects your understanding of risk?

| Answer Choices | Responses | |
|---|---|---|
| RISK—Chance of something happening that will have an impact on objectives | 21.43% | 21 |
| RISK—Event that would have a negative impact on the organization | 11.22% | 11 |
| RISK—Opportunity to make a profit or increase revenue | 0% | 0 |
| RISK—Effect of uncertainty on objectives | 32.65% | 32 |
| Combination of the probability of an event and its consequences | 31.63% | 31 |
| None of the above | 3.06% | 3 |
| **Total** | | **98** |

| # | Other (please specify) |
|---|---|
| 1 | Risk is a resource equivalent to funding, personnel, or material/materiel. Any savings can be achieved by simply increasing risk. Often claims are made that were not true savings, but simply embracing more risks. I define risk as one of many trade-offs to consider when making all policy decisions, especially funding or identifying efficiencies and/or enhanced effectiveness. |

| # | Other (please specify) |
|---|---|
| 2 | Any natural or man-made event that, unmitigated, will harm the organization. |
| 3 | Uncertainty about outcomes that can be either negative or positive. |
| 4 | All above definitions apply. |
| 5 | Risk: The potential for loss, harm, or missed opportunities in relation to achievement of our mission and strategic objectives. |
| 6 | Risks are threats that affect an organization's goals/objectives and the opportunities associated therewith. |

## Q12. What is your level of awareness about:

|  | Not familiar | Somewhat familiar | I have complete understanding | Total Respondents |
|---|---|---|---|---|
| ISO 31000 Risk Management Standard | 12.62% 13 | 43.69% 45 | 43.69% 45 | 103 |
| COSO Enterprise Risk Management Framework | 21% 21 | 40% 40 | 39% 39 | 100 |
| Government Accountability Office (GAO) Risk Management Framework | 37% 37 | 36% 36 | 28.00% 28 | 100 |
| Other (please specify below) | 26.09% 6 | 30.43% 7 | 43.48% 10 | |

| # | Other (please specify) |
|---|---|
| 1 | OMB A—123-Management's Responsibility for Internal Control |
| 2 | COBIT, ISO 27K |

*(continued)*

| # | Other (please specify) |
|---|---|
| 3 | I am an SME on risk challenges that agencies face regarding whether requirements should be accomplished by in-house agency personnel or by private sector vehicles; e.g., contracts or educational institutions. |
| 4 | I am familiar with all of these standards and use them on a day-to-day basis. |
| 5 | Managers' Internal Control Program (SECNAV 5200 series) |
| 6 | NIST Information Security risk framework |
| 7 | Other risk management frameworks |
| 8 | Risk IT, NIST 800–53, ISO 27000 |
| 9 | DoD Risk Management practices |
| 10 | ISACA Risk Management Framework |
| 11 | OMB Circular A-123 |
| 12 | BOBiT, ITIL |
| 13 | GAO Green Book |
| 14 | ANSI Z10 |
| 15 | Public Sector Risk Management Framework |
| 16 | ISO 9000 quality, ISO 14000 environment, AS4801 safety |
| 17 | Integrated Risk Management Framework—Canada |
| 18 | ONR 49000 ff. |
| 19 | OECG |
| 20 | Requirements of a knowledgeable owner |
| 21 | Project Management Institute, AACE International |
| 22 | COBIT, ISO 27K, ISO 20K |

## Q13. Which of the following do you prefer to use for ERM implementation?

| Answer Choices | Responses | |
|---|---|---|
| COSO ERM Framework | **18.45%** | 19 |
| ISO 31000 Risk Management Standard | **45.63%** | 47 |
| GAO Risk Management Framework | **16.50%** | 17 |
| Federal Manager's Financial Integrity Act (FMFIA) | **12.62%** | 13 |
| All of the above | **18.45%** | 19 |
| None of the above | **4.85%** | 5 |
| Other (please specify) | **17.48%** | 18 |

**Total Respondents: 103**

| # | Other (please specify) |
|---|---|
| 1 | I suggest we still not have an all-encompassing toolbox for managing risk. |
| 2 | We are just starting ERM. |
| 3 | DON MIC Program (SECNAV 5200 series) |
| 4 | Not using |
| 5 | Not familiar enough to make a judgment |
| 6 | We are developing a tailored program using best practices from COSO, GAO, and ISO. |
| 7 | ISACA Risk Management Framework |
| 8 | The most applicable to the situation. |
| 9 | OMB Circular A-123 |
| 10 | Customized by picking aspects of the above |
| 11 | We are still improving our traditional risk management program with ERM considered only sporadically. |
| 12 | A mix of the above that apply to my organization. |
| 13 | AS/NZS:4360 (original versions) |
| 14 | Public Administration training |
| 15 | ONR 49001 |
| 16 | ISO 55000—Asset management |
| 17 | My risk management is for projects, so use GAO. |
| 18 | TSA's Risk-Based security framework |

## Q14. What framework or standard has your organization adopted or considered to implement ERM? (Check all that apply.)

| Answer Choices | Responses | |
|---|---|---|
| COSO ERM (The Committee of Sponsoring Organizations of the Treadway Commission) | **22.33%** | 23 |
| ISO 31000 Risk Management Standard | **34.95%** | 36 |
| GAO Risk Management Framework | **15.53%** | 16 |
| All of the above | **11.65%** | 12 |
| None of the above | **31.07%** | 32 |

**Total Respondents: 103**

| # | Other (please specify) |
|---|---|
| 1 | US Department of Health and Human Services Program Integrity initiative |
| 2 | Hybrid framework of GAO, COSO, and ISO |
| 3 | MIC Program—required program |
| 4 | FMFIA |
| 5 | We don't officially have an ERM policy, but our current approach is a blend of the COSO and GAO frameworks (risk management and internal controls). |
| 6 | Not sure, implementation is still in the planning phase |
| 7 | Not sure. ERM is not formally implemented in our organization. |
| 8 | We are developing a tailored program using best practices from COSO, GAO, and ISO. |
| 9 | ISACA Risk Management Framework |
| 10 | This bureau does not yet have a formal ERM. |
| 11 | OMB A-123 |
| 12 | Unknown |
| 13 | Public Sector Risk Management Framework |
| 14 | I have proposed ISO 31000—organization is a bit deaf to this. |
| 15 | ONR 49001 |
| 16 | I am a consultant; oil and gas are primary clients. |
| 17 | RBS—Risk Based Security |
| 18 | It's a combination of the above and internal controls. |
| 19 | ISO is the one Risk Management is recommending. |
| 20 | Internal process with similarities to ISO 31000 |

## Q15. What is the scope of the ERM effort within your organization?

| Answer Choices | Responses | |
|---|---|---|
| ERM effort spans across a single program, project, or administrative area | **8.74%** | 9 |
| ERM effort spans across multiple programs and/or projects | **18.45%** | 19 |
| ERM effort cuts across the entire organization | **56.31%** | 58 |
| Has not been defined yet | **20.39%** | 21 |

**Total Respondents: 103**

| # | Other (please specify) |
|---|---|
| 1 | Note: Implementation is in the very early stages, but the program is designed to be organization-wide. |
| 2 | We are currently scoping our effort. |
| 3 | Note that the adopted RMgt policy scope is organization-wide; ERM implementation not yet embraced/overtly supported. |
| 4 | Two versions of ERM—Business Systems (fully implemented); ERM for operational decisions and risk exposure at ministerial level has not been formally implemented. |
| 5 | Most of my clients do not have a broad understanding of ERM. |

## Q16. What components are in place at your organization to aid in ERM implementation? (Check all that apply.)

| Answer Choices | Responses | |
|---|---|---|
| Risk Management Policy | **72.82%** | 75 |
| Change Management Plan | **17.48%** | 18 |
| Communications Plan | **37.86%** | 39 |
| ERM Strategic Plan | **36.89%** | 38 |
| Training and Education Plan | **45.63%** | 47 |
| Identified Governance Structure | **49.51%** | 51 |
| Written Endorsements from Senior Management | **41.75%** | 43 |
| Interagency Collaborative Workgroups | **25.24%** | 26 |
| IT and Database Systems; Dashboards | **31.07%** | 32 |

**Total Respondents: 103**

| # | Other (please specify) |
|---|---|
| 1 | ERM Program Office |
| 2 | Annual MIC Plan and Risk Assessments |
| 3 | These are the components within our specific organization. The parent organization has more of these components in place. |
| 4 | Enterprise Risk Management Committee |
| 5 | None of the above |
| 6 | In the beginning of considerations for ERM |
| 7 | IT Recovery Plan |
| 8 | Not sure, implementation is still in the planning phase |
| 9 | Link between strategic planning and strategic risks |
| 10 | Internal Control guidance following FMFIA. |
| 11 | A contract to help me create the framework. |
| 12 | Very early stages of ERM—juncture of GRC not fully comprehended; governance and internal audit split from RMgt, and all three managed from different areas—not integrated |
| 13 | Internal controls program |
| 14 | While they exist, each of these elements is still very basic at this time. |
| 15 | Risk Diagnostic, Risk Taxonomy, Significant Issues Dashboard, Potential Issues/Risks Master List, Socialization of potential risks/issues at the Management and Senior/Executive Level |
| 16 | Nothing formal yet |
| 17 | Program plan for implementation under development |

## Q17. What is the driving force behind ERM implementation at your organization?

| # | Responses |
|---|-----------|
| 1 | Compliance requirements |
| 2 | Executive management and Board of Trustees support |
| 3 | Changing economic scenario, especially long-drawn recession and slow growth of economy, rising youth unemployment |
| 4 | We deal with risk only when we must make policy decisions. Also when selecting options for weapons/systems/materiel procurement. As yet we do not have an enterprise-level outlook with a dedicated office. |
| 5 | Regulations |
| 6 | Leadership |
| 7 | My personal view [is] that focusing on internal control is too limiting. |
| 8 | Executive and Senior leadership and desired bureau and Department program efficiencies and priorities. |
| 9 | Higher HQ driving compliance |
| 10 | The Department is requiring all Bureaus under its domain to implement ERM. |
| 11 | Compliance with laws, rules, and regulations |
| 12 | Best practice |
| 13 | Senior leadership |
| 14 | Legislative oversight recommendation |
| 15 | To be in compliance with the Managers' internal control program, which is inspected by IG every three years. |
| 16 | Multiple-use agency and competing interests (internal vs. external) |
| 17 | It is good business management, as it enables our organization to meet its objectives and make better decisions. |
| 18 | Performance Excellence Program—GPRAMA |
| 19 | Business Continuity Planning is the current issue with visibility. Driven mostly by BoD and audit. |
| 20 | None |
| 21 | Achieve our objectives in an environment of fiscal constraint . . . risk-based decision making |
| 22 | N/A |

(continued)

## Q17. What is the driving force behind ERM implementation at your organization? (*Continued*)

| # | Responses |
|---|---|
| 23 | Good risk management |
| 24 | Compliance with Federal policy and regulations |
| 25 | The challenge of achieving the organization's strategic objectives in the face of substantial uncertainties. |
| 26 | Visible support by our CEO/Chancellor (senior leader) and our governance body (Board of Trustees) via the Board Audit Committee. Tone at the top! |
| 27 | Bond ratings |
| 28 | There are two sources—one is to address financial risks to government posed by offshore oil and gas operators and the other is to become more resilient in light of big policy and budget changes. |
| 29 | Alignment with practices at other governments. |
| 30 | Senior management |
| 31 | Answering on behalf of my public sector clients, the driving force is from an individual leader or a small team of leaders who see the value in a broader approach to managing risk. |
| 32 | Better decision making across the portfolio |
| 33 | Management's perspective |
| 34 | Auditability |
| 35 | The compliance of risk quality findings, coming from risk inspections. |
| 36 | High-profile issues that have led to much criticism of the agency from the Congress and the public |
| 37 | • Improve strategic decision making. • Identify risks and proactively manage them. • Increase organizational efficiency and effectiveness. • Promote accountability and integrity of the organization's work. • Use a common approach to evaluate operational and management risks. |
| 38 | Significant "negative" impact occurred within the business, which drove the implementation of ERM. In turn, executive leadership fully supported the implementation. |

| 40 | A data breach was the catalyst to establish an Office of Enterprise Risk Management—although it was already being considered. |
| 41 | cfg |
| 42 | Compliance and reporting |
| 43 | Business strategy |
| 44 | The University Senate |
| 45 | Grassroots knowledge and background in ERM from private sector prior work experience |
| 46 | Senior leadership |
| 47 | Having executive support to implement ERM |
| 48 | Senior leadership |
| 49 | We recently implemented an Internal Controls program over financial operations and want to expand to consider operations risks. |
| 50 | The desire to more accurately predict and plan for future risk issues. |
| 51 | I see it in individual program areas with leaders who are especially risk aware. |
| 52 | Leadership's desire to have a program. |
| 53 | Law enforcement organization with border enforcement responsibilities. |
| 54 | Very little is driving ERM. It just happens (somewhat) during the strategic planning and budget processes. |
| 55 | Compliance |
| 56 | Our Executive Director has embraced ERM and is championing it for the entire Department. |
| 57 | Contractual requirement for Risk Analysis and Management System |
| 58 | Central Government Agencies are pushing for it; value is being seen through our risk management support on major projects and providing an independent perspective. |
| 59 | Previous GAO audit. |
| 60 | Not fully supported because of lack of resourcing. |
| 61 | Decision making and risk intelligence |
| 62 | Financial considerations |

*(continued)*

## Q17. What is the driving force behind ERM implementation at your organization? *(Continued)*

| # | Responses |
|---|-----------|
| 63 | The awareness that the biggest risks we have other than hurricanes are not from pure risks, but from enterprise risks—funding, economic downturns, aging workforce and population, aging infrastructure, OPEB liabilities, etc. |
| 64 | There is none. |
| 65 | There isn't. |
| 66 | We are a risk management organization, so it would be silly if we didn't practice what we preach. |
| 67 | Reporting framework through Executive Risk Management Forum |
| 68 | Me. Then we got a new Director that has religion on ERM. |
| 69 | Better decision making in a more integrated manner; fragmentation currently exists. |
| 70 | Finance |
| 71 | Basic public administration best practices |
| 72 | Reactionary work; response to VAGO (Vic Auditor General's Office) Reports; Audit Committee priorities—not necessarily informed or driven by identified corporate risks/corporate risk register/risk management reporting. |
| 73 | To achieve organizational goals and minimize negative impacts. |
| 74 | Risk identification and impact analysis |
| 75 | N/A |
| 76 | Governance |
| 77 | CRO (me) |
| 78 | Legislation |
| 79 | Experience with disaster planning—at least one major financial impact affecting our organization annually for the past decade |
| 80 | Board need for information |
| 81 | Uncovering risks and opportunities in new projects, programs, etc. |
| 82 | ERM was original adopted by the University Board of Regents as part of the Audit/Controller program using the COSO framework. Now it is seen as a way to improve financial condition by reducing total cost of risk. |

| 83 | ?? |
| 84 | Using ERM helps us know where to focus/adjust our focus given resource constraints. |
| 85 | Some programs within the organization are implementing an ERM framework, and a few have practiced ERM for several years. The challenge is getting the entire organization on board. |
| 86 | External audit and other agency oversight. |
| 87 | Initial driver was examiner criticisms. |
| 88 | Best practices to implement ERM for effective and efficient risk management, especially with a discipline approach to monitoring risks. Getting ahead of the wave and setting an example for our member organizations. |
| 89 | I mainly look at projects. Finish date and CAPEX are the main concerns. |
| 90 | Congress and stakeholder groups |
| 91 | Streamline business processes and reduce the impact of change |
| 92 | Internal controls and having a clean audit |
| 93 | Mandate |
| 94 | Some chatter at working groups |
| 95 | Tone at the top. Getting a handle on the "what" that could happen. |
| 96 | Initially was compliance with recommendations from different types of audits and mandate, but now is the need to proactively identify threats and opportunities for better decision making. |
| 97 | It was being on GAO's High Risk List. |
| 98 | There is no driving force |
| 99 | Agency policy |
| 100 | Aversion to suffering liabilities for major strategic risks |
| 101 | CEO |
| 102 | IT Project missed POAM elements |
| 103 | Leadership |

## Q18. What have been some of your greatest challenges/obstacles in implementing ERM?

| # | Responses |
|---|-----------|
| 1 | Getting program and office-level buy-in. |
| 2 | Different business functions still lean toward working in silos in some areas (e.g., investments vs. benefits). |
| 3 | Organizational Leader's commitment to the approach; culture of firefighting and inaction |
| 4 | Senior managers want to look at a PowerPoint presentation and make a quick decision. They do not want to take the time to develop a new outlook and understanding of risks or other wicked problems. |
| 5 | Culture; Talent; Resources |
| 6 | Knowledge and tools |
| 7 | Getting program managers to realize that business as usual is a condition, not a virtue |
| 8 | Communicating and clearly demonstrating the value proposition for ERM. |
| 9 | Responsibility without corresponding authority |
| 10 | Culture change. |
| 11 | Buy-in and full support from upper leadership |
| 12 | Showing the value of ERM |
| 13 | Collaboration with others |
| 14 | Management direction has not been followed with implementation; resources scarce, knowledge of implementation lacking. |
| 15 | Accountability of the program and engagement by Senior Management. |
| 16 | Balancing Administration's priorities and agency-level priorities and Congressional interests |
| 17 | Lack of understanding about ERM—what it is and what are its benefits. |
| 18 | Lack of involvement from top leadership; lack of clear governance structure; low budget, no money for automated Risk Management Information System; inadequate communication and training; insufficient staffing; lack of a clear vision/plan |
| 19 | Resources |
| 20 | None |
| 21 | Language (some terms in ERM are not the language of business) and culture (some areas of our organization are stressed, overloaded because of cutbacks and resistant to "one more new thing or change") |

| 22 | Organization has not accepted the practice of ERM. |
| 23 | Management buy-in |
| 24 | Obtaining buy-in from customers that don't find ERM important to the organization |
| 25 | The necessary tone at the top exhibited by the most senior agency leader and management's tolerance for disciplined risk management practices. |
| 26 | Ensuring risk officer and risk considerations are a part of all strategic discussions and actions. |
| 27 | Time and resources |
| 28 | The primary challenge is a lack of understanding by BOEM leadership and management about the purpose of and possibilities associated with ERM. Another is a concern about the cost, and a third about capacity (do we have the skills to carry it out, do we need to contract out some aspect of it). |
| 29 | Lack of knowledge and motivation of senior executive. |
| 30 | Size of organization, risk-averse culture of organization |
| 31 | Again, on behalf of my public sector clients, the greatest challenges include senior management or board misunderstanding or lack of support, the lack of authority or stature of the risk manager, competition for resources, and time and the "ease" of staying with the status quo. |
| 32 | Understanding the purpose of ERM and how it can help with other RM efforts |
| 33 | Educating Management |
| 34 | None |
| 35 | The lack of standardization. We are a corporation that comes from a merger of 14 different companies, some public, some formerly private. |
| 36 | Prior to the events in #17, management did not see a need for an explicit ERM approach. ERM was viewed as an extra layer that was already being addressed indirectly through existing processes. |
| 37 | Stakeholder buy-in that ERM is not a paper exercise. Measuring the value-add of an ERM. |
| 38 | Getting employees to understand that ERM is dynamic and not static. |
| 39 | Not yet implemented |
| 40 | Too many conflicting initiatives across the Agency and too rapid growth in staffing within Agency |
| 41 | [unintelligible] |
| 42 | Buy-in from management |
| 43 | Senior management buy-in |

*(continued)*

261

## Q18. What have been some of your greatest challenges/obstacles in implementing ERM? (*Continued*)

| # | Responses |
|---|---|
| 44 | Overcoming the fear that risk management was all about not doing something because it was a risk rather than managing the risk so as to achieve an objective |
| 45 | Changeover of leadership driven by political cycle |
| 46 | Ensuring adequate participation in our deep dives |
| 47 | The fear that the IG will discipline executives who have self-identified high risk issues within their divisions |
| 48 | Difficulty in aligning to Strategic Plan. |
| 49 | Buy-in from program offices to fully understand value-add to their programs |
| 50 | Being able to accurately predict future risk issues. |
| 51 | Budget and funding shortfalls are taking a toll. People are focused on cutting costs and budgets, and it's difficult to fund staffing and programs to include formal ERM. |
| 52 | Lack of guidance or policy from OMB. |
| 53 | Bringing the team up to speed on the standards. |
| 54 | Senior leaders' lack of understanding and awareness of the benefits of ERM. |
| 55 | Access to top management |
| 56 | Measuring the benefits of mitigation measures. |
| 57 | Implementation across multiple programs |
| 58 | Hard to demonstrate value added and measure performance. How do you know if the negative event would have occurred had you not thought about it and put controls into place? |
| 59 | Getting people to embrace and actually tie decisions to risk-relating findings |
| 60 | —Executive ownership/support. —Lack of resources (personnel and technology). —Change management, communications, training. |
| 61 | Time and availability of staff to collaborate |
| 62 | Safety has not been integrated within the ERM efforts |
| 63 | Education on what Traditional Risk Management is. In the past, the RM department was a claims department or safety department for most of our County Departments. We are first working on having all colleagues embrace "we are all risk managers" from a pure risk basis. Without a fundamental understanding of Risk Management and the Risk Management process and techniques, there is a big obstacle in introducing the concept of Enterprise Risk Management. |

64 Getting support to even start an ERM program.

65 ERM is seen as a "buzz word" and a policy that is not much different from the existing city risk management policy.

66 Unknown

67 Lack of full commitment that might be caused by lack of buy-in

68 It's a big job for one person, and opposition of prior leadership.

69 Lack of serious commitment from senior management; the will is just not there in my opinion.

70 Communication

71 Getting people to quit thinking about it as ERM and accepting it is what distinguishes public administration from private business

72 CEO understanding and endorsement. Integration and/or close collaboration between Audit Committee, Governance, Internal Audit/Compliance, and Risk functions. One technical expert (me), and little education/ development of senior managers with regard to risk management approach (and necessity) in good/effective governance and service/outcome delivery.

73 Funding and long-term sustainability of RM processes.

74 —Time needed with staff—Bottom-up implementation strategy

75 A common Risk perception

76 Support from top management

77 Workload for effective implementation

78 No buy-in from management

79 1. Widely distributed workforce, 2. Development of primary responsibilities of government (Completed 2010)

80 A framework that is a good fit for health care

81 Decentralized environment

82 ERM program resides in Risk Management, and challenge is that Audit/Compliance office believes program should be in their department.

83 ??

84 Language: talking about managing risk as an organization (rather than "ERM"); the word "risk" can be loaded with imputed meanings, so we are careful to talk more of uncertainty in some cases than "risk" depending on the audience

85 Communicating the importance of ERM and getting management buy-in.

(continued)

## Q18. What have been some of your greatest challenges/obstacles in implementing ERM? (*Continued*)

| # | Responses |
|---|---|
| 86 | Balancing the need for risk details vs. the need for overall context and big-picture concerns; balancing the need for timely information vs. being sufficiently thorough; balancing the need for proactive risk assessments vs. competing with day-to-day operations. |
| 87 | I would have to say it is failure to: define risk appetite, make management accountable for risk ownership, lack of appropriate software tools, no ERM strategic plan in place, inexperienced ERM management. |
| 88 | Silos, unaware population, "what's in it for me?" "we already manage risks" |
| 89 | Corporate culture [does] not appreciate, maybe oppose risk analysis results so sometimes reject risk management even on specific projects |
| 90 | Agency-wide staff training. Being pushed hard to rollout. |
| 91 | Resources |
| 92 | Continuity of management direction |
| 93 | Change management; ERM managers don't have the right skill-set experience. |
| 94 | No executive support. |
| 95 | Getting buy-in from senior leadership. Explain what risk management is and is not, and developing evidence of risk management successes. |
| 96 | The people, because risk management is not in their corporate DNA. |
| 97 | Ensuring all employees/stakeholders no matter their position understand the importance of risk management, what it means, and how to identify potential issues/risks in performing daily activities. Also, employing a comprehensive approach across the organization is a challenge, as well as leadership taking ownership and being held accountable. |
| 98 | Other major enterprise-wide system changes have been happening over the last several years and there was no appetite to add another component. |
| 99 | Management commitment |
| 100 | Lack of shared understanding of risk, and ERM |
| 101 | Lack of clarity on who has what and why would impact rest of organization if/when not considered. Second, training the next guy. |
| 102 | Risk assessment; risk management plan; senior management caring about risk |
| 103 | Culture |

## Q19. What are or have been some of the greatest opportunities/benefits associated with implementing ERM?

| # | Responses |
|---|-----------|
| 1 | Showcasing effective risk mitigation strategies and accomplishments. |
| 2 | Risk is becoming everyday language, and our risk culture is being formed. |
| 3 | Being able to focus on high risk items, manage resources, and prepare in advance for some of the worst scenarios. |
| 4 | Co-creator of a 55-page instruction for helping SMEs throughout my agency select functions that should remain in-house vs. outsourcing where risk management was one of the significant factors. |
| 5 | Fewer surprises |
| 6 | Incorporating organizational assessment |
| 7 | Efficiency and accountability |
| 8 | Setting tone for risk management at the top; increasing awareness of risk management at all levels of the organization; increasing partnerships and collaborations for ERM success; and other benefits. |
| 9 | Recognizing the huge difference between systemic risk and risks faced due to "intelligent actors"/insider threats. |
| 10 | Transparency. |
| 11 | Getting ahead of issue and verifying our reliability in program areas. |
| 12 | Recognizing enterprise risk |
| 13 | Cross-agency communications |
| 14 | Potential to correct massive mischarging practices could lead to budgetary alignment and efficient use of existing resources. |
| 15 | Making staff/employees aware of reporting risks and to fix the areas before it becomes a major risk or identified by an outside source. |
| 16 | Obtaining commitment and accountability |
| 17 | ERM necessitates greater transparency across siloed organizations that previously did not communicate well or at all! |
| 18 | Improved risk awareness in program/project management |

(continued)

## Q19. What are or have been some of the greatest opportunities/ benefits associated with implementing ERM? *(Continued)*

| # | Responses |
|---|-----------|
| 19 | Still is being developed, but C-level execs seemed to be getting on-board more. Benefits will likely materialize in the form of reduced operating costs at some point. |
| 20 | None |
| 21 | ERM activity brings levels and functions together to create a place for discussion, knowledge sharing, and capture |
| 22 | N/A |
| 23 | ID Risk |
| 24 | Being able to bring a program into compliance with federal policy, rules, and regulations |
| 25 | Successfully having integrated effective risk management into capital investment decision making and policy development and administration. |
| 26 | Improved communication between departments on matters of risk and the potential second- and third-order effects outside of the immediate organizational proximity. |
| 27 | The "aha" factor once people get it |
| 28 | I think we have a great opportunity now that the Department of the Interior is about to release the new multi-year Strategic Plan, to establish our ERM framework, and I think it can also determine our policy priorities and the scope of any proposed regulations. |
| 29 | Confidence in financial statements. |
| 30 | Increased information sharing, better use of resources |
| 31 | More people understanding and managing organizational risk. Preparedness, resiliency. |
| 32 | Ability to articulate the impacts of decisions from a strategic perspective and facilitate cross-organizational communication |
| 33 | Less uncertainty, more peace of mind, more effective response to opportunities. |
| 34 | Work-in-progress |
| 35 | Everything has to be implemented, standardized, written, established. |
| 36 | Transparency, shared accountability, more thoughtful resource allocation |
| 37 | Increased risk awareness and breaking down the silos (creating the dialog) |
| 38 | Making the agency more effective and efficient in being good stewards of the taxpayer's money and reducing the waste within the organization. |
| 39 | N/A |

40  Strong support from the top. Improved relationship with IT staff (common goals). More recognition of risk throughout Agency.

41  [unintelligible]

42  Identifying and addressing long-standing risk areas

43  Increased opportunity; decreased loss.

44  The ability to gain government and private funding for significant research activities by ensuring the business case set out what the risks were and how they were going to be managed.

45  Alignment of strategy, risk, budget execution process to optimize resources to effectively manage priority risks

46  Opening up discussion about issues that impact all of the organization

47  The opportunities to reduce the enterprise's risk exposure to potential risks that would damage the reputation of the agency

48  Integrating the concept of "What keeps you up at night" to the highest levels of the organization.

49  Deeper understanding of our programs and internally developed risk management practices already in place

50  Having a voice to raise awareness of risk issues to senior leaders.

51  In a previous agency, the senior leadership had much more clarity of risk across the enterprise. They had a much clearer perspective of shared risk, risk interrelationships and interdependencies.

52  Leadership thoughtfully answers the question . . . What risks keep you up at night?

53  Knowledge is power, and familiarity with the standard helps to improve the operation.

54  Lots of opportunities exist within my organization to embrace ERM. Many challenges related to IT systems and budget constraints.

55  Establishing a common risk language

56  Elimination of silos and collaboration to identify and mitigate threats and embrace opportunities.

57  Integration of risk analysis across programs and communication structure for stakeholders

58  ERM unit has the single most horizontal view of the Agency and is relied on to present that perspective. We also provide an independent sober second look on things.

59  Leadership's willingness to increase rigor in risk analysis methods

60  —Awareness of COSO framework. —Objective setting. —Ensuring risks are properly mitigated. —Greater focus on program management (monitoring across the enterprise).

61  Seen as a benefit and has brought people together to talk about risk

62  Unknown

(continued)

## Q19. What are or have been some of the greatest opportunities/benefits associated with implementing ERM? (Continued)

| # | Responses |
|---|-----------|
| 63 | Holistic approach to ALL risk |
| 64 | N/A |
| 65 | ERM would mean that every employee at every level of the organization considers the frequency and severity of claims, accidents, and injuries and implements measures to mitigate predictable losses. |
| 66 | Unknown |
| 67 | Performance Monitoring tool that ensures that we do not implement for the sake of compliance, rather tie ERM to performance of an institution |
| 68 | The ability to get some senior leaders on board and to see the light. |
| 69 | Improve organizational decision making; accurately assess organization's needs anticipating potential risks and treatment efforts |
| 70 | Integration and risk reduction at a lower cost |
| 71 | None |
| 72 | Cross-team collaboration; identifying obstacles to achieving objectives; assurance/due diligence; planning for undesirable outcomes. |
| 73 | Achieving organizational objectives. |
| 74 | Showing interdependence of risks across the organization |
| 75 | Earthquake event |
| 76 | Process knowledge to enable improvements |
| 77 | Fulfilling massive compliance requirements |
| 78 | None |
| 79 | Clearly established priorities for service delivery. Conversion of paper records to electronics completed (5 years)—across functional areas. |
| 80 | Building awareness |
| 81 | Employees conducting risk assessments prior to implementing new programs, projects, etc. |
| 82 | Over the last seven years, total cost of risk has been reduced by over $700. Senior leadership understands that ERM is about efficiency and optimizing risk and we still have plenty of opportunity to improve. |
| 83 | ?? |

84  Helping colleagues understand how what they are doing fits in to ERM ("aha" moments) and seeing themselves and their challenges and strengths in managing risk

85  Starting with baby steps through the agency's internal control program.

86  ERM has created a "platform" for dialogue among the various executive leaders and functional directors.

87  Will eventually have a single framework or view of organizational risk. Assist management with understanding risks and the controls necessary to mitigate risk prior to the audit department or regulators performing their audits and examinations respectively. Audit may not have opportunity to help management as quickly as ERM would.

88  Implementing accountability, developing a terminology that we all use, discussing risk appetites as they relate to behavior, and aligning risk management with strategic planning.

89  When project management embraces the risk analysis results and goes on to develop good quality risk mitigations that are then implemented

90  Still assessing.

91  Better control and internal/external factors that can impact business processes and the use of resources.

92  Increased awareness of need for effective mitigation of activities funded outside of the Department.

93  Assist agency in managing risks during budget constraints

94  Prioritization of action plans.

95  People are talking about risk across different areas and are interested in proactively resolving problems

96  More accurate planning. Better decision making and results. Becoming risk aware and not averse.

97  Creating a monthly venue where potential risks/issues are discussed and vetted at the executive leadership level is a benefit.

98  *Will be ... once there is buy-in; the benefits that will follow will include greater understanding and ownership of risk and consequently, more accountability.

99  Visibility of risks, improved allocation of resources

100  Opportunity to implement true strategic management

101  Better management decisions, especially with regard to costs

102  Not a focus of management

103  Loss Control and Process Continuity

## Q20. Conceptual Skills: This is the strategic layer that requires the ability to understand all the organization's activities, how the pieces fit together, and how the organization can achieve its strategic goals.

| | Yes | No | Would Recommend | Total Respondents |
|---|---|---|---|---|
| (A) Planning: Determine appropriate goals for an enterprise; goal oriented; sees the big picture; maintains a global perspective. | 79.07%<br>68 | 13.95%<br>12 | 61.63%<br>53 | 86 |
| (B) Organizing: Creates an ERM department; staffing; build relationships with other stakeholders; create a risk management culture; leverage diversity. | 65.88%<br>56 | 17.65%<br>15 | 67.06%<br>57 | 85 |
| (C) Decision Making: Recognize and analyze problems and make difficult decisions under uncertain conditions in dynamic environments; use benchmarking to compare appropriate data; show good judgment | 78.57%<br>66 | 13.10%<br>11 | 58.33%<br>49 | 84 |
| (D) Management Process: Know the basic five-step management process of creating a program, analyzing opportunities, identifying solutions, the decision process, and system administration. | 82.35%<br>70 | 12.94%<br>11 | 54.12%<br>46 | 85 |
| (E) Ethical Judgment: Know ethical theories; demonstrate a high level of ethical behavior, as evidenced by compliance with the fiduciary duties of care (competency and due diligence), disclosure (transparency), and loyalty. | 83.53%<br>71 | 7.06%<br>6 | 56.47%<br>48 | 85 |
| (F) Organizational Architect: Able to build business relationships, strategic alliances, and partnerships as well as being able to secure mutual benefit from such arrangements. | 76.47%<br>65 | 14.12%<br>12 | 58.82%<br>50 | 85 |
| (G) Strategic Thinking: Employ a sense of vision to create new innovative concepts, products, and solutions. | 87.06%<br>74 | 4.71%<br>4 | 55.29%<br>47 | 85 |

**Q21. Technical Skills:** This is the operational layer, where many of the traditional duties and specialized skills of risk managers come into play. Some skills may not be applicable, and responses depend on individual experience and the work environment.

| | Yes | No | Would Recommend | Total Respondents |
|---|---|---|---|---|
| (A) Risk Management Process: Understand the risk management model; adapt a model to the organization's needs; understand how risk creates value. Know the risk management process of creating a risk program, analyzing risks, identifying solutions, using a decision process, and system administration. | 91.86% 79 | 4.65% 4 | 53.49% 46 | 86 |
| (B) Risk Analysis: Link risk initiatives into critical business drivers; perform risk identification, measurement, and analysis applying statistical concepts; create valid risk forecasts; perform risk mapping and risk profiling; determine the cost of risk. | 83.53% 71 | 8.24% 7 | 57.65% 49 | 85 |
| (C) Risk Control: The ability to apply risk control theories to create prevention, reduction, enablement, and enhancement tactics; can create emergency response and business continuity plans. | 80% 68 | 9.41% 8 | 56.47% 48 | 85 |
| (D) Risk Financing: Thoroughly understand risk retention plans and risk financing transfers, including insurance, alternative risk financing, and hybrid plans; prepare allocation to cost centers. | 45.24% 38 | 40.48% 34 | 47.62% 40 | 84 |

*(continued)*

271

**Q21. Technical Skills: This is the operational layer, where many of the traditional duties and specialized skills of risk managers come into play. Some skills may not be applicable, and responses depend on individual experience and the work environment. (*Continued*)**

| | Yes | No | Would Recommend | Total Respondents |
|---|---|---|---|---|
| (E) Enterprise Risk Management (ERM): Understand the techniques and processes for optimizing risk-taking decisions within an organization. | 77.38%<br>65 | 15.48%<br>13 | 59.52%<br>50 | 84 |
| (F) Project Management: Understand how to successfully design and implement projects; can prepare risk management reports. | 72.94%<br>62 | 16.47%<br>14 | 52.94%<br>45 | 85 |
| (G) Vendor Relations: Establish and maintain agent/broker relationships; develop other vendor relationships. | 50%<br>42 | 32.14%<br>27 | 48.81%<br>41 | 84 |
| (H) Risk Management Information Systems (RMIS): Implement and operate comprehensive RMIS systems or databases; information repositories. | 54.12%<br>46 | 32.94%<br>28 | 57.65%<br>49 | 85 |

## Q22. Core Competency Skills: These skills are sometimes considered "soft" interpersonal or personal skills, but they are also in fact the basic business management skills.

| | Yes | No | Would Recommend | Total Respondents |
|---|---|---|---|---|
| INTERPERSONAL | 90.20% 46 | 3.92% 2 | 52.94% 27 | 51 |
| (A) Leadership: Ability to influence others' behavior toward the enterprise's goals; having a high emotional intelligence; can build trust while maintaining confidentiality. | 88.89% 72 | 4.94% 4 | 58.02% 47 | 81 |
| (B) Motivator: Ability to inspire others to pursue the enterprise's objectives. | 88.10% 74 | 7.14% 6 | 54.76% 46 | 84 |
| (C) Negotiations: Ability to listen and to manage conflicts and achieve compromise while meeting meaningful goals and respecting other parties' perspectives. | 88.10% 74 | 8.33% 7 | 52.38% 44 | 84 |
| (D) Consensus Builder: Ability to merge many ideas into a cohesive plan. | 89.29% 75 | 5.95% 5 | 54.76% 46 | 84 |
| (E) Team Builder: Ability to unify workers to achieve a common goal. | 85.54% 71 | 4.82% 4 | 57.83% 48 | 83 |
| PERSONAL | 84.44% 38 | 0% 0 | 53.33% 24 | 45 |
| (A) Motivated: Inspired to succeed and the ability to help others achieve their goals as well as being driven to deliver on goals. | 94.05% 79 | 3.57% 3 | 46.43% 39 | 84 |
| (B) Innovative: Ability to be creative and inquisitive; seek new solutions to challenges; and able to be adaptable, flexible, and open to change. | 90.36% 75 | 2.41% 2 | 56.63% 47 | 83 |
| (C) Experienced: Possesses adequate practical experience in appropriate disciplines. | 81.48% 66 | 6.17% 5 | 55.56% 45 | 81 |

(continued)

## Q22. Core Competency Skills: These skills are sometimes considered "soft" interpersonal, or personal skills, but they are also in fact the basic business management skills. (Continued)

| | Yes | No | Would Recommend | Total Respondents |
|---|---|---|---|---|
| (D) Communication: Ability to listen and understand others' points of view and to articulate tactfully and respectfully one's own perspective orally, in writing, and in presentations. | 95.18%<br>79 | 1.20%<br>1 | 51.81%<br>43 | 83 |
| (E) Consultative: Ability to advise the organization's various divisions on how they can manage their particular risks. | 87.95%<br>73 | 6.02%<br>5 | 49.40%<br>41 | 83 |
| BUSINESS SKILLS | 88.10%<br>37 | 2.38%<br>1 | 47.62%<br>20 | 42 |
| (A) Accounting: Understand the basic accounting concepts of transaction recognition, matching, and conservatism, and the ability to prepare financial reports. | 46.34%<br>38 | 43.90%<br>36 | 46.34%<br>38 | 82 |
| (B) Economics: Understand micro- and macro-economics, demand and supply, equilibriums, income, employment, and fiscal policies, money and banking, and resource allocation. | 42.50%<br>34 | 43.75%<br>35 | 42.50%<br>34 | 80 |
| (C) Budget/Finance: Know the government budget process; know capital structuring, capital budgeting, working capital management, analyzing financial statements, ratio analysis, the time value of money, portfolio theory, capital market transfers, asset/liability matching, and financial engineering. | 62.65%<br>52 | 30.12%<br>25 | 45.78%<br>38 | 83 |
| (D) Legal: Understand the legal components of the risk management industry. | 67.07%<br>55 | 20.73%<br>17 | 52.44%<br>43 | 82 |
| (E) Compliance: Know the fiduciary duties to identify, disclose, and manage an organization's risks. | 78.57%<br>66 | 15.48%<br>13 | 48.81%<br>41 | 84 |
| (F) Human Resource: Understand labor demand and supply, government employment processes, diversity management, training and development, and compensation and benefits. | 62.50%<br>50 | 25%<br>20 | 48.75%<br>39 | 80 |
| (G) Management: Plan, organize, lead, control, and allocate resources. | 81.71%<br>67 | 12.20%<br>10 | 47.56%<br>39 | 82 |

| Competency | % | n | % | n | % | n | Total |
|---|---|---|---|---|---|---|---|
| (H) Information Technology: Understand the essential components and requirements so as to assist in designing a Risk Management Information System (RMIS); networking. | 57.32% | 47 | 30.49% | 25 | 51.22% | 42 | 82 |
| (I) Strategic Planning: Understand/know SWOT (Strengths, Weaknesses, Opportunities, Threats) analysis; keep up with key government trends and developments; collaborate with key external agencies; able to adopt industry practices into governmental operations. | 87.80% | 72 | 6.10% | 5 | 57.32% | 47 | 82 |
| (J) Change Management: Implement change; think about how and when the changes should occur; involve the stakeholders in those decisions. Minimize adverse consequences and facilitate acceptance and use of the changed structures and processes. Clearly define what is changing: Determine the precise scope and focus of the changes (including the employees affected). Plan and implement specific steps to ensure change is made: Determine the specific activities to be undertaken as part of change management. Monitor the implementation and effectiveness of the change: Provide for performance monitoring, feedback, evaluation, and mid-course corrections. | 79.27% | 65 | 9.76% | 8 | 60.98% | 50 | 82 |
| (K) Operations: Knowledge of how a business functions, process design, capacity planning and scheduling, inventory management, and quality control. | 81.71% | 67 | 13.41% | 11 | 47.56% | 39 | 82 |
| (L) Statistics: Understand data collection, description, modeling, probability, hypothesis testing, regression, time series analysis, decision analysis, trend analysis, and forecasting. | 61.73% | 50 | 22.22% | 18 | 55.56% | 45 | 81 |
| (M) Security: Securing the physical assets and premises of the enterprise. Ensuring personal security of staff as well as of intellectual property and data management systems. | 57.50% | 46 | 26.25% | 21 | 51.25% | 41 | 80 |
| (N) Safety: Protecting the physical well-being of personnel against work-related accidents, injuries, or other debilitations. | 60.49% | 49 | 24.69% | 20 | 50.62% | 41 | 81 |
| (O) Audit: Review the accuracy of an organization's internal control systems and financial operations. | 64.20% | 52 | 28.40% | 23 | 48.15% | 39 | 81 |

## Q23. Do you have any additional comments about your experience in implementing ERM?

| # | Responses |
|---|---|
| 1 | It largely requires a top-down influence but also involves bottom-up implementation on the ground to be successful. |
| 2 | Many risk decisions involve fundamental changes in outlook at a very basic level, an event referred to as "triple look learning" by Organizational Development (OD) practitioners. When risk mitigation involves basic/strategy changes in outlook and processes, senior managers will often avoid the change required due to the in-depth challenges. Ultimately this leads to a layering of problems that are difficult to identify; i.e., "wicked problems." Once the perception of a problem is wicked, that in turn creates difficulties in identifying the risks. Ultimately, risk management becomes an endless loop with no beginning or end and managers who are gun-shy in addressing risk issues. |
| 3 | It's a long and winding road subject to support that ebbs and flows based on administration (subject to change every 4–8 yrs.), and agency leadership, i.e., Directors with a strong private sector business background are much more likely to support ERM than a Director with exclusive public sector experience. |
| 4 | Unfortunately, my knowledge and certification have not been actively utilized in my organization—I am functionally disconnected from the implementing group, though I identified myself as a resource in this effort. |
| 5 | Add: Strategic decision-making skills. This is a skill set I utilize every day as I determine who to reach out to for input and partnership as I develop our ERM program, as well as how to communicate the value of ERM to decision makers within our organization. This is also an area where I have a lot of growth opportunity as an ERM professional and a manager. |
| 6 | N/A |
| 7 | No |
| 8 | Understanding of the Government Accountability Office Green Book; frameworks established by the Committee of Sponsoring Organizations of the Treadway Commission (COSO), Internal Control Integrated Framework (May 2013) and Enterprise Risk Management Integrated Framework (September 2014); understanding of the Open Compliance and Ethics Group (OCEG) Redbook; and, ISO 31000. |
| 9 | Most organizations devote too little attention to the science behind qualitative risk analysis, and thus many of the risk assessments are of questionable value. |
| 10 | The ability to identify preexisting or parallel risk management activities and processes and translate/graft them into the larger ERM program model for an organization is key and will help build support for ERM from senior leaders/ stakeholders of other initiatives. |
| 11 | I have not yet implemented ERM at my organization, or rather we have not, but I completed training on ISO 31000, will receive a certificate as an internal controls risk analyst soon. I will also present my vision for ERM in my organization to our Deputy Director next week. I don't know if this is the last question, but the questions on the first page forced you to select two answers even when you wanted "other" or none. |
| 12 | ERM demands more leadership skill than technical skill. Some of the business skills listed are "nice to know" but not necessary if you have appropriate subject matter experts involved. |

13. All management decision makers are involved in managing risk. As such, they should receive formal training in ERM frameworks such as ISO 31000, 31004, and 31010.

14. Many of the above need to be understood and practiced by Line Managers, who must be accountable for managing risk in their area of control. The Risk Management Practitioner needs to understand the challenges so as to be able to provide advice and service to the relevant Line Manager.

15. Please consider briefing results of this study at an upcoming AFERM—Association for Federal Enterprise Risk Management meeting, or the Annual Summit.

16. Some of the above skills should be part of the specific program office and/or specialist. ERM should be "baked in" to the business rather than concentrated in the ERM office. The program offices must own their risks.

17. No

18. While a downturn in the economy creates new ERM risks and ERM is needed during these times, it is also a time that the public sector does not have the resources to implement ERM. I am interested in an ERM 101—walk before we run—phase-in approach to ERM. Showing value to various operating departments will be key—purchasing, finance, utilities, law enforcement, facilities, legal, and elected officials.

19. CEO endorsement/involvement is critical. Expectation that a risk lens is used for operational and strategic decision making must become a business expectation and competency for senior managers. Clear accountability, with objective measures should be part of this process.

20. No

21. I have implemented and/or designed ERM for over 60 organizations: the key skill set that is not touched on in this survey is being able to adapt, tailor, and scale every ERM activity to the organization you are working with and its culture. Also, my experience in implementation tells me that demonstrating the value of ERM as a continuous activity and skill strength is essential—links to performance measures can help to demonstrate value in ERM. Lastly, many organizations (public sector among them) are developing "corporate risk profiles" intended to inform the planning and priority setting for the organization: trouble is, that often when the profiles are developed, no one compares what the organization is currently focused on and helps leadership to see the implications of the corporate risk profile in terms of what adjustments need to be made going forward to existing plans and priorities. Better linkage is possible and very helpful with the CRP.

22. No

23. Our approach to ERM is based on the ISO 31000, and therefore we see it as a prevention process to help us to proactively make decisions about risk to reduce it or take over the opportunities that might enhance our work and the mission. Therefore we do not see risk management as an oversight process but more as a business performance process. We do have oversight already in place through ethics, internal/external auditor, information security, and physical security processes and entities.

24. The majority of our management team consists of engineers with only the most rudimentary of management training.

25. Senior Management sponsor required

# ABOUT THE AUTHOR

**Karen Hardy** is an expert risk management professional with extensive experience in the public sector. Dr. Hardy has designed and implemented ERM in multiple government agencies and is often sought after for advice on how to initiate ERM. She has served in the role of deputy director for risk management at a cabinet-level agency and has developed and implemented multiple agency risk management policies.

Dr. Hardy is a cofounder of the Association for Federal Enterprise Risk Management, has served as board vice president, and serves on the U.S. Technical Advisory Group for ISO 31000. She established and chaired the U.S. federal government's first Interagency ERM Council and has served as a senior advisor on risk management for the Office of Management and Budget, Executive Office of the President.

She has published articles in numerous national and international publications, including Canada's *Public Sector Digest*. Dr. Hardy has been a guest lecturer at the Brookings Institution in Washington, D.C., and has been a presenter at many events, including World Risk Day and World Standards Day. She holds a doctor of education degree from Nova Southeastern University in organizational leadership and human resource development.

# INDEX

Page references followed by *fig* indicate an illustrated figure; followed by *t* indicate a table; followed by *e* indicate an exhibit.

primary source for federal managers, 139; private sector use of the, 152; RIMs Risk Maturity Model (RMM) adaptability to, 184; risk assessment component of, 120; strategic plan emphasis of the, 97; three dimensions of, 139

Credibility risk management, 88

Cyber critical infrastructure protection (cyber CIP) profile, 16–17

**D**

Dali, Alex, 143–149

Data breach, 20

Davis, K., 176

Deen, Paula, 22

Deepwater Horizon explosion (2010), 8

Defense Special Weapons Agency, 83

den Dekker, Peter, 3*t*

Department of Agriculture (USDA): Agricultural Marketing Service of the, 17; Animal and Plant Health Inspection Service of the, 17; Food Safety Inspection Service (FSIS), 17; salmonella outbreak public health alert issued by, 25–26

Department of Defense (DoD), 82–84

Department of Energy, 83

Department of Homeland Security (DHS): challenges of applying strategic risk management, 165*e*–166*e*; NFIP management role of the, 14; risk management as defined by, 166*e*; security risk management by, 83, 85

Department of Justice: JPMorgan Chase mortgage case settlement with the, 26; on largest-ever hacking scheme busted, 23

Department of Labor: on "bright outlook" occupations, 2–3; new rule to strengthen mine safety, 19; O-NET Online of, 3

Department of Veterans Affairs (VA), 15

*Determining Performance and Accountability Challenges and High Risks* (GAO), 12

Detroit bankruptcy, 23

Dow Jones, 23

**E**

EF5 tornado, 21

E-Government Act, 95

Electronic Records Archives (ERA), 97

Enterprise Risk Management Control Program (NIH), 90–94

Enterprise risk management (ERM): action plans and tips for federal agencies, 223–226; assessing organization readiness for ERM implementation, 48*t*; building on the evolution of risk management, 36–38; comparing traditional risk management to, 38–42*t*; core competencies of, 209–221; current state in government, 5, 7; definitions and concepts of, 27–28, 161, 227–228; ERM Core Competency Survey (2014) on key components of, 217–218, 220; ERM maturity models, 181–193*t*, 229; expansion in federal space, 1; financial audit requirement of effective, 27; global recognition of, 1; growing demand for, 4; holistic, 5; how organizational culture impacts implementation of, 173–175; internal auditor role in, 194–207; internal control linked to, 44, 54–55; mapping risks to strategic outcomes in, 123–124e; purpose of, 124; RIMS on appropriate behaviors of, 177; risk communication using framework of, 109–110; Standard & Poor's (S&P) analysis of, 168–169, 170–171; state of Washington's 7 Steps to ERM process, 31–32; status in the government, 29–30; strategic risk management component of, 160–164, 165e–166e; understanding the limitations of, 30–31. *See also* Risk management frameworks

ERM action plans: ninety-day, 223–224; sample implementation plans, 224–225; words of wisdom on strategic, 225–226

ERM Core Competency Survey (2014), 195

ERM Core Competency Survey competency skill sets: business skills, 210*fig*, 211, 214*t*, 215, 218–219, 221; conceptual skills, 210*fig*, 214*t*, 215, 218, 220–221; ERM components in place to aid ERM implementation, 212*t*; interpersonal skills, 210*fig*, 211, 214*t*, 215, 218, 221; personal skills, 210*fig*, 211, 214*t*, 215, 218, 221; Risk Manager Core Competency Model on, 210*fig*, 211; skills and ERM training of the respondents, 214*t*–215; state and local government view of, 218–219; summary of skill recommendations by all respondents, 215; technical skills, 210*fig*–211, 214*t*, 215, 218, 220–221

ERM Core Competency Survey for the Public Sector (2014): description of the, 35, 209; federal versus state and local government views of ERM, 216–221; respondents on conceptual, technical, and core competency skills, 210–211.

*See also* Core competencies; Risk Manager Core Competency Model (RIMS)

ERM Core Competency Survey respondents: demographics of, 211, 216, 219; on ERM resources available to the, 212–213, 217, 219; federal versus state and local government views of ERM, 216–221; summary of skill recommendations by all, 215; on their ERM practice, 213–214; top three ERM components in state and local vs. federal government, 211, 212*t*

ERM implementation plans: getting started, 224; operating an ERM program, 225; organizing for ERM, 224

ERM maturity models: Aon Risk Maturity Index (RMI), 184–185, 186*t*; to assess agency's level of ERM maturity, 229; Canada Treasury Board Risk Management Capability Model, 188e–193t; Capability Maturity Model Integration (CMMI), 182; origins and development of, 181–182; RIMS Risk Maturity Model (RMM), 183–184; risk maturity rating by industry, 187*fig*; SEI Capability Maturity Model (CMM), 182–184; State of Washington's Risk Maturity Model (ERMMM), 185–186, 188. *See also* Maturity Model tools

Ernst & Young (EY) survey report, 152

Ethical threats/opportunities, 120e

European hail/floods insurance costs, 25

Evaluation: GAO Internal Control Management and Evaluation Tool for, 68, 70–80, 120, 177; Program Assessment Rating Tool (PART) for, 154; PSC Audit of the Integrated Risk

Health Inspection Service (USDA), 17;
FDA Food Safety Modernization Act
(FSMA) on, 17–18; as high-risk area,
17–18

Food Safety Inspection Service (FSIS), 17

Foster Farms, 25–26

*Framework on the Management of Risk*
(2000) [Canadian government], 195

Freddie Mac crisis (2008), 26, 175

Frigo and Anderson's Strategic Risk
Management Framework, 152

Frigo, Mark L., 152

Fukushima Daiichi nuclear plant
(Japan), 26

**G**

Gallagher, Arthur J., 37

GAO (Government Accountability
Office): criteria for removing high-risk
designation by, 11–13; description
and responsibilities of the, 130–131;
*Determining Performance and
Accountability Challenges and High Risks*
guidance document used by, 12; director
for strategic issues at the, 5; High Risk
List (1990–2013) of, 10*t*–11; NARA audit
by the, 9, 96–98; NIH Risk Management
Program review the, 90; reporting on the
potential of the GPRA Modernization
Act, 157; risk as defined by the, 34*t*; Risk
Management Framework, 120, 121;
*Standards for Internal Control in the
Federal Government* ("Green Book") by
the, 54, 55–67, 129. *See also* Evaluation
Tool (GAO)

GAO Internal Control Management and
Evaluation Tool: control activities
and major factors, 75–77; control

environment standard and major
factors, 70–72; description and
function of, 68; information and
communications and major factors,
77–78; monitoring and major factors,
78–80; risk assessment component
of, 120; risk assessment standard and
major factors, 72–75; *Sample Risk
Culture Survey* drawn from statements
of, 177. *See also* GAO (Government
Accountability Office)

GAO Risk Management Framework:
advantages of using, 131; assessment
component of, 120, 121; comparing to
other frameworks, 128*e*; designing and
implementing ERM using, 131–135;
illustrated diagram of, 131*fig*; increasing
use of the, 228; ISO 31000 standard
similarity to, 137; Matrix for, 132*t*–134*t*;
origins and development of, 129–130;
phases of the, 130; principles of, 135;
risk assessment component of, 120, 121

Ginnie Mae (GNMA), 85–86

Gjerdrum, Dorothy, 136

Global Institute for Risk Management
Standards (G31000), 1, 143, 149

Glossary: key performance terminology,
164*e*–165*e*; risk management
terminology, 110–111

Goldman Sachs, 26

Governance and strategic direction
threats/opportunities, 115*e*–116*e*

Government Auditing Standards, 2003
Revision, 129

*Government Executive* magazine, 1

Government National Mortgage
Association (GNMA) "Ginnie Mae,"
85–86

Inspector General (IG), 68

Institute of Internal Auditors (IIA), 28, 149, 161, 194, 227. *See also* Internal auditors

Institute of Risk Management (IRM), 141

Integrated Risk Management Framework (Canada), 29, 35–36, 49*e*–53*e*, 195

Internal auditors: ERM Core Competency Survey (2014) on, 195; ERM role that should not be taken by, 194–195; how they add value to ERM, 194; Public Safety Canada Audit of Integrated Risk Management case study on, 195, 196–207. *See also* Institute of Internal Auditors (IIA)

Internal control: assessing structures of, 68; definition of, 54; ERM link to organization's, 44, 54–55; GAO's *Standards for Internal Control in the Federal Government* ("Green Book") on, 54, 55–67

Internal control standards summaries: control activities, 69, 75–77; control environment, 68–69, 70–72; information and communications, 69, 77–80; monitoring, 69; risk assessment, 69, 72–75

International Risk Management Standard. *See* ISO 31000 (International Risk Management Standard)

Interpersonal skills: ERM Core Competency Survey (2014) on, 215, 218, 221; Risk Management Training Rubric on, 214*t*; Risk Manager Core Competency Model on, 210*fig*, 211

IRS Business Systems Modernization, 10, 12

ISO 31000 (International Risk Management Standard): advantages for national governments to adopt, 147–148; Alex Dali interview on his expanded view of, 143–149; ANSI adoption of the, 1, 36, 136; comparing to other frameworks, 127*e*–129*e*, 144, 146; definition of risk by the, 34*t*; description of, 135–137; ERM Core Competency Survey for the Public Sector (2014) findings on, 217; future in foreign national government operations, 148–149; illustrated diagram of, 135*fig*; increasing use of the, 228; internal ERM audit use of the, 195; NIH's adherence to the, 91–92, 93; private sector use of the, 152; risk assessment component of, 120; Risk Evaluation and Risk Analysis stages of the Risk Management Framework of the, 54; risk management architecture of, 137; strategic plan emphasis of the, 97; world map of, 145*fig*

ISO Guide 73.2009, Risk Management Vocabulary, 138

ITABHI Corporation, 29

**J**

Japanese Typhoon Wipha disaster, 26

J.C. Penney Co, Inc., 23, 168*e*

Jersey shore boardwalk fire, 25

JetBlue, 23

JPMorgan Chase mortgage case settlement, 26

JWTIntelligence, 87–88

**K**

Kaplan and Mike's communication framework, 106, 109

Molasses spill (Hawaii's Honolulu Harbor), 24–25

Monitoring and evaluation: Canada Treasury Board Risk Management Capability Model on, 192*t*; definition of, 110; Public Safety Canada Audit of Integrated Risk Management findings on PSC's, 206*t*; standard used for, 69, 78–80

Monitoring standard: description of, 69; Evaluation Tool on major factors of, 78–80

Morgan Stanley, 26

Mortgage backed securities (MBS), 85

**N**

NASA (National Aeronautics and Space Administration), 16, 83

NASDAQ, 23

National Archives and Records Administration (NARA): Electronic Records Archives (ERA) acquisition by, 97; GAO audit of the, 9, 96–98; Modern Records Program of the, 100

National Archives and Records Administration (NARA) case study: background information on the, 95–98; best practices for risk management, 100–103; GAO audit of NARA, 96–98; identified risks and best practices, 98–100; performance audit conclusions of the, 103; recommendations for executive action, 104

National Association of Corporate Directors' Blue Ribbon Report on Risk Governance, 167

National Disaster Risk Reduction and Management Council, 26

National Flood Insurance Program (NFIP), 12, 14–15

National Football League (NFL) concussion settlement, 24

National Forum for Risk Management in the Public Sector, 141

National Incident Command's Flow Rate Technical Group, 8

National Institutes of Health, 9

National Institutes of Health (NIH) case study: aligning risk management program designs with GAO's framework, 91–92; background of, 90–91; best practices of the, 94–95; insights for program enhancements, 92–94; ISO 31000 adherence during, 91–92, 93; new ERM Program replacing the Management Control Program, 90–94; NIH risk management goals, 89–90; NIH Risk Management Program, 90

National Performance Review/ National Partnership for Reinventing Government (1993–2000), 154

National Security Agency, 83

National Transportation Safety Board (NTSB), 86–87

New CFO Management Agenda, 46

Newstrom, J. W., 176

New York's Metropolitan Transportation Authority cat bond, 23–24

Ninety-day action plans, 223–224

Nook (Barnes & Noble Inc.), 168*e*

North Carolina State University's Center for Enterprise Risk Management, 35

North Dakota oil spill, 25

NTSB's Most Wanted List, 87

President's Commission on Risk
Management, 129
President's Management Agenda
(2001), 154
Preventive Health and Health Services
Block Grant (PHHSBG), 157
PricewaterhouseCoopers, 144
Privacy and information stewardship
threats/opportunities, 118*e*
Private sector: "At Risk" Brands report
(24/7 Wall St.), 168*e*; COSO ERM
Integrated Framework, 152; Frigo and
Anderson's Strategic Risk Management
Framework used in the, 152; increasing
adoption and practice of ERM in the,
227–229; ISO 31000 use by the, 152;
Results-Driven Strategy used by the,
167; return driven strategy (RDS) used
by the, 151; risk and performance
management in the, 151–152; risk
maturity rating by industry, 187*fig*
Program Assessment Rating Tool
(PART), 154
Program design and delivery threats/
opportunities, 118*e*
Public health: CDC credibility and
reputation management risk, 88–89;
Food and Drug Administration (FDA)
responsibilities for, 82; high-risk area
of protecting, 16; salmonella outbreak
alert, 25–26
Public Safety Canada Audit of Integrated
Risk Management case study: assessing
strategic risks, 200–201; audit findings,
recommendations, and management
responses, 197–199; on governance
structures, 203–205; identifying
strategic risks, 199–200; preparation

and background of the, 195; on
PSC's key risks related to integrated
risk management, 206*t*, 207; on
risk-informed decision making and
culture, 205–207; specific use risk tools
examined in, 201–203; summary of
findings and lines of inquiry, 196–197
Public Sector Risk Management LinkedIn
group, 211
Public sector. *See* Canadian government;
Federal government
Public Service in Canada (PSC): Integrated
Risk Management Framework used by
the, 29, 35–36, 49*e*–53*e*, 195, 196–207;
Integrated Risk Management Policy
approved by, 195; Public Safety Canada
Audit of Integrated Risk Management
by, 195, 196–207; risk as defined by, 34*t*.
*See also* Canadian government
PWGSC, 146

## R

Rainfall floods (Colorado), 24
"Recent Risk Events" (RIMS), 5, 9, 18–26
"Reputation and Its Risks" (*Harvard
Business Review*), 89
Reputation risk management: description
and example of, 88; risk statements on
threats/opportunities, 119*e*
Residual risk, 111
Resources: ERM Core Competency Survey
(2014) findings on, 212–213, 217, 219;
management of threats/opportunities,
119*e*–120*e*
Results-Driven Strategy, 167
Return driven strategy (RDS), 151
Ridge, Tom, 166*e*
RIMS Fellow Advisory Council, 209

RIMS Risk Maturity Model (RMM), 183–184

Risk: definitions of, 33, 34*t*, 110; identifying federal government performance, 159–160*fig*; overview of the emerging, 7–10; policies for managing various types of government, 41*t*–42*t*; residual, 111; risk treatment used to modify, 111; selected white collar occupational groups and potential, 39*t*–40*t*; societal direct and indirect exposures to, 8–9; "white spaces" left open for interpreting impact of, 29

Risk and Insurance Management Society (RIMS): on appropriate ERM behaviors, 177; on building a risk culture, 173; ERM as defined by, 28, 161; "Recent Risk Events" by, 5, 9, 18–20; RIMS Fellow Advisory Council of, 209; RIMS Risk Maturity Model (RMM), 183–184; Risk Manager Core Competency Model of, 209

Risk and performance management: glossary of key performance terms, 164*e*–165*e*; government approaches to, 151–152, 153–160; private sector approaches to, 151–152, 167–170; special challenge of homeland security, 165*e*–166*e*; Standard & Poor's ERM analysis of, 170–171; strategic risk management component of, 160–164, 165*e*–166*e*

Risk appetite, 110

Risk assessment: ANSI Risk Assessment Techniques Standard, 121–122; as component of any risk management framework, 120–131; COSO ERM Integrated Framework, 68; definition of, 110; GAO Internal Control Management and Evaluation Tool, 68, 70–80, 120, 177; OMB Circular A-123 promulgating use of, 229; standard used for, 69, 72–75; techniques for, 120–124*e*. *See also* Evaluation

Risk assessment standard: description of, 69; Evaluation Tool on major factors of, 72–75

Risk assessment techniques: assessing key risks, 122; mapping risks to strategic outcomes, 123–124*e*; overview of the, 120–122; Risk Matrix tool, 122–123

Risk Assessment Techniques Standard (ANSI), 121–122

Risk communication: Canada Treasury Board Risk Management Capability Model on, 193*t*; communication threats/opportunities, 114*e*–115*e*; ERM framework for facilitating, 109–110; glossary of risk management terms used in, 110–111; Kaplan and Mike's framework for, 106, 109; organizational structure determining approach to, 105–106; Treasury Board of Canada Secretariat's risk taxonomy used for, 106, 107*t*–108*t*

Risk culture: ERM Core Competency Survey (2014) findings on, 217, 219–220; McKinsey & Company's Working Paper on building a, 175–176; methods for influencing changes in, 176*t*; sample survey on, 177*e*–180*e*. *See also* Organizational culture

Risk economy, 106

Risk executive, 216

Risk management: agency hiring activities related to, 2*t*–3*t*; comparing ERM to

Competency Survey for the Public Sector (2014)

Risk manager self-identification, 216

Risk Management Framework (GAO). *See* GAO Risk Management Framework

Risk maps: mapping risks to strategic outcomes, 123; State of Washington Risk Map, 123–124*e*

Risk Matrix, 122–123

Risk Maturity Model (ERMMM) [Washington], 185–186, 188

Risk maturity rating by industry, 187*fig*

Risk owners: definition of, 111; ERM Core Competency Survey on self-identification as, 216

Risk profiles: definition of, 111; GAO High Risk List selected, 13–18

Risk statement inventory: business processes, 114*e*; capital infrastructures, 114*e*; change management, 117*e*–118*e*; communications, 114*e*–115*e*; conflict of interest, 115*e*; financial management, 115*e*; governance and strategic direction, 115*e*–116*e*; human resources management, 116*e*; information management, 116*e*–117*e*; information technology, 117*e*; knowledge management, 116*e*; legal considerations, 117*e*; policy development and implementation, 118*e*; political considerations, 119*e*; privacy and information stewardship, 118*e*; program design and delivery, 118*e*; project management, 119*e*; reputational considerations, 119*e*; resource management, 119*e*–120*e*; stakeholders and partnerships, 120*e*; values and ethics, 120*e*

Risk statements: description of, 111; the event and potential negative impact of event elements of a, 112; IF/THEN format used for writing, 111–112; inventory of, 113, 114*e*–120*e*; key factors of specific and broader, 113; process for developing, 112–113

Risk taxonomy: description and function of a, 106; Treasury Board of Canada Secretariat, 106, 107*t*–108*t*

Risk treatment, definition of, 111

Royal Bank of Scotland, 24

Russian meteor explosion, 19

## S

Salmonella Heidelberg bacteria, 25

Salmonella outbreak, 25–26

*Sample Risk Culture Survey,* 177*e*–180*e*

Santander, 24

Sarbanes-Oxley Act (2002), 43, 184

Schanzer, David H., 166

Schein, Edgar, 174, 176

Sears, 22

Securities and Exchange Commission (SEC), 167

Security risk management: Department of Homeland Security (DHS) responsibility for, 83; DoD risk management responsibility for, 82–83; Information Analysis and Infrastructure Protection (IAIP) responsibility for, 84; Office for Domestic Preparedness (ODP) responsibility for, 83; since September 11th terrorist attacks, 83, 84–85; Target data breach (2013) issue of, 152; U.S. Coast Guard responsibility for, 83

Sentinel Initiative (2008) [FDA], 82

management since 9/11 attacks, 83,
84–85, 166e
Tesco chain (UK supermarket), 18
Tesoro Logistics, 25
Threats/opportunities. *See* Risk statements
Tornado risk management, 21, 87
Train derailment (Spain), 23
Transparency: Canada's Integrated Risk
Management Framework application
for, 50e; Obama administration focus
on, 4; strategic risk management (SRM)
on importance of, 161
Transportation safety risk management,
86–87
Treasury Board of Canada Secretariat's
risk taxonomy, 106, 107t–108t
24/7 Wall St. "At Risk" Brands
Report, 168e
Typhoon Wipha (Japan), 26

**U**
Upper Big Branch Mine explosion
(2010), 19
USAJOBS.gov, 2
U.S. Coast Guard, 83
U.S. Geological Survey, 20
U.S. Postal Service (USPA): external risk
management by the, 87–88; financial

sustainability issue of, 18; Mail Service
Updates site of the, 87; Performance
Plan established by the, 88
U.S. Securities and Exchange Commission
(SEC), 167
U.S. Technical Advisory Group
(US TAG), 136

**V**
Values threats/opportunities, 120e
Vermont's patent trolls law, 21
Volvo, 168e

**W**
Walmart, 22
Washington bridge collapse, 21
Washington. *See* State of Washington
Wells Fargo, 26
West Fertilizer Company explosion
(Texas), 20
White collar occupational groups risks,
39t–40t
Willis, 25
WNBA (Women's National Basketball
Association), 168e
Working Paper (McKinsey & Company),
175–176
World Health Organization, 20